MARKETING FOR THE MANUFACTURER

THE BUSINESS ONE IRWIN/APICS LIBRARY OF INTEGRATED RESOURCE MANAGEMENT

Customers and Products

Marketing for the Manufacturer   *J. Paul Peter*

Field Service Management: An Integrated Approach to Increasing Customer Satisfaction   *Arthur V. Hill*

Effective Product Design and Development: How to Cut Lead Time and Increase Customer Satisfaction   *Stephen R. Rosenthal*

Logistics

Integrated Production and Inventory Management: Revitalizing the Manufacturing Enterprise   *Thomas E. Vollmann, William L. Berry, and D. Clay Whybark*

Purchasing: Continued Improvement through Integration   *Joseph Carter*

Integrated Distribution Management: Competing on Customer Service, Time and Cost   *Christopher Gopal and Harold Cypress*

Manufacturing Process

Integrative Facilities Management   *John M. Burnham*

Integrated Process Design and Development   *Dan L. Shunk*

Integrative Manufacturing: Transforming the Organization through People, Process and Technology   *Scott Flaig*

Support Functions

Managing Information: How Information Systems Impact Organizational Strategy   *Gordon B. Davis and Thomas R. Hoffmann*

Managing Human Resources: Integrating People and Business Strategy   *Lloyd Baird*

Managing for Quality: Integrating Quality and Business Strategy   *Howard Gitlow*

World-Class Accounting and Finance   *Carol J. McNair*

MARKETING FOR THE MANUFACTURER

J. Paul Peter
McManus-Bascom Professor in Marketing
University of Wisconsin—Madison
Madison, Wisconsin

BUSINESS ONE IRWIN
Homewood, Illinois 60430

This publication is designed to provide accurate and
authoritative information in regard to the subject matter
covered. It is sold with the understanding that neither the
author nor the publisher is engaged in rendering legal, accounting,
or other professional services. If legal advice or other expert
assistance is required, the services of a competent
professional person should be sought.

*From a Declaration of Principles jointly adopted by a Committee
of the American Bar Association and a Committee of Publishers.*

Sponsoring editor: Jeffrey A. Krames
Project editor: Susan Trentacosti
Production manager: Bette K. Ittersagen
Art coordinator: Mark Malloy
Compositor: Graphic World, Inc.
Typeface: 11/13 Times Roman
Printer: Arcata Graphics/Kingsport

Library of Congress Cataloging-in-Publication Data

Peter, J. Paul.
     Marketing for the manufacturer/J. Paul Peter.
          p.   cm.—(The Business One Irwin/APICS library of integrated
     resource management)
     Includes index.
     ISBN 1-55623-648-4
     1. Marketing.   2. Manufacturer—Marketing.   I. Title.
II. Series.
HF5415.P4417   1992
670'.68'8—dc20   92–5874

Printed in the United States of America
1 2 3 4 5 6 7 8 9 0 K 9 8 7 6 5 4 3 2

FOREWORD

Marketing for the Manufacturer is one book in a series that addresses the most critical issue facing manufacturing companies today: integration—the identification and solution of problems that cross organizational and company boundaries—and, perhaps more importantly, the continuous search for ways to solve these problems faster and more effectively! The genesis for the series is the commitment to integration made by the American Production and Inventory Control Society (APICS). I attended several brainstorming sessions a few years ago in which the primary topic of discussion was, "What jobs will exist in manufacturing companies in the future—not at the very top of the enterprise and not at the bottom, but in between?" The prognostications included:

- The absolute number of jobs will decrease, as will the layers of management. Manufacturing organizations will adopt flatter organizational forms with less emphasis on hierarchy and less distinction between white collars and blue collars.
- Functional "silos" will become obsolete. The classical functions of marketing, manufacturing, engineering, finance, and personnel will be less important in defining work. More people will take on "project" work focused on continuous improvement of one kind or another.
- Fundamental restructuring, meaning much more than financial restructuring, will become a way of life in manufacturing enterprises. The primary focal points will be a new market-driven emphasis on creating value with customers, as well as greatly increased flexibility, a new business-driven attack on global markets which includes new deployment of information technology, and fundamentally new jobs.
- Work will become much more integrated in its orientation. The payoffs will increasingly be made through connections across organizational and company boundaries. Included are customer and

vendor partnerships, with an overall focus on improving the value-added chain.

- New measurements that focus on the new strategic directions will be required. Metrics will be developed, similar to the cost of quality metric, that incorporate the most important dimensions of the environment. Similar metrics and semantics will be developed to support the new uses of information technology.

- New "people management" approaches will be developed. Teamwork will be critical to organizational success. Human resource management will become less of a "staff" function and more closely integrated with the basic work.

Many of these prognostications are already a reality. APICS has made the commitment to *leading* the way in all of these change areas. The decision was both courageous and intelligent. There is no future for a professional society not committed to leading-edge education for its members. Based on the Society's past experience with the Certification in Production and Inventory Management (CPIM) program, the natural thrust of APICS was to develop a new certification program focusing on integration. The result, Certification in Integrated Resource Management (CIRM) is a program composed of 13 building block areas which have been combined into four examination modules, as follows:

Customers and products
  Marketing
  Field service
  Product design and development
Manufacturing processes
  Industrial facilities management
  Process design and development
  Manufacturing (production)
Logistics
  Production and inventory control
  Procurement
  Distribution
Support functions
  Total quality management
  Human resources
  Finance and accounting
  Information systems

As can be seen from this topical list, one objective in the CIRM program is to develop educational breadth. Managers increasingly *must* know the underlying basics in each area of the business: who are the people who work there, what are day-to-day *and* strategic problems, what is state-of-the-art practice, what are the expected improvement areas, and what is happening with technology? This basic breadth of knowledge is an absolute prerequisite to understanding the potential linkages and joint improvements.

But it is the linkages, relationships, and integration that are even more important. Each examination devotes approximately 40 percent of the questions to the connections *among* the 13 building block areas. In fact, after a candidate has successfully completed the four examination modules, he or she must take a fifth examination (Integrated Enterprise Management), which focuses solely on the interrelationships among all functional areas of an enterprise.

The CIRM program has been the most exciting activity on which I have worked in a professional organization. Increasingly, manufacturing companies face the alternative of either proactive restructuring to deal with today's competitive realities, or just sliding away—giving up market share and industry leadership. Education must play a key role in making the necessary changes. People working in manufacturing companies need to learn many new things and "unlearn" many old ones.

There were very limited educational materials available to support CIRM. There were textbooks in which basic concepts were covered and bits and pieces which dealt with integration, but there simply was no coordinated set of materials available for this program. That has been the job of the CIRM series authors, and it has been my distinct pleasure as series editor to help develop the ideas and facilitate our joint learning. All of us have learned a great deal, and I am delighted with every book in the series. But the spirit of continuous improvement is built into the CIRM program and into the book series. The next editions will be even better!

Thomas E. Vollmann
Series Editor

PREFACE

This book is designed for training manufacturers about the marketing function in organizations. The basic philosophy underlying it is that manufacturing managers of the future need to develop integrated solutions to problems that cross traditional functional boundaries. In order to do so, these managers need to understand both the tools and concepts of other functional areas. This book is devoted to providing an understanding of the tools and concepts in the field of marketing.

The book explains to manufacturing managers how people trained in marketing view their functional role in an organization and the strategic areas in which marketing personnel are trained to believe they have decision-making responsibility. The first three parts of the book emphasize this by focusing on marketing's role in strategic planning, understanding target markets, and developing marketing mixes. The topics covered in these parts are identical to those taught in marketing courses in colleges and universities across the country.

Second, the book investigates relationships between marketing and other functional areas, particularly manufacturing. The last two parts of the book have this emphasis. Part 4 provides an overview of some of the emerging ideas about marketing-manufacturing interfaces and Part 5 contains four cases and lessons from them designed to focus attention on marketing strategy concerns and relationships between marketing and manufacturing.

Each chapter of the text contains a variety of figures and highlights designed to assist the reader in understanding important issues in marketing analysis. It is hoped that the book will provide manufacturing managers with an understanding of marketing and its role in organizations.

J. Paul Peter

CONTENTS

PART 5
CASES IN MARKETING MANAGEMENT

PART 1

INTRODUCTION TO MARKETING

CHAPTER 1
Strategic Planning and the Marketing Management Process

CHAPTER 1

STRATEGIC PLANNING AND THE MARKETING MANAGEMENT PROCESS

The purpose of this introductory chapter is to present the marketing management process and outline what marketing managers must *manage* if they are to be effective. In doing so, it will also present a framework around which the remaining chapters are organized. Our first task is to review the organizational philosophy known as the marketing concept, since it underlies much of the thinking presented in this book. The remainder of this chapter will focus on the process of strategic planning and its relationship to the process of marketing planning.

THE MARKETING CONCEPT

Simply stated, the marketing concept means that *an organization should seek to make a profit by serving the needs of customer groups*. The concept is very straightforward and has a great deal of commonsense validity. Perhaps this is why it is often misunderstood, forgotten, or overlooked.

The purpose of the marketing concept is to rivet the attention of marketing managers on serving broad classes of customer needs (customer orientation), rather than on the firm's current products (production orientation) or on devising methods to attract customers to current products (selling orientation). Thus, effective marketing starts with the recognition of customer needs and then works backward to devise products and services to satisfy these needs. In this way, marketing managers can satisfy customers more efficiently in the present and anticipate changes in customer needs more accurately in the future. It is hoped that the end result is a more efficient market in which the customer is better satisfied and the firm is more profitable

---

HIGHLIGHT 1–1
Basic Elements of the Marketing Concept

1. Companywide managerial awareness and appreciation of the consumer's role as it is related to the firm's existence, growth, and stability. As Drucker has noted, business enterprise is an organ of society; thus, its basic purpose lies outside the business itself. And the valid definition of business purpose is the creation of customers.
2. Active, companywide managerial awareness of, and concern with, interdepartmental implications of decisions and actions of an individual department. That is, the firm is viewed as a network of forces focused on meeting defined customer needs, and comprising a system within which actions taken in one department or area frequently result in significant repercussions in other areas of the firm. Also, it is recognized that such actions may affect the company's equilibrium with its external environment, for example, its customers, its competitors.
3. Active, companywide managerial concern with innovation of products and services designed to solve selected consumer problems.
4. General managerial concern with the effect of new products and service introduction on the firm's profit position, both present and future, and recognition of the potential rewards which may accrue from new product planning, including profits and profit stability.
5. General managerial appreciation of the role of marketing intelligence and other fact-finding and reporting units within, and adjacent to the firm, in translating the general statements presented above into detailed statements of profitable market potentials, targets, and action. Implicit in this statement is not only an expansion of the traditional function and scope of formal marketing research, but also assimilation of other sources of marketing data, such as the firm's distribution system and its advertising agency counsel, into a potential marketing intelligence service.
6. Companywide managerial effort, based on participation and interaction of company officers, in establishing corporate and departmental objectives that are understood by and acceptable to these officers, and that are consistent with enhancement of the firm's profit position.

Source: Robert L. King, "The Marketing Concept: Fact or Intelligent Platitude," *The Marketing Concept in Action,* Proceedings of the 47th National Conference (Chicago: American Marketing Association, 1964), p. 657. For an up-to-date discussion of the marketing concept, see Franklin S. Houston, "The Marketing Concept: What It Is and What It Is Not," *Journal of Marketing,* April 1986, pp. 81–87.

The principle task of the marketing function operating under the marketing concept is not to manipulate customers to do what suits the interests of the firm, but rather to find effective and efficient means of making the business do what suits the interests of customers. This is not

---

HIGHLIGHT 1–2
Ten Key Principles for Marketing Success

Principle 1. Create Customer Want Satisfaction.
Principle 2. Know Your Buyer Characteristics.
Principle 3. Divide the Market into Segments.
Principle 4. Strive for High Market Share.
Principle 5. Develop Deep and Wide Product Lines.
Principle 6. Price Position Products and Upgrade Markets.
Principle 7. Treat Channels as Intermediate Buyers.
Principle 8. Coordinate Elements of Physical Distribution.
Principle 9. Promote Performance Features.
Principle 10. Use Information to Improve Decisions.

Source: Fred C. Allvine, Excerpt from *Marketing: Principles and Practices*, p. viii, by Fred C. Allvine, copyright © 1987 by Harcourt Brace Jovanovich, Inc., reprinted by permission of the publisher.

to say that all firms practice marketing in this way. Clearly, many firms still emphasize only production and sales. However, effective marketing, as defined in this text, requires that consumer needs come first in organizational decision making.

One qualification to this statement deals with the question of a conflict between consumer wants and societal needs and wants. For example, if society deems clean air and water as necessary for survival, this need may well take precedence over a consumer's want for goods and services that pollute the environment.

WHAT IS MARKETING?

One of the most persistent conceptual problems in marketing is its definition.[1] The American Marketing Association has recently defined marketing as "the process of planning and executing conception, pricing, promotion, and distribution of ideas, goods, and services to create

---

[1]See Reinhard Angelmar and Christian Pinson, "The Meaning of Marketing," *Philosophy of Science,* June 1975, pp. 208–14.

exchanges that satisfy individual and organizational objectives."[2] Although this broad definition allows the inclusion of nonbusiness exchange processes (i.e., persons, places, organizations, ideas) as part of marketing, the primary emphasis in this text is on marketing in the business environment. However, this emphasis is not meant to imply that marketing concepts, principles, and techniques cannot be fruitfully employed in other areas of exchange. In fact, some discussions of nonbusiness marketing take place later in the text.

WHAT IS STRATEGIC PLANNING?

Before a production manager, marketing manager, and personnel manager can develop plans for their individual departments, hopefully, some larger plan or blueprint for the *entire* organization has been developed. Otherwise, on what would the individual departmental plans be based?

In other words, there is a larger context for planning activities. Let us assume that we are dealing with a large business organization that has several business divisions and several product lines within each division (e.g., General Electric, Philip Morris). Before any marketing planning can be done by individual divisions or departments, a plan has to be developed for the *entire* organization.[3] Then objectives and strategies established at the top level provide the context for planning in each of the divisions and departments by divisional and departmental managers. These lower-level managers develop their plans within the constraints developed at the higher levels.[4]

Strategic Planning and Marketing Management

Many of today's most successful business organizations are here today because many years ago they offered the right product at the right time to a rapidly growing market. The same can also be said for nonprofit and

---

[2]Peter D. Bennett, *Dictionary of Marketing Terms* (Chicago: American Marketing Association, 1988), p. 115.

[3]John H. Grant and William R. King, *The Logic of Strategic Planning* (Boston: Little, Brown, 1982), chap. 1. This section is based on J. H. Donnelly, Jr., J. L. Gibson, and J. M. Ivancevich, *Fundamentals of Management*, 7th ed. (Homewood, Ill: Richard D. Irwin, 1990), chap. 5.

[4]L. Rosenberg and C. D. Schewe, "Strategic Planning: Fulfilling the Promise," *Business Horizons*, July–August 1985, pp. 54–63.

governmental organizations. Many of the critical decisions of the past were made without the benefit of strategic thinking or planning. Whether these decisions were based on wisdom or were just luck is not important. They resulted in a momentum which has carried these organizations to where they are today. However, present-day managers are increasingly recognizing that wisdom and intuition alone are no longer sufficient to guide the destinies of their large organizations in today's ever-changing environment. These managers are turning to strategic planning.[5]

Strategic planning includes all of the activities that lead to the development of a clear organzational mission, organizational objectives, and appropriate strategies to achieve the objectives for the entire organization. Figure 1–1 presents the process of strategic planning. It indicates that the organization gathers information about the changing elements of its environment. This information is useful in aiding the organization to adapt better to these changes through the process of strategic planning.[6] The strategic plan(s)[7] and supporting plan are then implemented in the environment. The results of this implementation are fed back as new information so that continuous adaptation can take place.

The Strategic Planning Process

The output of the strategic planning process is the development of a strategic plan. Figure 1–1 indicates four components of a strategic plan: mission, objectives, strategies, and portfolio plan. Let us carefully examine each one.

---

[5]C. Anderson and C. P. Zeithaml, "Stage of the Product Life Cycle, Business Strategy, and Business Performance," *Academy of Management Journal*, March 1984, pp. 5–24.

[6]The process depicted in Figure 1–1 is a generally agreed upon model of the strategic planning process, although some may include or exclude a particular element. For example, see A. A. Thompson and A. J. Strickland III, *Strategic Management: Concepts and Cases*, 6th ed. (Homewood, Ill: Richard D. Irwin, 1990), and Philip Kotler, *Marketing Management: Analysis, Planning, and Control*, 6th ed. (Englewood Cliffs, N.J.: Prentice Hall, 1988).

[7]The process may differ depending on the type of organization or management approach, or both. For certain types of organizations, one strategic plan will be sufficient. Some manufacturers with similar product lines or limited product lines will develop only one strategic plan. However, organizations with widely diversified product lines and widely diversified markets may develop strategic plans for units or divisions. These plans usually are combined into a master strategic plan.

FIGURE 1–1
The Strategic Planning Process

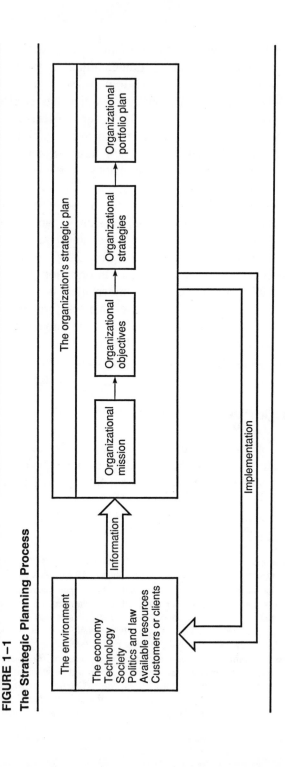

Organizational Mission

Every organization's environment supplies the resources that sustain the organization, whether it is a business organization, a college or university, or a governmental agency. In exchange for these resources, the organization must supply the environment with goods and services at an acceptable price and quality. In other words, every organization exists to accomplish something in the larger environment, and that purpose or mission is usually clear at the start. However, as time passes and the organization expands, the environment changes, and managerial personnel change, one or more things are likely to occur. First, the original purpose may become irrelevant as the organization expands into new products, new markets, and even new industries. Second, the original mission remains relevant but some managers begin to lose interest in it. Finally, changes in environment may make the original mission inappropriate. The result of any or all of these three conditions is a "drifting"

HIGHLIGHT 1–3
Some Actual Mission Statements

Organization	Mission
1. Office equipment manufacturer	We are in the business of problem solving. Our business is to help solve administrative, scientific, and human problems.
2. Credit union	To produce a selected range of quality services to organizations and individuals to fulfill their continuing financial needs.
3. Large conglomerate	Translating new technologies into commercially salable products.
4. Consumer products paper company	The development and marketing of inedible food store products.
5. State department of health	Administering all provisions of law relating to public health laws and regulations of the State Board of Health, supervising and assisting county and regional boards and departments of health, and doing all other things reasonably necessary to protect and improve the health of the people.
6. Appliance manufacturer	A willingness to invest in any area of suitable profit and growth potential in which the organization has or can acquire the capabilities.

organization, without a clear mission or purpose to guide critical decisions. When this occurs, management must search for a purpose or restate the original purpose.

The mission statement of an organization should be a long-run vision of what the organization is trying to become: the unique aim that differentiates the organization from similar ones. Note that the need is not a stated purpose, such as "to fulfill the educational needs of college students," that will enable stockholders and managers to feel good or to use for good public relations. The need is for a stated mission that will provide direction and significance to all members of the organization regardless of their level in the organization.

The basic questions that must be answered when an organization decides to examine and restate its mission are: "What is our business?" "What should it be?" While such questions may appear simple, they are in fact such difficult and critical ones that the major responsibility for answering them must lie with top management.[8] In developing a statement of mission, management must take into account three key elements:[9]

1. *The organization's history.* Every organization—large or small, profit or nonprofit—has a history of objectives, accomplishments, mistakes, and policies. In formulating a mission the critical characteristics and events of the past must be considered.

2. *The organization's distinctive competences.* While there are many things an organization may be able to do, it should seek to do what it can do best. Distinctive competences are things that an organization does well: so well in fact that they give it an advantage over similar organizations. Procter & Gamble could probably enter the synthetic fuel business but such a decision would certainly not take advantage of its major distinctive competence: knowledge of the market for low-priced, repetitively purchased

---

[8]Lewis W. Walker, "The CEO and Corporate Strategy in the Eighties: Back to Basics," *Interfaces,* January–February 1984, pp. 3–9; Peter Drucker, *Management: Tasks, Responsibilities, Practices* (New York: Harper & Row, 1974), chap. 7.

[9]Kotler, *Marketing Management,* chap. 2.

consumer products. No matter how appealing an opportunity may be, the organization must have the competences to capitalize on that opportunity.[10]

3. *The organization's environment.* The organization's environment dictates the opportunities, constraints, and threats that must be identified before a mission statement is developed. Technological developments in the communications field may have a negative impact on travel and should certainly be considered in the mission statement of a large motel chain.[11]

However, it is extremely difficult to write a useful and effective mission statement. It is not uncommon for an organization to spend one or two years developing a useful mission statement. When completed, an effective mission statement will be: *focused on markets rather than products, achievable, motivating, and specific.*[12]

Focused on Markets Rather Than Products.   The customers or clients of an organization are critical in determining its mission. Traditionally, many organizations defined their business in terms of what they made, "our business is glass," and in many cases they named the organization for the product or service (e.g., National Cash Register, Harbor View Savings and Loan Association). Many of these organizations have found that, when products and technologies become obsolete, their mission is no longer relevant and the name of the organization may no longer describe what it does. Thus, a more enduring way of defining the mission is needed. In recent years, therefore, a key feature of mission statements has been an *external* rather than *internal* focus. In other words, the mission statement should focus on the broad class of needs that the organization is seeking to satisfy (external focus), *not* on the physical product or service

[10]For a study of the relationship between corporate distinctive competencies and performance in 185 firms, see M. A. Hitt and R. D. Ireland, "Corporate Distinctive Competence, Strategy and Performance," *Strategic Management Journal*, July–September 1985, pp. 273–93.

[11]See C. Smart and I. Vertinsky, "Strategy and the Environment: A Study of Corporate Responses to Crises," *Strategic Management Journal*, April–June 1984, pp. 199–214. This study of the largest U.S. and Canadian companies examines the relationship between a firm's external environment and its repertoire of strategic responses to cope with crisis.

[12]Drucker, *Management*, pp. 77–89; Kotler, *Marketing Management*, chap. 2.

that the organization is offering at present (internal focus). This has been clearly stated by Peter Drucker. He argues:

> A business is not defined by the company's name, statutes, or articles of incorporation. It is defined by the want the customer satisfies when he buys a product or service. To satisfy the customer is the mission and purpose of every business. The question "What is our business?" can, therefore, be answered only by looking at the business from the outside, from the point of view of customer and market.[13]

While Drucker was referring to business organizations, the same necessity exists for both nonprofit and governmental organizations.[14] That necessity is to state the mission in terms of serving a particular group of clients or customers and meeting a particular class of need.

Achievable.   While the mission statement should "stretch" the organization toward more effective performance, it should, at the same time, be realistic and achievable. In other words, it should open a vision of new opportunities but should not lead the organization into unrealistic ventures far beyond its competences.

Motivational.   One of the side (but very important) benefits of a well-defined mission is the guidance it provides employees and managers working in geographically dispersed units and on independent tasks. It provides a shared sense of purpose outside the various activities taking place within the organization. Therefore, such end results as sales, patients cared for, and reduction in violent crimes can then be viewed as the result of careful pursuit and accomplishment of the mission and not as the mission itself.[15]

Specific.   As we mentioned earlier, public relations should not be the primary purpose of a statement of mission. It must be specific to provide direction and guidelines to management when they are choosing

---

[13]Drucker, *Management*, p. 79.

[14]Paul C. Nutt, "A Strategic Planning Network for Nonprofit Organizations," *Strategic Management Journal*, January–March 1984, pp. 57–76; Peter Smith Ring and James L. Perry, "Strategic Management in Public and Private Organizations: Implications of Distinctive Contexts and Constraints," *Academy of Management Review*, April 1985, pp. 276–86.

[15]"Who's Excellent Now," *Business Week*, November 5, 1984, pp. 76–88.

between alternative courses of action.[16] In other words, "to produce the highest quality products at the lowest possible cost" sounds very good, but it does not provide direction for management.

Organizational Objectives

Organizational objectives are the end points of an organization's mission and are what it seeks through the ongoing, long-run operations of the organization. The organizational mission is distilled into a finer set of specific and achievable organizational objectives. These objectives must be *specific, measurable, action commitments* by which the mission of the organization is to be achieved.

As with the statement of mission, organizational objectives are more than good intentions. In fact, if formulated properly, they can accomplish the following:

1. They can be converted into specific actions.
2. They will provide direction. That is, they can serve as a starting point for more specific and detailed objectives at lower levels in the organization. Each manager will then know how his or her objectives relate to those at higher levels.
3. They can establish long-run priorities for the organization.
4. They can facilitate management control because they serve as standards against which overall organizational performance can be evaluated.

Organizational objectives are necessary in any and all areas that may influence the performance and long-run survival of the organization. Peter Drucker believes that objectives should be established in at least eight areas of organizational performance. These are market standing, innovations, productivity, physical and financial resources, profitability, manager performance and responsibility, worker performance and attitude, and social responsibility.[17]

The above list of objectives is by no means exhaustive. An organization may very well have additional ones. The important point is that management must translate the organizational mission into specific

---

[16]Drucker, *Management*, p. 87.

[17]Peter Drucker, *The Practice of Management* (New York: Harper & Row, 1954); and reemphasized in Drucker's *Management*.

FIGURE 1–2
Sample Organizational Objectives (Manufacturing Firm)

Area of Performance	Possible Objective
1. Market standing	To make our brands number one in their field in terms of market share.
2. Innovations	To be a leader in introducing new products by spending no less than 7 percent of sales for research and development.
3. Productivity	To manufacture all products efficiently as measured by the productivity of the work force.
4. Physical and financial resources	To protect and maintain all resources—equipment, buildings, inventory, and funds.
5. Profitability	To achieve an annual rate of return on investment of at least 15 percent.
6. Manager performance and responsibility	To identify critical areas of management depth and succession.
7. Worker performance and attitude	To maintain levels of employee satisfaction consistent with our own and similar industries.
8. Social responsibility	To respond appropriately whenever possible to societal expectations and environmental needs.

---

objectives that will support the realization of the mission. The objectives may flow directly from the mission or be considered subordinate necessities for carrying out the mission of the organization. Figure 1–2 presents some examples of organizational objectives. Note that they are broad statements that serve as guides and that they are of a continuing nature. They specify the end points of an organization's mission and the results that it seeks in the long run both externally and internally. Most important, however, the objectives in Figure 1–2 are *specific, measurable, action commitments* on the part of the organization.

Organizational Strategies

Hopefully, when an organization has formulated its mission and developed its objectives, it knows where it wants to go. The next managerial task is to develop a "grand design" to get there. This grand design constitutes

FIGURE 1–3
Organizational Growth Strategies

Products / Markets	Present Products	New Products
Present Customers	Market penetration	Product development
New Customers	Market development	Diversification

the organizational strategies. The role of strategy in strategic planning is to identify the general approaches that the organization will utilize to achieve its organizational objectives. It involves the choice of major directions the organization will take in pursuing its objectives.

Achieving organizational objectives comes about in two ways. It is accomplished by better managing what the organization is presently doing and/or finding new things to do. In choosing either or both of these paths, the organization then must decide whether to concentrate on present customers or to seek new ones, or both. Figure 1–3 presents the available strategic choices. It is known as a product/market matrix and indicates the strategic alternatives available to an organization for achieving its objectives. It indicates that an organization can grow in a variety of ways by concentrating on present or new products and on present or new customers.[18]

Market Penetration Strategies.   These organizational strategies focus on improving the position of the organization's present products with its present customers. For example:

- A dairy concentrates on getting its present customers to purchase more of its products.
- A charity seeks to increase contributions from present contributors.

---

[18]Originally discussed in the classic H. Igor Ansoff, *Corporate Strategy* (New York: McGraw-Hill, 1965).

- A bank concentrates on getting present depositors to use additional services.

A market penetration strategy might involve devising a marketing plan to encourage customers to purchase more of a product. Tactics used to carry out the strategy could include price reductions, advertising that stresses the many benefits of the product, packaging the product in different-sized packages, or making the product available at more locations.

HIGHLIGHT 1–4
Some Commonly Used Performance Standards

Effectiveness Standards

A. Sales Criteria.
1. Total sales.
2. Sales by product or product line.
3. Sales by geographic region.
4. Sales by salesperson.
5. Sales by customer type.
6. Sales by market segment.
7. Sales by size of order.
8. Sales by sales territory.
9. Sales by intermediary.
10. Market share.
11. Percentage change in sales.

B. Customer Satisfaction.
1. Quantity purchased.
2. Degree of brand loyalty.
3. Repeat purchase rates.
4. Perceived product quality.
5. Brand image.
6. Number of letters of complaint.

Efficiency Standards

C. Costs.
1. Total costs.
2. Costs by product or product line.
3. Costs by geographic region.
4. Costs by salesperson.
5. Costs by customer type.
6. Costs by market segment.
7. Costs by size of order.
8. Costs by sales territory.
9. Costs by intermediary.
10. Percentage change in costs.

Effectiveness-Efficiency Standards

D. Profits.
1. Total profits.
2. Profits by product or product line.
3. Profits by geographic region.
4. Profits by salesperson.
5. Profits by customer type.
6. Profits by market segment.
7. Profits by size of order.
8. Profits by sales territory.
9. Profits by intermediary.

Source: Reprinted by permission from *Marketing: Principles and Strategies,* by Charles D. Schewe, p. 593. © 1987 by McGraw-Hill.

Likewise, a production plan might be developed to produce more efficiently what is being produced at present. Implementation of such a plan could include increased production runs, the substitution of preassembled components for individual product parts, or the automation of a process that previously was performed manually. In other words, market penetration strategies concentrate on improving the efficiency of various functional areas in the organization.

Market Development Strategies.   Following this strategy, an organization would seek to find new customers for its present products. For example:

- A manufacturer of industrial products may decide to develop products for entrance into consumer market.
- A governmental social service agency may seek individuals and families who have never utilized the agency's services.
- A manufacturer of automobiles decides to sell automobiles in Eastern Europe because of the recent transition to a free market system.

Product Development Strategies.   In choosing either of the remaining two strategies, the organization in effect, seeks new things to do. With this particular strategy, the new products developed would be directed to present customers. For example:

- A candy manufacturer may decide to offer a low-calorie candy.
- A social service agency may offer additional services to present client families.
- A college or university may develop programs for senior citizens.

Diversification.   An organization diversifies when it seeks new products for customers it is not serving at present. For example:

- A discount store purchases a savings and loan association.
- A cigarette manufacturer diversifies into real estate development.
- A college or university establishes a corporation to find commercial uses for the results of faculty research efforts.

On what basis does an organization choose one (or all) of its strategies? Of extreme importance are the directions set by the mission statement. Management should select those strategies consistent with its mission and capitalize on the organization's distinctive competencies which will lead to a sustainable competitive advantage.[19] A sustainable competitive advantage can be based on either the assets or skills of the organization. Technical superiority, low-cost production, customer service/product support, location, financial resources, continuing product innovation, and overall marketing skills are all examples of distinctive competencies that can lead to a sustainable competitive advantage.[20] For example, Honda is known for providing quality automobiles at a reasonable price. Each succeeding generation of Honda cars has shown marked quality improvement over previous generations. This, in turn, has led to the Honda Accord's becoming the leading selling car in the United States. The key to sustaining a competitive advantage is to continually focus and build on the assets and skills that will lead to long-term performance gains.

Organizational Portfolio Plan

The final phase of the strategic planning process is the formulation of the organizational portfolio plan. In reality, most organizations at a particular time are a portfolio of businesses, that is, product lines, divisions, schools. To illustrate, an appliance manufacturer may have several product lines (e.g., televisions, washers and dryers, refrigerators, stereos) as well as two divisions, consumer appliances and industrial appliances. A college or university will have numerous schools (e.g., education, business, law, architecture) and several programs within each school. Some widely diversified organizations such as Philip Morris, are in numerous unrelated businesses, such as cigarettes, food products, land development, industrial paper products, and a brewery.

Managing such groups of businesses is made a little easier if resources are plentiful, cash is plentiful, and each is experiencing growth and profits. Unfortunately, providing larger and larger budgets each year to all businesses is seldom feasible. Many are not experiencing growth, and profits and resources (financial and nonfinancial) are becoming more and more scarce. In such a situation, choices must be made, and some

---

[19]N. Venkatramen and J. C. Camillus, "Exploring the Concept of 'Fit' in Strategic Management," *Academy of Management Review,* July 1984, pp. 513–25; H. Mintzberg and J. A. Waters, "Of Strategies, Deliberate and Emergent," *Strategic Management Journal,* July–September 1985, pp. 257–72.

[20]D. Aaker, "Managing Assets and Skills: The Key to a Sustainable Competitive Advantage," *California Management Review,* Winter 1989, pp. 91–106.

method is necessary to help management make the choices. Management must decide which businesses to build, maintain, or eliminate, or which new businesses to add.[21] Indeed, much of the recent activity in corporate restructuring has centered around decisions relating to which groups of businesses management should focus on.

Obviously, the first step in this approach is to identify the various division's product lines and so on that can be considered a "business." When identified, these are referred to as *strategic business units* (SBUs) and have the following characteristics:

- They have a distinct mission.
- They have their own competitors.
- They are a single business or collection of related businesses.
- They can be planned independently of the other businesses of the total organization.

Thus, depending on the type of organization, an SBU could be a single product, product line, division; a department of business administration; or a state mental health agency. Once the organization has identified and classified all of its SBUs, some method must be established to determine how resources should be allocated among the various SBUs. These methods are known as *portfolio models*. For those readers interested, the appendix of this chapter presents two of the most popular portfolio models, the Boston Consulting Group model and the General Electric model.

The Complete Strategic Plan

Figure 1–1 indicates that at this point the strategic planning process is complete, and the organization has a time-phased blueprint that outlines its mission, objectives, and strategies. Completion of the strategic plan facilitates the development of marketing plans for each product, product line, or division of the organization. The marketing plan serves as a subset of the strategic plan in that it allows for detailed planning at a

---

[21]There are several portfolio models; each has its detractors and supporters. The interested reader should consult Richard G. Hamermesh and Roderick E. White, "Manage Beyond Portfolio Analysis," *Harvard Business Review,* January–February 1984, pp. 103–9, and J. A. Seeger, "Revising the Images of BCG's Growth/Share Matrix," *Strategic Management Journal,* January–March 1984, pp. 93–97.

target market level. Several marketing plans, each one targeted toward a specific market, will evolve from the strategic plan. For example, separate marketing plans would be developed for the various markets that a firm, which produces consumer appliances and industrial electrical products, competes in. Given a completed strategic plan, each area knows exactly where the organization wishes to go and can then develop objectives, strategies, and programs that are consistent with the strategic plan.[22] This important relationship between strategic planning and marketing planning is the subject of the final section of this chapter.

THE MARKETING MANAGEMENT PROCESS

Marketing management can be defined as "the analysis, planning, implementation, and control of programs designed to bring about desired exchanges with target markets for the purpose of achieving organizational objectives. It relies heavily on designing the organization's offering in terms of the target market's needs and desires and on using effective pricing, communication, and distribution to inform, motivate, and service the market."[23] It should be noted that this definition is entirely consistent with the marketing concept, since it emphasizes the serving of target market needs as the key to achieving organizational objectives. The remainder of this section will be devoted to a discussion of the marketing management process in terms of the model in Figure 1–4.

Organizational Mission and Objectives

Marketing activities should start with a clear understanding of the organization's mission and objectives. These factors provide marketing management direction by specifying the industry, the desired role of the firm in the industry (such as research-oriented innovator, custom-batch specialist, or mass producer, and hopefully, a precise statement of what the firm is trying to accomplish). However, since written mission statements and objectives are often ambiguous or ill-defined, the marketing

---

[22]R. A. Linneman and H. E. Klein, "Using Scenarios in Strategic Decision Making," *Business Horizons*, January–February 1985, pp. 64–74.

[23]Kotler, *Marketing Management*, p. 14.

FIGURE 1–4
Strategic Planning and Marketing Planning

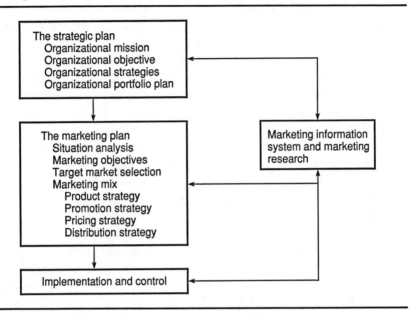

manager may have to consult with other members of top management to determine precisely what the firm is trying to accomplish, both overall and during a specific planning period. For example, a commonly stated organizational objective is "growth." Obviously, this objective is so general that it is practically useless. On the other hand, a statement such as "sustained growth of 14 percent in profits before taxes" provides a quantitative goal which the marketing manager can use for determining desired sales levels and the marketing strategies to achieve them. In addition, the marketing manager must monitor any changes in mission or objectives and adapt marketing strategies to meet them.

Situation Analysis

With a clear understanding of organizational objectives and mission, the marketing manager must then analyze and monitor the position of the firm and, specifically, the marketing department, in terms of its past, present, and future situation. Of course, the future situation is of primary concern. However, an analysis of past trends and current situation are most useful for predicting the future situation.

The situation analysis can be divided into six major areas of concern: (1) the cooperative environment; (2) the competitive environment; (3) the economic environment; (4) the social environment; (5) the political environment; and (6) the legal environment. In analyzing each of these environments, the marketing executive must search both for opportunities and for constraints or threats to achieving objectives. Opportunities for profitable marketing often arise from changes in these environments that bring about new sets of needs to be satisfied. Constraints on marketing activities, such as limited supplies of scarce resources, also arise from these environments.

The Cooperative Environment.   The cooperative environment includes all firms and individuals who have a vested interest in the firm's accomplishing its objectives. Parties of primary interest to the marketing executive in this environment are (1) suppliers; (2) resellers; (3) other departments in the firm; and (4) subdepartments and employees of the marketing department. Opportunities in this environment are primarily related to methods of increasing efficiency. For example, a company might decide to switch from a competitive bid process of obtaining materials to a single source that is located near the company's plant. Likewise, members of the marketing, engineering, and manufacturing functions may utilize a teamwork approach to developing new products versus a sequential approach. Constraints consist of such things as unresolved conflicts and shortages of materials. For example, a company manager may believe that a distributor is doing an insufficient job of promoting and selling the product, or a marketing manager may feel that manufacturing is not taking the steps needed to produce a quality product.

The Competitive Environment.   The competitive environment includes primarily other firms in the industry that rival the organization for both resources and sales. Opportunities in this environment include such things as (1) acquiring competing firms; (2) offering demonstrably better value to consumers and attracting them away from competitors; and (3) in some cases, driving competitors out of the industry. For example, one airline purchases another airline, a bank offers depositors a free checking account with no minimum balance requirements, or a grocery chain engages in an everyday low-price strategy that competitors can't meet. The primary constraints in these environments are the demand stimulation activities of competing firms and the number of consumers who cannot be lured away from competition.

HIGHLIGHT 1–5
Some Important Federal Regulatory Agencies

Agencies	Responsibilities
Federal Trade Commission (FTC)	Enforces laws and develops guidelines regarding unfair business practices.
Food and Drug Administration (FDA)	Enforces laws and develops regulations to prevent distribution and sale of adulterated or misbranded foods, drugs, cosmetics, and hazardous consumer products.
Consumer Product Safety Commission (CPSC)	Enforces the Consumer Product Safety Act—which covers any consumer product not assigned to other regulatory agencies.
Interstate Commerce Commission (ICC)	Regulates interstate rail, bus, truck, and water carriers.
Federal Communications Commission (FCC)	Regulates interstate wire, radio, and television.
Environmental Protection Agency (EPA)	Develops and enforces environmental protection standards.
Office of Consumer Affairs (OCA)	Responds to consumers' complaints.

The Economic Environment. The state of the macroeconomy and changes in it also bring about marketing opportunities and constraints. For example, such factors as high inflation and unemployment levels can limit the size of the market that can afford to purchase a firm's top-of-the-line product. At the same time, these factors may offer a profitable opportunity to develop rental services for such products or to develop less expensive models of the product. In addition, changes in technology can provide significant threats and opportunities.

For example, in the communications industry, technology has developed to a level where it is now possible to provide cable television using phone lines. Obviously such a system poses a severe threat to the existence of the cable industry as it exists today.

The Social Environment. This environment includes general cultural and social traditions, norms, and attitudes. While these values change slowly, such changes often bring about the need for new products and services. For example, a change in values concerning the desirability of large families brought about an opportunity to market better methods of birth control. On the other hand, cultural and social values also place constraints on marketing activities. As a rule, business practices that are contrary to social values become political issues, which are often resolved by legal constraints. For example, public demand for a cleaner environment has caused the government to require that automobile manufacturers' products meet certain average gas mileage and emission standards.

The Political Environment. The political environment includes the attitudes and reactions of the general public, social and business critics, and other organizations, such as the Better Business Bureau. Dissatisfaction with such business and marketing practices as unsafe products, products that waste resources, and unethical sales procedures can have adverse effects on corporation image and customer loyalty. However, adapting business and marketing practices to these attitudes can be an opportunity. For example, these attitudes have brought about markets for such products as unbreakable children's toys, high-efficiency air conditioners, and more economical automobiles.

The Legal Environment. This environment includes a host of federal, state, and local legislation directed at protecting both business competition and consumer rights. In past years, legislation reflected social and political attitudes and has been primarily directed at constraining business practices. Such legislation usually acts as a constraint on business behavior, but again can be viewed as providing opportunities for marketing safer and more efficient products. In recent years, there has been less emphasis on creating new laws for constraining business practices. As an example, deregulation has become more common as evidenced by recent events in the airlines, financial services, and telecommunications industries.

Marketing Planning

In the previous sections it was emphasized that (1) marketing activities must be aligned with organizational objectives; and (2) marketing opportunities are often found by systematically analyzing situational environments. Once an opportunity is recognized, the marketing executive

---

HIGHLIGHT 1–6
Key Elements in the Marketing Plan

People
- What is the target market for the firm's product(s)? What is its size and growth potential?

Profit
- What is the expected profit from implementing the marketing plan? What are the other objectives of the marketing plan, and how will their achievement be evaluated?

Personnel
- What personnel will be involved in implementing the marketing plan? Will only intrafirm personnel be involved, or will other firms, such as advertising agencies or marketing research firms, also be employed?

Product
- What product(s) will be offered? What variations in the product will be offered in terms of style, features, quality, branding, packaging, and terms of sale and service? How should products be positioned in the market?

Price
- What price or prices will products be sold for?

Promotion
- How will information about the firm's offerings be communicated to the target market?

Place
- How, when, and where will the firm's offerings be delivered for sale to the target market?

Policy
- What is the overall marketing policy for dealing with anticipated problems in the marketing plan? How will unanticipated problems be handled?

Period
- For how long a time is the marketing plan to be in effect? When should the plan be implemented, and what is the schedule for executing and evaluating marketing activities?

---

must then plan an appropriate strategy for taking advantage of the opportunity. This process can be viewed in terms of three interrelated tasks: (1) establishing marketing objectives; (2) selecting the target market; and (3) developing the marketing mix.

Establishing Objectives.   Marketing objectives usually are derived from organizational objectives; in some cases where the firm is totally marketing-oriented, the two are identical. In either case objectives must be specified and performance in achieving them should be measurable. Marketing objectives are usually stated as standards of performance (e.g., a certain percentage of market share or sales volume) or as tasks to be achieved by given dates. While such objectives are useful, the marketing concept emphasizes that profits rather than sales should be the overriding objective of the firm and marketing department. In any case, these objectives provide the framework for the marketing plan.

Selecting the Target Markets.   The success of any marketing plan hinges on how well it can identify consumer needs and organize its resources to satisfy them profitably. Thus, a crucial element of the marketing plan is selecting the group or segments of potential consumers the firm is going to serve with each of its products. Four important questions must be answered:

1. What do consumers need?
2. What must be done to satisfy these needs?
3. What is the size of the market?
4. What is its growth profile?

Present target markets and potential target markets are then ranked according to *(a)* profitability; *(b)* present and future sales volume; and *(c)* the match between what it takes to appeal successfully to the segment and the organization's capabilities. Those that appear to offer the greatest potential are selected. Chapters 3, 4, and 5 are devoted to discussing consumer behavior, industrial buyers, and market segmentation.

Developing the Marketing Mix.   The marketing mix is the set of controllable variables that must be managed to satisfy the target market and achieve organizational objectives. These controllable variables are usually classified according to four major decision areas: product, price, promotion, and place (or channels of distribution). The importance of these decision areas cannot be overstated and, in fact, the major portion of this text is devoted to analyzing them. Chapters 6 and 7 are devoted to product and new product strategies; Chapters 8 and 9 to promotion strategies in terms of both nonpersonal and personal selling; Chapter 10 to distribution strategies; and Chapter 11 to pricing strategies. Thus, it should be clear to the reader that the marketing mix is the core of the marketing management process.

The output of the foregoing process is the marketing plan. It is a formal statement of decisions that have been made on marketing activities; it is a blueprint of the objectives, strategies, and tasks to be performed.

Implementation and Control of the Marketing Plan

Implementing the market plan involves putting the plan into action and performing marketing tasks according to the predefined schedule. Even the most carefully developed plans often cannot be executed with perfect timing. Thus, the marketing executive must closely monitor and coordinate implementation of the plan. In some cases, adjustments may have to be made in the basic plan because of changes in any of the situational environments. For example, competitors may introduce a new product. In this event, it may be desirable to speed up or delay implementation of the plan. In almost all cases, some minor adjustments or "fine tuning" will be necessary in implementation.

Controlling the marketing plan involves three basic steps. First, the results of the implemented marketing plan are measured. Second, these results are compared with objectives. Third, decisions are made on whether the plan is achieving objectives. If serious deviations exist between actual and planned results, adjustments may have to be made to redirect the plan toward achieving objectives.

Marketing Information Systems and Marketing Research

Throughout the marketing management process current, reliable, and valid information is needed to make effective marketing decisions. Providing this information is the task of the marketing decision support system (MDSS) and marketing research. These topics are discussed in detail in Chapter 2.

THE RELATIONSHIP BETWEEN THE STRATEGIC PLAN AND THE MARKETING PLAN

Strategic planning is clearly a top-management responsibility. However, marketing managers and mid-level managers in the organization are indirectly involved in the process in two important ways: (1) they often influence the strategic planning process by providing inputs in the form of information and suggestions relating to their particular products, product lines, and areas of responsibility; and (2) they must be aware of what the process of strategic planning involves as well as the results because everything they do, the marketing objectives and strategies they develop, must be derived from the strategic plan. There is rarely a strategic planning question or decision that does not have marketing implications.

Thus, if strategic planning is done properly, it will result in a clearly defined blueprint for managerial action at all levels in the organization. Figure 1–5 illustrates the hierarchy of objectives and strategies using one possible objective and two strategies from the strategic plan (above the dotted line) and illustrating how these relate to elements of the marketing plan (below the dotted line). Many others could have been developed, but our purpose is to illustrate how the marketing plan must be derived from and contribute to the achievement of the strategic plan.

FIGURE 1–5
Relating the Marketing Plan to the Strategic Plan

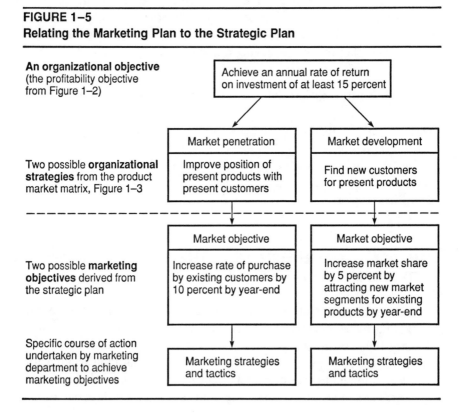

LESSONS FOR THE MANUFACTURER

This chapter provides an overview of the marketing planning process and its role in overall strategic planning. It provides several lessons for manufacturers. First, marketing's role in organizations is primarily externally oriented, and its major function is creating exchanges between the company and organizational buyers and/or consumers. While the relationships among marketing and other functional areas in an organization are clearly important, they are not the major focus of marketing analysis. In this chapter, internal relationships among functional areas are considered to be part of the cooperative environment and analyzed to find opportunities for and threats to achieving organizational objectives. While there has been little research on the relationships among marketing and other functional areas, marketing writers sometimes refer to interfunctional relationships as "internal marketing."

Second, while there is no question that marketing is a very important organizational function and that satisfying consumer needs at a profit (the marketing concept) is an effective organizational strategy, marketing writers and executives sometimes confuse the marketing function with the overall organizational strategy. While the marketing mix includes product, price, promotion, and channels of distribution, it is clear that marketing personnel do not have sole responsibility for making all of the decisions in all of these areas. Clearly, other functional areas, including manufacturing, finance, and human resources, have much to say about what is to be produced, what price should be charged for it, how it is to promoted, and what channels of distribution will be used. Thus, it should not be surprising if marketing personnel do not fully understand the importance of the manufacturing function or the problems faced in manufacturing quality products. Given the increasing importance of cross-functional management systems and teamwork among functions, this insight should be useful for helping manufacturing personnel understand the way marketing personnel think about business problems.

Finally, the information in this chapter provides manufacturing personnel with an overview of the key elements of marketing planning. In addition to establishing marketing objectives, the main tasks of marketing are viewed as selecting appropriate target markets and developing marketing mixes. These tasks are accomplished by developing knowledge of an organization's customers through marketing research, which should provide key inputs into product design and development. In addition, joint efforts by marketing and manufacturing personnel to understand the strengths and weaknesses of the company and its products in comparison with competitors can be valuable for improving technology, distribution, customer satisfaction, and new product rollouts.

APPENDIX: PORTFOLIO MODELS

Portfolio models have become a valuable aid to marketing managers in their efforts to develop effective marketing plans. The use of these models has become widespread as marketing managers face a situation that can best be described as "more products, less time, and less money." More specifically, (1) as the number of products a firm produces expands, the time available for developing marketing plans for each product decreases; (2) at a strategic level, management must make resource allocation decisions across lines of products and, in diversified organizations, across different lines of business; and (3) when resources are limited (which they usually are), the process of deciding which strategic business units (SBUs) to emphasize becomes very complex. In such situations, portfolio models can be very useful.

Portfolio analysis is not a new idea. Banks manage loan portfolios seeking to balance risks and yields. Individuals who are serious investors usually have a portfolio of various kinds of investments (common stocks, preferred stocks, bank accounts, and the like), each with different characteristics of risk, growth, and rate of return. The investor seeks to manage the portfolio to maximize whatever objectives he or she might have. Applying this same idea, most organizations have a wide range of products, product lines, and businesses, each with different growth rates and returns. Similar to the investor, managers should seek a desirable balance among alternative SBUs. Specifically, management should seek to develop a business portfolio that will assure long-run profits and cash flow.

Portfolio models can be used to classify SBUs to determine the future cash contributions that can be expected from each SBU as well as the future resource requirements that each will require. Remember, depending on the organization, an SBU could be a single product, product line, division, or distinct business. While there are many different types of portfolio models, they generally examine the competitive position of the SBU and the chances for improving the SBU's contribution to profitablility and cash flow.

There are several portfolio analysis techniques. Two of the most widely used are discussed in this appendix. To truly appreciate the concept of portfolio analysis, however, we must briefly review the development of portfolio theory.

A REVIEW OF PORTFOLIO THEORY

The interest in developing aids for managers in the selection of strategy was spurred by an organization known as the Boston Consulting Group over 25 years ago. Its ideas, which will be discussed shortly, and many of those that followed were based on the concept of experience curves.

Experience curves are similar in concept to learning curves. Learning curves were developed to express the idea that the number of labor hours it takes to produce one unit of a particular product declines in a predictable manner as the number of units produced increases. Hence, an accurate estimation of how long it takes to produce the hundredth unit is possible if the production time for the 1st and 10th unit are known.

The concept of experience curves was derived from the concept of learning curves. Experience curves were first widely discussed in the ongoing Profit Impact of Marketing Strategies (PIMS) study conducted by the Strategic Planning Institute. The PIMS project studies 150 firms with more than 1,000 individual business units. Its major focus is on determining which environmental and internal firm variables influence the firm's return on investment (ROI) and cash flow. The researchers have concluded that seven categories of variables appear to influence the return on investment: (1) competitive position; (2) industry/market environment; (3) budget allocation; (4) capital structure; (5) production processes; (6) company characteristics; and (7) "change action" factors.[24]

The experience curve includes all costs associated with a product and implies that the per-unit cost of a product should fall, due to cumulative experience, as production volume increases. In a given industry, therefore, the producer with the largest volume and corresponding market share should have the lowest marginal cost. This leader in market share should be able to underprice competitors, discourage entry into the market by potential competitors, and, as a result, achieve an acceptable return on investment. The linkage of experience to cost to price to market share to ROI is exhibited in Figure A–1. The Boston Consulting Group's view of the experience curve led the members to develop what has become known as the BCG Portfolio Model.

---

[24]George S. Day and David B. Montgomery, "Diagnosing the Experience Curve," *Journal of Marketing*, Spring 1983, pp. 44–58.

FIGURE A–1
Experience Curve and Resulting Profit Curve

THE BCG MODEL

The BCG is based on the assumption that profitability and cash flow will be closely related to sales volume. Thus, in this model, SBUs are classified in terms of their relative market share and the growth rate of the market the SBU is in. Using these dimensions, products are either classified as stars, cash cows, dogs, or question marks. The BCG model is presented in Figure A–2.

- *Stars* are SBUs with a high share of a high-growth market. Because high-growth markets attract competition, such SBUs are usually cash users because they are growing and because the firm needs to protect their market share position.
- *Cash cows* are often market leaders, but the market they are in is not growing rapidly. Because these SBUs have a high share of a low-growth market, they are cash generators for the firm.
- *Dogs* are SBUs that have a low share of a low-growth market. If the SBU has a very loyal group of customers, it may be a source of profits and cash. Usually, dogs are not large sources of cash.
- *Question marks* are SBUs with a low share of a high-growth market. They have great potential but require great resources if the firm is to successfully build market share.

As you can see, a firm with 10 SBUs will usually have a portfolio that includes some of each of the above. Having developed this analysis, management

FIGURE A–2
The Boston Consulting Group Portfolio Model

	Relative Market Share	
	High	Low
High	Stars	Question marks
Low	Cash cows	Dogs

Market Growth Rate

must determine what role each SBU should assume. Four basic objectives are possible:

1. *Build share.* This objective sacrifices immediate earnings to improve market share. It is appropriate for promising question marks whose share has to grow if they are ever to become stars.

2. *Hold share.* This objective seeks to preserve the SBU's market share. It is very appropriate for strong cash cows to ensure that they can continue to yield a large cash flow.

3. *Harvest.* Here, the objective seeks to increase the product's short-term cash flow without concern for the long-run impact. It allows market share to decline in order to maximize earnings and cash flow. It is an appropriate objective for weak cash cows, weak question marks, and dogs.

4. *Divest.* This objective involves selling or divesting the SBU because better investment opportunities exist elsewhere. It is very appropriate for dogs and those question marks the firm cannot afford to finance for growth.

Major criticisms of the BCG Portfolio Model have revolved around its focus on market share and market growth as the primary indicators of profitability. In addition, the BCG model assumes that the major source of SBU financing comes from internal means. While the above criticisms are valid ones, the usefulness of the BCG model in assessing the strategic position of SBUs has enabled it to continue to be utilized extensively by managers across all industries.

THE GENERAL ELECTRIC MODEL

Although the BCG model can be useful, it does assume that market share is the sole determinant of an SBU's profitability. Also, in projecting market growth rates, a manager should carefully analyze the factors that influence sales and any opportunities for influencing industry sales.

Some firms have developed alternative portfolio models to incorporate more information about market opportunities and competitive positions. The GE model is one of these. The GE model emphasizes all the potential sources of strength, not just market share, and all of the factors that influence the long-term attractiveness of a market, not just its growth rate. As Figure A–3 indicates, all SBUs are classified in terms of *business strength and industry attractiveness*. Figure A–4 presents a list of items that can be used to position SBUs in the matrix.

Industry attractiveness is a composite index made up of such factors as those listed in Figure A–4. For example: *market size*—the larger the market the more attractive it would be; *market growth*—high-growth markets are more attractive than low-growth markets; *profitability*—high-profit-margin markets are more attractive than low-profit-margin industries.

Business strength is a composite index made up of such factors as those listed in Figure A–4. For example: *market share*—the higher the SBU's share of market, the greater its business strength; *quality leadership*—the higher the SBU's quality compared to competitors, the greater its business strength; *share compared with leading competitor*—the closer the SBU's share to the market leader, the greater its business strength.

Once the SBUs are classified, they are placed on the grid (Figure A–3). Priority "A" SBUs (often called *the green zone*) are those in the three cells at the upper left, indicating that these are SBUs high in both industry attractiveness and business strength, and that the firm should "build share." Priority "B" SBUs (often called *the yellow zone*) are those medium in both industry attractiveness and business strength. The firm will usually decide to "hold share" on these SBUs. Priority "C" SBUs are those in the three cells at the lower right (often called *the red zone*). These SBUs are low in both industry attractiveness and business strength. The firm will usually decide to *harvest* or *divest* these SBUs.

FIGURE A–3
The General Electric Portfolio Model

		Business Strength		
---	---	Strong	Average	Weak
	High	A	A	B
Industry Attractiveness	Medium	A	B	C
	Low	B	C	C

FIGURE A–4
Components of Industry Attractiveness and Business Strength at GE

Industry Attractiveness	Business Strength

Market size
Market growth
Profitability
Cyclicality
Ability to recover from inflation
World scope
	Market position:
	  Domestic market share
	  World market share
	  Share growth
	  Share compared with leading competitor
	Competitive strengths:
	  Quality leadership
	  Technology
	  Marketing
	  Relative profitability

Whether the BCG, the GE model, or a variation of these models is used, some analyses must be made of the firm's current portfolio of SBUs as part of any strategic planning effort. Marketing must get its direction from the organization's strategic plan.

PART 2

UNDERSTANDING TARGET MARKETS

CHAPTER 2

MARKETING DECISION SUPPORT SYSTEMS AND MARKETING RESEARCH

It is obvious that the American business system has been capable of producing a vast quantity of goods and services. However, in the past two decades the American business system has also become extremely capable of producing massive amounts of information and data. In fact, the last decade has often been referred to as the "Information Era" and the "Age of Information."

This situation is a complete reverse from what previously existed. In the past, marketing executives did not have to deal with an over-supply of information for decision-making purposes. In most cases they gathered what little data they could and hoped that their decisions would be reasonably good. In fact, it was for this reason that marketing research came to be recognized as an extremely valuable staff function. It provided marketing management with information where previously there had been little or none and, thereby, alleviated to a great extent the paucity of information for marketing decision making. However, marketing management in many companies has failed to store marketing information, and much valuable marketing information is lost when marketing personnel change jobs or companies.

Today, marketing managers often feel buried by the deluge of information and data that comes across their desks. How can it be, then, that so many marketing managers complain that they have insufficient or inappropriate information on which to base their everyday operating decisions? Specifically, most of these complaints fall into the following categories:

1. There is too much marketing information of the wrong kind and not enough of the right kind.

2. Marketing information is so dispersed throughout the company that great effort is usually needed to locate simple facts.
3. Vital information is sometimes suppressed by other executives or subordinates for personal reasons.
4. Vital information often arrives too late to be useful.
5. Information often arrives in a form that provides no idea of its accuracy, and there is no one to turn to for confirmation.

Marketing management requires current, reliable information before it can function efficiently. Because of this need, and the information explosion of the past decade, many large corporations have banked their total marketing knowledge in computers. Well-designed marketing decision support systems (MDSS) can eliminate corporate losses of millions of dollars from lost information and lost opportunities.

This chapter is concerned with marketing decision support systems and marketing research. Since the two concepts are easily confused, it is important initially to distinguish one from the other. In general terms,

---

HIGHLIGHT 2–1
Suggestions for Developing an MDSS

The following is a list of suggestions to aid in the effective implementation of an MDSS.

1. Develop small systems first before coordinating them into an overall system.
2. Develop systems relevant to current management practices and organizational structures.
3. Develop decision support system skills internally and do not rely too heavily on outside experts.
4. Involve users of the system in its design and implementation.
5. Build a flexible system to meet the information needs of various levels of management and types of managers.
6. Monitor early usage of the system to ensure success and make sure future users of the system are aware of the success.
7. Build the system in an evolutionary manner, adding complex models only after data storage and retrieval systems are successfully in place.

Source: From *Principles of Marketing*, 3rd ed., by Thomas C. Kinnear and Kenneth L. Bernhardt. Copyright © 1990, 1986 by Scott, Foresman and Company. Reprinted by permission of HarperCollins Publishers.

a marketing decision support system is concerned with the continuous gathering, processing, and utilization of pertinent information for decision-making purposes. The primary objective of the MDSS is to ensure that right information is available to the right decision maker at the right time. Marketing research, on the other hand, usually focuses on a specific marketing problem with the objective of providing information for a particular decision. As such, marketing research is an integral part of the overall marketing decision support system but usually is project oriented rather than a continuous process.

MARKETING DECISION SUPPORT SYSTEMS

A marketing decision support system is a new type of marketing information system. This type of information system is designed to support all phases of marketing decision making—from problem identification to choosing the relevant data to work with, picking the approach to be used in making the decision, and evaluating alternative courses of action. This type of information system can be defined as:

> a coordinated collection of data, system tools, and techniques with supporting software and hardware by which an organization gathers and interprets relevant information from business and the environment and turns it into a basis for making management decisions.[1]

Figure 2–1 illustrates the concept of an MDSS. There are two main changes depicted in this figure: (1) the conversion of data to information; and (2) the conversion of information to action. The first conversion is the task of the marketing information center, while the second is the major purpose of marketing decision making.

The Marketing Information Center

Although the growth of the concept of a marketing decision support system has been fairly recent, most experts agree that a single, separate marketing information center must exist to centralize responsibility for marketing information within the firm. This is necessary because both

---

[1]Peter D. Bennett, ed., *Dictionary of Marketing Terms* (Chicago: American Marketing Association, 1988), p. 53.

FIGURE 2–1
The Marketing Decision Support System

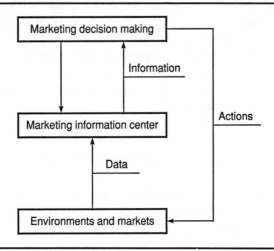

the users and suppliers of such information are widely scattered throughout the organization, and some unit is needed to oversee the entire operation.

The general purpose of this organizational unit is to maintain, as
well as to improve and upgrade, the accuracy, completeness, and timeliness of information for marketing management decisions. Operationally,
this means that the information center must gather raw data from various
environments and markets and process them so they can be obtained and
analyzed by marketing executives. Data must be gathered from both
internal and external sources. Internally, such data as sales, costs, and
profits, as well as other company reports, need to be converted to information and stored in the computer. Externally, data from trade journals,
magazines, newspapers, government publications, and other sources of
pertinent information used by marketing executives for decision making
also must be converted and stored.

A critical point here is that the MDSS converts raw data into information that marketing management can actually use for making intelligent
decisions. An MDSS must produce information in a form marketing
executives can understand, when it is needed, and have it under the
manager's control. In other words, a key distinction that separates an
MDSS from other types of marketing information systems is that an
MDSS has the direct and primary objective of supporting marketing

---

FIGURE 2–2
Examples of MISs and MDSSs

A Marketing Information System (MIS) at Savin Corporation

Savin Corporation has installed a computer terminal in each of its warehouses to keep track of every item in its inventory. The system identifies the quantity on hand, the location and movement of stock, and the status of all orders. The system is used to plan shipments, locate single items in inventory, and locate customer records.

*A Marketing Information System (MIS) at United Services
Automobile Association*

The United Services Automobile Association, the nation's eighth largest insurer of passenger cars, purchased a $4 million system that now contains virtually all of the company's written records. When a customer reports an accident, an adjuster can call up the customer's file, check the coverage, and keep track of all the paperwork through the final settlement of the claim. The company figures that it used to take five people a day-and-a-half to perform tasks that one person now handles in 20 minutes.

A Marketing Decision Support System (MDSS) at Crocker National Bank

The Crocker National Bank in San Francisco has purchased desk-top terminals for most of its top-level executives. Each terminal is tapped into the huge computers that record all bank transactions. The executives are able to make comparisons, analyze problems, and prepare charts and tables in response to simple commands. For example, they can analyze emerging trends in deposits and loans and monitor the influence of various interest rates and loan maturities.

A Marketing Decision Support System (MDSS) at Gould, Inc.

Gould, Inc., has developed a decision support system to help managers retrieve, manipulate, and display information needed for making decisions. The system combines large visual display and video terminals with a computerized information system. The system is designed solely to assist managers to make comparisons and analyze problems for decision-making purposes. The MDSS instantly prepares tables and color charts in response to simple commands.

---

management decision making.[2] Figure 2–2 provides examples of two firms with conventional MISs and two firms with MDSSs to illustrate this important difference.

---

[2]See Gilbert A. Churchill, Jr., *Marketing Research: Methodological Foundations* (Hinsdale, Ill.: Dryden Press, 1987), chap. 18. Also see George M. Zinkhan, Erich A. Joachimsthaler, and Thomas C. Kinnear, "Individual Differences and Marketing Decision Support System Usage and Satisfaction," *Journal of Marketing Research*, May 1987, pp. 208–14.

Marketing Decision Making

Earlier we stated that the main purpose of marketing executives is to convert information to actions through the process of decision making. Note that, in Figure 2–1, two up-and-down arrows connect marketing decision making with the marketing information center. These arrows represent an important aspect of the MDSS (i.e., it is an *interactive system* in which marketing executives sit at computer terminals and actively analyze information and convert it to actions).

In previous types of marketing information systems, the information center often attempted to prepare reports to meet the individual needs of different marketing executives at different levels in the organization. More often than not, such attempts provided too much information of the wrong kind and not enough information of the right kind. However, in addition to the flexibility, timeliness, and detail provided by an MDSS, such problems do not occur because marketing executives themselves retrieve and manipulate the information.

Many experts believe that, in a few years, most marketing executives will be sharing their desk space with a personal computer. Personal computers have the capability of increasing both the productivity of marketing managers and the quality of their decisions. First, the capacity of the computers to extract, process, and analyze data swiftly and accurately is awesome. Second, computers have gotten smaller, faster, and smarter in a shorter time than any other technological innovation in history. A desktop personal computer can solve ordinary arithmetic problems 18 times faster than the world's first large-scale computer built less than 50 years ago (weighing 30 tons). Finally, computers have become extremely inexpensive in comparison to earlier models. Just 30 years ago a medium-sized computer cost a quarter of a million dollars. A firm can now buy a desk-top computer with three times the memory capacity for less than $2,000. While it may take some time for marketing executives to learn to use the equipment, the potential for better, more profitable decision making may outweigh the brief inconvenience.

MARKETING RESEARCH

Marketing research should be an integral part of a marketing decision support system. In essence, marketing research combines insights and intuition with the research process to provide information for making marketing decisions. In general, marketing research can be defined as:

> the function that links the consumer, customer, and public to the marketer through information—information used to identify and define marketing opportunities and problems; generate, refine, and evaluate marketing actions; monitor marketing performance; and improve understanding of marketing as a process. Marketing research specifies the information required to address these issues; designs the method for collecting information; manages and implements the data collection process; analyzes the results; and communicates the findings and their implications.[3]

Today's marketing managers should understand the role of research in decision making. It cannot be overstated that *marketing research is an aid to decision making and not a substitute for it.* In other words, marketing research does not make decisions but it can substantially increase the probability that the best decision will be made. Unfortunately, too often marketing managers view marketing research reports as the final answer to their problems. Instead, marketing managers should recognize that (1) even the most carefully controlled research projects can be fraught with pitfalls and (2) decisions should be made in the light of their own knowledge and experience and other factors that are not explicitly considered in the research project. The problems that the Coca-Cola Company faced when it dropped its original formula and introduced New Coke were brought about by both faulty marketing research and a failure of Coke executives to use sound judgment in interpreting the research results.[4]

Although marketing research does not make decisions, it is a direct means of reducing risks associated with managing the marketing mix and long-term marketing planning. In fact, a company's return on investment from marketing research is a function of the extent to which research output reduces the risk inherent in decision making. For example, marketing research can play an important role in reducing new product failure costs by evaluating consumer acceptance of a product prior to full-scale introduction.

---

[3]Peter D. Bennett, ed., *Dictionary of Marketing Terms* (Chicago: American Marketing Association, 1988), pp. 117–18.

[4]For a complete discussion of these issues, see Robert F. Hartley, *Marketing Mistakes,* 4th ed. (New York: John Wiley & Sons, 1989), pp. 221–36.

HIGHLIGHT 2–2
Marketing Research that Influenced Marketing Strategies

Marketing research can be a useful aid in decision making. Below are several examples of marketing research that helped firms develop their marketing strategies.

Eastman Kodak Company

The Eastman Kodak Company was faced with flat sales and needed to devise a strategy to improve sales performance. The company knew that amateur photographers goof on more than 2 billion pictures a year and had its technical researchers look at 10,000 photos to see what kinds of things users were doing wrong. The study led to a number of design ideas for the Kodak disc camera that helped eliminate almost one half of the out-of-focus and underexposed shots. The disc camera has been one of the most successful products in Kodak history.

M&M/Mars Candy Company

In an attempt to determine the proper weight for its candy bars, M&M/Mars Candy Company conducted a 12-month test in 150 stores. For the test it altered the size of its products across the stores but kept the prices constant. It found that, in those stores where the dimensions were increased, sales went up 20 to 30 percent. As a result of this research, the company decided to change almost its entire product line.

American Express

American Express was disappointed with its inability to attract female cardholders. A group of American Express executives listened in on a market research panel of women discussing credit cards. The panel members indicated that they were very familiar with American Express and thought highly of it, but few saw it as a card for them. It seemed that the prestige image promoted for years using various celebrities appealed more to men than to women. Based on this research, the company developed a new ad campaign that did away with celebrities and emphasized that American Express is "part of a lot of interesting lives."

Mercedes Benz

When Mercedes Benz made its initial foray into the U.S. market, it conducted consumer surveys. The research showed that people wanted a no-nonsense car with distinct quality, engineering, design, and performance. This research served as the basis for selecting models to be introduced in the United States and also influenced print ads to emphasize facts, rather than gimmickry.

Source: Adapted from Gilbert A. Churchill, Jr., *Marketing Research: Methodological Foundations,* 4th ed. (Hinsdale, Ill.: Dryden Press, 1987), pp. 3–4.

In a highly competitive economy a firm's survival depends on the marketing manager's ability to make sound decisions, to outguess competitors, to anticipate consumer needs, to forecast business conditions, and to plan for company growth. Marketing research is one tool to help accomplish these tasks. Research is also vital for managerial control, because without appropriate data, the validity of past decisions on the performance of certain elements in the marketing system (e.g., the performance of the sales force or advertising) cannot be evaluated reliably.

Although many of the technical aspects of marketing research, such as sampling design or statistical analysis, can be delegated to experts, the process of marketing research begins and ends with the marketing manager. In the beginning of a research project it is the marketing manager's responsibility to work with researchers to define the problem carefully. When the research project is completed, the application of the results in terms of decision alternatives rests primarily with the marketing manager.[5] For these reasons, and since the marketing manager must be able to communicate with researchers throughout the course of the project, it is vital for managers to understand the research process from the researcher's point of view.

The Research Process

Marketing research can be viewed as a systematic process for obtaining information to aid in decision making. Although there are many different types of marketing research, the framework illustrated in Figure 2–3 represents a general approach to defining the research process. Each element of this process will be briefly discussed.

Purpose of the Research
The first step in the research process is to determine explicitly the purpose of the research. This may well be much more difficult than it sounds. Quite often a situation or problem is recognized as needing research, yet

---

[5]For a discussion of the use of research findings in marketing decision making, see Rohit Deshpande, "The Organizational Context of Market Research Use," *Journal of Marketing*, Fall 1982, pp. 91–101. Also see Rohit Deshpande and Gerald Zaltman, "A Comparison of Factors Affecting Use of Marketing Information in Consumer and Industrial Firms," *Journal of Marketing Research*, February 1987, pp. 114–19.

FIGURE 2–3
The Five Ps of the Research Process

the nature of the problem is not clear or well defined. Thus, an investigation is required to clarify the problem or situation. This investigation includes such things as interviewing corporate executives, reviewing records, and studying existing information related to the problem. At the end of this stage the researcher should know (1) the current situation; (2) the nature of the problem; and (3) the specific question or questions the research is to find answers to—that is, why the research is being conducted.

Plan of the Research
The first step in the research plan is to formalize the specific purpose of the study. Once this is accomplished, the sequencing of tasks and responsibilities for accomplishing the research are spelled out in detail. This stage is critical since decisions are made that determine the who, what, when, where, and how of the research study.

An initial decision in this stage of the process is the type of data that will be required. The two major types of data are primary and secondary. Primary data is data that must be collected from original sources for the purposes of the study. Secondary data is information that has been previously collected for some other purpose but can be used for the purposes of the study.

HIGHLIGHT 2–3
A Comparison of Five Methods of Marketing Research

	Definition	Advantages	Disadvantages
Observation	Systematic description of behavior.	Documents the variety of on-going behavior. Unobtrusive observation captures what happens naturally, when no experimenter is present.	Time consuming. Requires careful training of observers. Observer may interfere with behavior and alter what is happening.
Case study	In-depth description of a single person, family, or organization.	Focuses on the complexity and uniqueness of the individual.	May lack generalizability. Data may reflect the interests and perspective of the investigator.
Survey research	Asking questions to a comparatively large number of people about their opinions, attitudes, or behavior.	Permits data collection from large numbers of subjects.	The way questions are asked can influence the answers. Survey response may not be directly related to behavior.
Experimentation	An analysis of cause-effect relations by manipulating some conditions and holding others constant.	Permits statements about causality. Permits control and isolation of specific variables.	Laboratory findings may not be applicable to other settings.
Correlational research	Assessing the strength of relationship among variables.	Determines whether information on variable A can be used to predict variable B.	Difficult to infer causality. Cannot detect nonlinear relationships.

Source: Adapted from P. R. Newman and B. M. Newman, *Principles of Psychology* (Homewood, Ill.: Dorsey Press, 1983), p. 28.

If the research project requires primary data, decisions have to be made concerning the following issues:

1. How will the data be collected? Personal interviews? Mail questionnaires? Telephone interviews?
2. How much data is needed?
3. What measures will be used, and how will they be checked for reliability and validity?[6]
4. Who will design the measures and collect the data?
5. Where will the data be collected? Nationally? Regionally? Locally? At home? At work?
6. When and for how long will data be collected?

If secondary data will suffice for the research question(s), similar decisions have to be made. However, since the data are already in existence, the task is much simpler (and cheaper). For example, most of the sources of secondary data listed in Section 5 of this text are available in a public or university library.

In addition to determining data requirements, the research plan also specifies the method of data analysis, procedures for processing and interpreting the data, and the structure of the final report. In other words, the entire research project is sequenced, and responsibility for the various tasks is assigned. Thus, the research plan provides the framework for the coordination and control of the entire project.

When the research plan is fully specified, the time and money costs of the project are estimated. If management views the benefits of the research as worth the costs, the project proceeds to the next phase. A sample research plan is presented in Figure 2–4.

Performance of the Research
Performance is used here in the narrow sense: of preparing for data collection and actually collecting the data. It is at this point that the research plan is put into action.

---

[6]For sources of information and discussion of reliability and validity issues, see J. Paul Peter and Gilbert A. Churchill, Jr., "The Relationships among Research Design Choices and Psychometric Properties of Rating Scales: A Meta-Analysis," *Journal of Marketing Research,* February 1986, pp. 1–10.

HIGHLIGHT 2–4
Types of Questions that Marketing Research Can Help Answer

I. *Planning.*
   A. What kinds of people buy our product? Where do they live? How much do they earn? How many of them are there?
   B. Is the market for our product increasing or decreasing? Are there promising markets that we have not yet reached?
   C. Are there markets for our products in other countries?

II. *Problem Solving.*
   A. Product
      1. Which, of various product designs, is likely to be the most successful?
      2. What kind of packaging should we use for our product?
   B. Price
      1. What price should we charge for our new product?
      2. As production costs decline, should we lower our prices or try to develop a higher-quality product?
   C. Place
      1. Where, and by whom, should our product be sold?
      2. What kinds of incentives should we offer to induce dealers to push our product?
   D. Promotion
      1. How effective is our advertising? Are the right people seeing it? How does it compare with the competition's advertising?
      2. What kinds of sales promotional devices—coupons, contests, rebates, and so forth—should we employ?
      3. What combination of media—newspapers, radio, television, magazines—should we use?

III. *Control.*
   A. What is our market share overall? In each geographic area? By each customer type?
   B. Are customers satisfied with our product? How is our record for service? Are there many returns?
   C. How does the public perceive our company? What is our reputation with dealers?

Source: Gilbert A. Churchill, Jr., *Basic Marketing Research* (Hinsdale, Ill.: Dryden Press, 1988), p. 8.

The preparations obviously depend on the type of data desired and method of data collection. For primary research, questions and questionnaire items must be pretested and validated. In addition, preparations for

---

FIGURE 2–4
Sample Research Plan

I. *Tentative project title.*
II. *Statement of the problem.*
One or two sentences to outline or to describe the general problem under consideration.
III. *Define and delimit the problem.*
Here the writer states the purpose(s) and scope of the problem. *Purpose* refers to goals or objectives. Closely related to this is *justification.* Sometimes this is a separate step, depending on the urgency of the task. *Scope* refers to the actual limitations of the research effort; in other words, what is *not* going to be investigated. Here is the point where the writer spells out the various hypotheses to be investigated or the questions to be answered.
IV. *Outline.*
Generally, this is a tentative framework for the entire project by topics. It should be flexible enough to accommodate unforeseen difficulties, show statistical tables in outline form, and also show graphs planned. Tables should reflect the hypotheses.
V. *Method and data sources.*
The types of data to be sought (primary, secondary) are briefly identified. A brief explanation of how the necessary information or data will be gathered (e.g., surveys, experiments, library sources) is given. *Sources* refer to the actual depositories for the information, whether from government publications, company records, actual people, and so forth. If measurements are involved, such as consumers' attitudes, the techniques for making such measurements are stated. All of the techniques (statistical and nonstatistical) should be mentioned and discussed about their relevance for the task at hand. The nature of the problem will probably indicate the types of techniques to be employed, such as factor analysis, depth interviews, or focus groups.
VI. *Sample design.*
This provides the limits of the universe or population to be studied and how it will be listed (or prepared). The writer specifies the population, states the sample size, whether sample stratification will be employed, and how. If a nonrandom sample is to be used, the justification and the type of sampling strategy to be employed, such as convenience sample, are stated.
VII. *Data collection forms.*
The forms to be employed in gathering the data should be discussed and, if possible, included in the plan. For surveys, this will involve either a questionnaire or an interview schedule. For other types of methods, the forms could include IBM cards, inventory forms, psychological tests, and so forth. The plan should state how these instruments have been or will be validated, and the reader should be given some indication of their reliability and validity.
VIII. *Personnel requirements.*
This provides a complete list of all personnel who will be required, indicating exact jobs, time duration, and expected rate of pay. Assignments should be made indicating each person's responsibility and authority.

FIGURE 2–4   *(concluded)*

IX. *Phases of the study with a time schedule.*
This is a detailed outline of the plan to complete the study. The entire study should be broken into workable pieces. Then, considering the person who will be employed in each phase, their qualifications and experience, and so forth, the time in months for the job is estimated. Some jobs may overlap. This plan will help in estimating the work months required. The overall time for the project should allow for time overlaps on some jobs.
Illustration:
1. Preliminary investigation—two months.
2. Final test of questionnaire—one month.
3. Sample selection—one month.
4. Mail questionnaires, field follow-up, and so forth—four months.
5. Additional phases.
X. *Tabulation plans.*
This is a discussion of editing and proof of questionnaires, card punching, and the type of computer analysis. An outline of some of the major tables required is very important.
XI. *Cost estimate for doing the study.*
Personnel requirements are combined with time on different phases to estimate total personnel costs. Estimates on travel, materials, supplies, drafting, computer charges, and printing and mailing costs must also be included. If an overhead charge is required by the administration, it should be calculated and added to the subtotal of the above items.

---

mail surveys include such things as sample selection, questionnaire printing, and envelope and postage considerations. For telephone or personal interviews, such things as interviewer scoring forms, instructions, and scheduling must be taken care of. For secondary data, such things as data recording procedures and instructions need attention.

In terms of actual data collection, a cardinal rule is to obtain and record the maximal amount of useful information, subject to the constraints of time, money, and interviewee privacy. Failure to obtain and record data clearly can obviously lead to a poor research study, while failure to consider the rights of subjects or interviewees raises both ethical and practical questions. Thus, both the objectives and constraints of data collection must be closely monitored.

Processing Research Data

Processing research data includes the preparation of data for analysis and the actual analysis of the data. Preparations include such things as editing and structuring the data, and perhaps coding and preparing it for computer analysis. Data sets should be clearly labeled to ensure that they are not misinterpreted or misplaced. The data are then analyzed according to the procedure specified in the research plan and are interpreted according to standard norms of the analysis.

Preparation of Research Report

The research report is a complete statement of everything accomplished relative to the research project and includes a writeup of each of the previous stages. Figure 2–5 illustrates the types of questions the researcher should ask prior to submitting the report to the appropriate decision maker.

The importance of clear and unambiguous report writing cannot be overstressed, since the research is meaningless if it cannot be communicated. Often the researcher must trade off the apparent precision of scientific jargon for everyday language that the decision maker can understand. It should always be remembered that research is an aid for decision making and not a substitute for it.

Problems in the Research Process

Although the foregoing discussion presented the research process in a simplified framework, this does not mean that conducting research is a simple task. There are many problems and difficulties that must be overcome if a research study is to be of value. For example, consider the difficulties in one type of marketing research, *test marketing*.

The major goal of most test marketing is to measure new product sales on a limited basis where competitive retaliation and other factors are allowed to operate freely. In this way, future sales potential can be estimated. Test market research is a vital element in new product marketing. Listed below are a number of problem areas that can invalidate test market study results.[7]

1. Representative test areas are improperly selected from the standpoint of size, geographical location, population characteristics, and promotional facilities.

---

[7]For a discussion of some general problems in marketing research, see Alan G. Sawyer and J. Paul Peter, "The Significance of Statistical Significance Testing in Marketing Research," *Journal of Marketing Research,* May 1983, pp. 122–33.

FIGURE 2–5
Six Criteria for Evaluating Marketing Research Reports

---

1. Under what conditions was the study made? The report should provide:
   a. Full statement of the problems to be investigated by the study.
   b. Source of financing for the study.
   c. Names of organizations participating in the study, together with their qualifications and vested interests.
   d. Exact time period covered in data collection.
   e. Definitions of terms employed.
   f. Copies of data collection instruments.
   g. Source of collateral data.
   h. Complete statement of method.
2. Has the questionnaire been well designed?
3. Has the interviewing been adequately and reliably done?
4. Has the best sampling plan been followed, or has the best experimental design been used?
5. Was there adequate supervision and control over the editing, coding, and tabulating?
6. Have the conclusions been drawn in a logical and forthright manner?

---

2. Sample size and design are incorrectly formulated because of ignorance, budget constraints, or an improper understanding of the test problem.

3. Pretest measurements of competitive brand's sales are not made, which means that the researcher has no realistic base to use for comparison purposes.

4. Attempts are not made to control the cooperation and support of test stores. Consequently, certain package sizes might not be carried, or pricing policies might not be adhered to.

5. Test market products are overadvertised or overpromoted during the test.

6. The full effect of such sales-influencing factors as sales force, season, weather conditions, competitive retaliation, shelf space, and so forth are not fully evaluated.

7. Market test periods are too short to determine whether the product is fully accepted by consumers or only tried on a limited basis.

Similar problems could be listed for almost any type of marketing research. However, the important point to be recognized is that careful planning, coordination, and control are imperative if the research study is to accomplish its objective.

HIGHLIGHT 2–5
Techniques of Collecting Survey Data

Personal Interview	Mail	Telephone
Advantages		
Most flexible means of obtaining data.	Wider and more representative distribution of sample possible.	Representative and wider distribution of sample possible.
Identity of respondent known.	No field staff.	No field staff.
Nonresponse generally very low.	Cost per questionnaire relatively low.	Cost per response relatively low.
Distribution of sample controllable in all respects.	People may be more frank on certain issues (e.g., sex).	Control over interviewer bias easier; supervisor present essentially at interview.
	No interviewer bias; answers in respondent's own words.	Quick way of obtaining information.
	Respondent can answer at his or her leisure, has time to "think things over."	Nonresponse generally very low. Callbacks simple and economical.
	Certain segments of population more easily approachable.	
Disadvantages		
Likely to be most expensive of all.	Bias due to nonresponse often indeterminate.	Interview period not likely to exceed five minutes.
Headaches of interviewer supervision and control.	Control over questionnaire may be lost.	Questions must be short and to the point; probes difficult to handle.
Dangers of interviewer bias and cheating.	Interpretation of omissions difficult.	Certain types of questions cannot be used.
	Cost per return may be high if nonresponse very large.	Nontelephone owners as well as those without listed numbers cannot be reached.
	Certain questions, such as extensive probes, cannot be asked.	
	Only those interested in the subject may reply.	
	Not always clear who replies.	
	Certain segments of population not approachable (e.g., illiterates).	
	Probably slowest of all.	

LESSONS FOR THE MANUFACTURER

A marketing decision support system is that part of the overall decision support system that serves the marketing function. Much of the information in this system, including consumer profiles, sales and profit information, and environmental trend analysis, is clearly useful for manufacturing decision making. For example, analysis of sales and profit information is critical for making sales forecasts, which influence production scheduling and other production decisions. Analysis of consumer profiles, including their attitudes toward the company's products and those of competitors, is critical for determining what types of product alterations could be useful for attracting and holding customers.

The role of marketing research in successful organizations is critical for manufacturing. It has become so important that many manufacturing companies now have their own marketing research departments rather than hiring outside companies to do their research work. Marketing research provides a major input into decisions involving product characteristics, design, and engineering since many companies recognize that producing what consumers want is more efficient and effective than producing products and then seeing whether consumers will purchase them. Leading edge companies, like DEC, have created teams of marketing, engineering, and manufacturing personnel to better integrate the processes involved in researching markets and designing and building products that customers want. This approach helps avoid problems that occur when each function performs its tasks independently and has a "throw it over the wall" mentality.

ADDITIONAL READINGS

Aaker, David A., and George S. Day. *Marketing Research*. 4th ed. New York: John Wiley, 1990.

Boyd, Harper W., Jr.; Ralph Westfall; and Stanley F. Stasch. *Marketing Research: Text and Cases*. 7th ed. Homewood, Ill.: Richard D. Irwin, 1989.

Churchill, Gilbert A., Jr. *Marketing Research: Methodological Foundations*. 4th ed. Hinsdale, Ill.: Dryden Press, 1987.

————. *Basic Marketing Research*. Hinsdale, Ill.: Dryden Press, 1988.

Dillon, William R.; Thomas J. Madden; and Neil H. Firtle. *Marketing Research in a Marketing Environment*. 2nd ed. Homewood, Ill.: Richard D. Irwin, 1990.

Green, Paul E.; Donald S. Tull; and Gerald Albaum. *Research for Marketing Decisions*. 5th ed. Englewood Cliffs, N.J.: Prentice Hall, Inc., 1988.

Peterson, Robert A. *Marketing Research*. 2nd ed. Plano, Tex.: Business Publications Inc., 1988.

Tull, Donald S., and Del I. Hawkins. *Marketing Research: Measurement and Method*. 5th ed. New York: Macmillan, 1990.

CHAPTER 3

CONSUMER BEHAVIOR

The marketing concept emphasizes that profitable marketing begins with the discovery and understanding of consumer needs and then develops a marketing mix to satisfy these needs. Thus, an understanding of consumers and their needs and purchasing behavior is integral to successful marketing.

Unfortunately, there is no single theory of consumer behavior that can totally explain why consumers behave as they do. Instead, there are numerous theories, models, and concepts making up the field. In addition, the majority of these notions have been borrowed from a variety of other disciplines, such as sociology, psychology, social psychology, and economics, and must be integrated to understand consumer behavior.

This chapter examines some of the many influences on consumer behavior in terms of the buying process. The reader may wish to examine Figure 3–1 closely, since it provides the basis for this discussion.

The chapter will proceed by first examining the buying process and then discussing the group, product class, and situational influences on this process.

THE BUYING PROCESS

The buying process can be viewed as a series of five stages: need, recognition, alternative search, alternative evaluation, purchase decision, and postpurchase feelings. In this section, each of these stages will be discussed. It should be noted at the outset that this is a general model for depicting a logical sequence of buying behavior. Clearly, individuals will vary from this model because of personal differences in such things as personality, self-concept, subjective perceptions of information, the product, and the purchasing situation. However, the model provides a useful framework for organizing our discussion of consumer behavior.

FIGURE 3–1
An Overview of the Buying Process

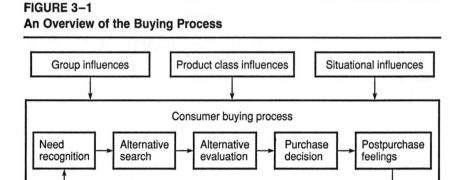

Need Recognition

The starting point for this model of the buying process is the recognition of an unsatisfied need by the consumer. Any number of either internal or external stimuli may activate needs or wants and recognition of them. Internal stimuli are such things as feeling hungry and wanting some food, feeling a headache coming on and wanting some Excedrin, or feeling bored and looking for a movie to go to. External stimuli are such things as seeing a McDonald's sign and then feeling hungry or seeing a sale sign for winter parkas and remembering that last year's coat is worn out.

It is the task of marketing managers to find out what needs and wants a particular product can and does satisfy and what unsatisfied needs and wants consumers have for which a new product could be developed. In order to do so, marketing managers should understand what types of needs consumers may have. A well-known classification of needs was developed many years ago by Abraham Maslow and includes five types.[1] Maslow's view is that lower-level needs, starting with physiological and safety must be attended to before higher-level needs can be satisfied. Maslow's hierarchy is described below.

---

[1]A. H. Maslow, *Motivation and Personality* (New York: Harper & Row, 1954); also see James F. Engel, Roger D. Blackwell, and Paul W. Miniard, *Consumer Behavior,* 6th ed. (Hinsdale: Dryden Press, 1990), chap. 17 for further discussion of need recognition.

Physiological Needs. This category consists of the primary needs of the human body, such as food, water, and sex. Physiological needs will dominate when all needs are unsatisfied. In such a case, none of the other needs will serve as a basis for motivation.

Safety Needs. With the physiological needs met, the next higher level assumes importance. Safety needs consist of such things as protection from physical harm, ill health, economic disaster, and avoidance of the unexpected.

Belongingness and Love Needs. These needs are related to the social and gregarious nature of humans and the need for companionship. This level in the hierarchy is the point of departure from the physical or quasi-physical needs of the two previous levels. Nonsatisfaction of this level of need may affect the mental health of the individual.

Esteem Needs. These needs consist of both the need for the self-awareness of importance to others (self-esteem) and actual esteem from others. Satisfaction of these needs leads to feelings of self-confidence and prestige.

Self-actualization Needs. This need can be defined as the desire to become more and more what one is, to become everything one is capable of becoming. This means that the individual will fully realize the potentialities of given talents and capabilities. Maslow assumes that satisfaction of these needs is only possible after the satisfaction of all the needs lower in the hierarchy.

While the hierarchy arrangement of Maslow presents a convenient explanation, it is probably more realistic to assume that the various need categories overlap. Thus, in affluent societies, many products may satisfy more than one of these needs. For example, gourmet foods may satisfy both the basic physiological need of hunger as well as esteem and status needs for those who serve gourmet foods to their guests.

Alternative Search

Once a need is recognized, the individual then searches for alternatives for satisfying the need. There are five basic sources from which the individual can collect information for a particular purchase decision.

1. *Internal sources*. In most cases the individual has had some previous experience in dealing with a particular need. Thus, the individual will usually "search" through whatever stored information and experience is in his or her mind for dealing with the need. If a previously acceptable product for satisfying the need is remembered, the individual may purchase with little or no additional information search or evaluation. This is quite common for routine or habitual purchases.

2. *Group sources*. A common source of information for purchase decisions comes from communication with other people, such as family, friends, neighbors, and acquaintances. Generally, some of these (i.e., relevant others) are selected which the individual views as having particular expertise for the purchase decision. Although it may be quite difficult for the marketing manager to determine the exact nature of this source of information, group sources of information often are considered to be the most powerful influence on purchase decisions.

3. *Marketing sources*. Marketing sources of information include such factors as advertising, salespeople, dealers, packaging, and displays. Generally, this is the primary source of information about a particular product. These sources of information will be discussed in detail in the promotion chapters of this text.

4. *Public sources*. Public sources of information include publicity, such as a newspaper article about the product, and independent ratings of the product, such as *Consumer Reports*. Here product quality is a highly important marketing management consideration, since such articles and reports often discuss such features as dependability and service requirements.

5. *Experiential sources*. Experiential sources refer to handling, examining, and perhaps trying the product while shopping. This usually requires an actual shopping trip by the individual and may be the final source consulted before purchase.

Information collected from these sources is then processed by the consumer.[2] However, the exact nature of how individuals process

---

[2]For a detailed review of research on external search, see Sharon E. Beatty and Scott M. Smith, "External Search Effort: An Investigation Across Several Product Categories," *Journal of Consumer Research*, June 1987, pp. 83–95.

HIGHLIGHT 3–1
How Much Do American Consumers Consume?

It may be difficult for many people to appreciate how much Americans purchase and consume. For example, did you know that *in an average day,* Americans . . .

- Eat 5.8 million pounds of chocolate candy.
- Use 550,000 pounds of toothpaste and gargle 69,000 gallons of mouthwash.
- Buy 190,000 watches, about half of which are for gifts.
- Eat 228,000 bushels of onions.
- Buy 120,000 new radios and 50,000 new television sets.
- Eat 47 million hot dogs.
- Buy over 5.6 million books and 970,000 tapes.
- Buy 99,000 fishing licenses and 78,000 hunting licenses.
- Buy over 30,000 automobiles.
- Spend $200,000 to buy roller skates.
- Spend $40 million on automobile repairs and replacements for damage caused by rust.
- Wear more than 3 million pounds of rubber off their tires, enough to make 250,000 new tires.
- Buy 38,000 Ken and Barbie dolls.
- Buy about 35 million paper clips and 4 million eraser-tipped wooden pencils.
- Buy 12,000 new refrigerators and 10,000 new kitchen ranges.
- And last but not least, snap up 82,000 mousetraps?

Source: Excerpted from Tom Parker, *In One Day* (Boston: Houghton Mifflin, 1984) Copyright © 1984 by Tom Parker. Reprinted by permission of Houghton Mifflin Co.; and Randolph E. Schmid, "Face It: You're a Statistic," *Wisconsin State Journal,* May 17, 1988, p. 1D.

information to form evaluations of products is not fully understood. In general, information processing is viewed as a four-step process in which the individual is (1) exposed to information; (2) becomes attentive to the information; (3) understands the information; and (4) retains the information.[3]

---

[3]For further discussion of information processing, see J. Paul Peter and Jerry C. Olson, *Consumer Behavior and Marketing Strategy,* 2nd ed. (Homewood, Ill.: Richard D. Irwin, 1990), chap. 3.

HIGHLIGHT 3–2
Some Determinants of the Extent of Consumers' Information Search

Market Environment

Number of alternatives.
Complexity of alternatives.
Marketing mix of alternatives.
Stability of alternatives on the market (new alternatives).
Information available.

Situational Variables

Time pressure.
Social pressure (family, peers, boss).
Financial pressure.
Organizational procedures.
Physical and mental condition.
Ease of access to information sources.

Potential Payoff/Product Importance

Price.
Social visibility.
Perceived risk.
Differences among alternatives.
Number of crucial attributes.
Status of decision-making activity (in family, organization, society).

Knowledge and Experience

Stored knowledge.
Rate of product use.
Previous information.
Previous choices (number and identity).
Satisfaction.

Individual Differences

Training.
Approach to problem solving (compulsiveness, open-mindedness, pre-planning, innovativeness).
Approach to search (enjoyment of shopping, sources of information, etc.).
Involvement.
Demographics (age, income, education, marital status, household size, social class, occupation).
Personality/lifestyle variables (self-confidence, etc.).

Conflict and Conflict-Resolution Strategies

Source: Reprinted with permission from "Individual Differences in Search Behavior for a Nondurable," by William L. Moore and Donald R. Lehmann, from the *Journal of Consumer Research,* December 1980, pp. 296–307. For a summary of empirical research on these and other search determinants, see Sharon E. Beatty and Scott M. Smith, "External Search Effort: An Investigation across Several Product Categories," *Journal of Consumer Research,* June 1987, pp. 83–95.

Alternative Evaluation

During the process of collecting information or, in some cases, after information is acquired, the consumer then evaluates alternatives based on what has been learned. One approach to describing the evaluation process can be found in the logic of attitude modeling.[4] The basic logic can be described as follows:

1. The consumer has information about a number of brands in a product class.
2. The consumer perceives that at least some of the brands in a product class are viable alternatives for satisfying a recognized need.
3. Each of these brands has a set of attributes (color, quality, size, and so forth).
4. A set of these attributes are relevant to the consumer, and the consumer perceives that different brands vary in terms of how much of each attribute they possess.
5. The brand that is perceived as offering the greatest number of desired attributes in the desired amounts and desired order will be the brand the consumer will like best.
6. The brand the consumer likes best is the brand the consumer will intend to purchase.

Purchase Decision

If no other factors intervene after the consumer has decided on the brand that is intended for purchase, the actual purchase is a common result of search and evaluation. Actually, a purchase involves many decisions, which include product type, brand, model, dealer selection, and method of payment, among other factors. In addition, rather than purchasing, the consumer may make a decision to modify, postpone, or avoid purchase based on an inhibitor to purchase, or a perceived risk.

---

[4]For a summary of research on attitude modeling, see Blair H. Sheppard, Jon Hartwick, and Paul R. Warshaw, "The Theory of Reasoned Action: A Meta-Analysis of Past Research with Recommendations for Modification and Future Research." *Journal of Consumer Research*, December 1988, pp. 325–43.

Traditional risk theorists believe that consumers tend to make risk-minimizing decisions based on their *perceived* definition of the particular purchase. The perception of risk is based upon the possible consequences and uncertainties involved. Consequences may range from economic loss, to embarrassment if a new food product does not turn out well, to actual physical harm. Perceived risk may be either functional (related to financial and performance considerations) or psychosocial (related to whether the product will further one's self- or reference group image). The amount of risk a consumer perceives in a particular product depends on such things as the price of the product and whether other people will see the individual using the product.

The perceived risk literature emphasizes that consumers generally try to reduce risk in their decision making. This can be done by either reducing the possible negative consequences or by reducing the uncertainty. The possible consequences of a purchase might be minimized by purchasing in small quantities or by lowering the individual's aspiration level to expect less in the way of results from the product. However, this cannot always be done. Thus, reducing risk by attempting to increase the certainty of the purchase outcome may be the more widely used strategy. This can be done by seeking additional information regarding the proposed purchase. In general, the more information the consumer collects prior to purchase, the less likely postpurchase dissonance is to occur.

Postpurchase Feelings

In general, if the individual finds that a certain response achieves a desired goal or satisfies a need, the success of this cue-response pattern will be remembered. The probability of responding in a like manner to the same or similar situation in the future is increased. In other words, the response has a higher probability of being repeated when the need and cue appear together again, and thus it can be said that learning has taken place. Frequent reinforcement increases the habit potential of the particular response. Likewise, if a response does not satisfy the need adequately, the probability that the same response will be repeated is reduced.

For some marketers this means that, if an individual finds a particular product fulfills the need for which it was purchased, the probability is high that the product will be repurchased the next time the need arises. The firm's promotional efforts often act as the cue. If an individual repeatedly purchases a product with favorable results, loyalty may develop toward the particular product or brand. This loyalty can result in habitual purchases, and such habits are often extremely difficult for competing firms to alter.

Although many studies in the area of buyer behavior center around the buyer's attitudes, motives, and behavior before and during the purchase decision, emphasis has also been given to study of behavior after the purchase. Specifically, studies have been undertaken to investigate postpurchase dissonance, as well as postpurchase satisfaction.[5]

The occurrence of postdecision dissonance is related to the concept of cognitive dissonance. This theory states that there is often a lack of consistency or harmony among an individual's various cognitions, or attitudes and beliefs, after a decision has been made—that is, the individual has doubts and second thoughts about the choice made. Further, it is more likely that the intensity of the anxiety will be greater when any of the following conditions exist:

1. The decision is an important one psychologically or financially, or both.

2. There are a number of forgone alternatives.

3. The forgone alternatives have many favorable features.

These factors can relate to many buying decisions. For example, postpurchase dissonance might be expected to be present among many purchasers of such products as automobiles, major appliances, and homes. In these cases, the decision to purchase is usually an important one both financially and psychologically, and there are usually a number of favorable alternatives available.

When dissonance occurs after a decision has been made, the individual may attempt to reduce it by one or more of the following methods:

1. By seeking information that supports the wisdom of the decision.

2. By perceiving information in a way to support the decision.

3. By changing attitudes to a less favorable view of the forgone alternatives.

4. By avoiding the importance of the negative aspects of the decision and enhancing the positive elements.

---

[5]For further discussion of consumer satisfaction, see Richard L. Oliver and John E. Swan, "Consumer Perceptions of Interpersonal Equity and Satisfaction in Transactions: A Field Survey Approach," *Journal of Marketing*, April 1989, pp. 21–35; Richard L. Oliver and John E. Swan, "Equity and Disconfirmation Perceptions as Influences on Merchant and Product Satisfaction," *Journal of Consumer Research*, December 1989, pp. 372–83.

HIGHLIGHT 3–3
A Summary of American Cultural Values

It is important for marketers to understand cultural values and to create and adapt products to the values held by consumers. Below is a description of American cultural values and their relevance to marketing.

Value	General Features	Relevance to Marketing
Achievement and success	Hard work is good; success flows from hard work	Acts as a justification for acquisition of goods ("You deserve it")
Activity	Keeping busy is healthy and natural	Stimulates interest in products that are time-savers and enhance leisure-time activities
Efficiency and practicality	Admiration of things that solve problems (e.g., save time and effort)	Stimulates purchase of products that function well and save time
Progress	People can improve themselves; tomorrow should be better	Stimulates desire for new products that fulfill unsatisfied needs; acceptance of products that claim to be "new" or "improved"
Material comfort	"The good life"	Fosters acceptance of convenience and luxury products that make life more enjoyable
Individualism	Being one's self (e.g., self-reliance, self-interest, and self-esteem)	Stimulates acceptance of customized or unique products that enable a person to "express his or her own personality"
Freedom	Freedom of choice	Fosters interest in wide product lines and differentiated products
External conformity	Uniformity of observable behavior; desire to be accepted	Stimulates interest in products that are used or owned by others in the same social group
Humanitarianism	Caring for others, particularly the underdog	Stimulates patronage of firms that compete with market leaders

---

HIGHLIGHT 3–3 *concluded*

Value	General Features	Relevance to Marketing
Youthfulness	A state of mind that stresses being young at heart or appearing young	Stimulates acceptance of products that provide the illusion of maintaining or fostering youth
Fitness and health	Caring about one's body, including the desire to be physically fit and healthy	Stimulates acceptance of food products, activities, and equipment perceived to maintain or increase physical fitness

---

Source: Leon G. Schiffman and Leslie Lazar Kanuck, *Consumer Behavior,* 4th ed., © 1991, p. 424. Adapted by permission of Prentice Hall, Englewood Cliffs, New Jersey.

Dissonance could, of course, be reduced by admitting that a mistake had been made. However, most individuals are reluctant to admit that a wrong decision has been made. Thus, it is more likely that a person will seek out supportive information to reduce dissonance.

These findings have much relevance for the marketer. In a buying situation, when a purchaser becomes dissonant it is reasonable to predict such a person would be highly receptive to advertising and sales promotion that supports the purchase decision. Such communication presents favorable aspects of the product and can be useful in reinforcing the buyer's wish to believe that a wise purchase decision was made. For example, purchasers of major appliances or automobiles might be given a phone call or sent a letter reassuring them that they have made a wise purchase.[6]

GROUP INFLUENCES ON CONSUMER BEHAVIOR

Behavioral scientists have become increasingly aware of the powerful effects of the social environment and personal interactions on human behavior. In terms of consumer behavior, culture, social class, and

---

[6]For additional discussion of postpurchase feelings and behavior, see Mary C. Gilly and Betsy D. Gelb, "Post-Purchase Consumer Processes and the Complaining Consumer," *Journal of Consumer Research,* December 1982, pp. 323–28; Jagdip Singh, "Consumer Complaint Intentions and Behavior: Definitional and Taxonomical Issues," *Journal of Marketing,* January 1988, pp. 93–107.

reference group influences have been related to purchase and consumption decisions. It should be noted that these influences can have both direct and indirect effects on the buying process. By direct effects we mean direct communication between the individual and other members of society concerning a particular decision. By indirect effects we mean the influence of society on an individual's basic values and attitudes as well as the important role that groups play in structuring an individual's personality.

Cultural and Subcultural Influences

Culture is one of the most basic influences on an individual's needs, wants, and behavior, since all facets of life are carried out against the background of the society in which an individual lives. Cultural antecedents affect everyday behavior, and there is empirical support for the notion that culture is a determinant of certain aspects of consumer behavior.

Cultural values are transmitted through three basic organizations: the family, religious organizations, and educational institutions, and, in today's society, educational institutions are playing an increasingly greater role in this regard. Marketing managers should adapt the marketing mix to cultural values and constantly monitor value changes and differences in both domestic and international markets. To illustrate, one of the changing values in America is the increasing emphasis on achievement and career success. This change in values has been recognized by many business firms that have expanded their emphasis on time-saving, convenience-oriented products.

In a nation as large as the United States the population is bound to lose a significant amount of its homogeneity, and thus subcultures arise. In other words, there are subcultures in the American culture where people have more frequent interactions than with the population at large and thus tend to think and act alike in some respects. Subcultures are based on such things as geographic areas, religions, nationalities, ethnic groups, and age. Many subcultural barriers are decreasing because of mass communication, mass transit, and a decline in the influence of religious values. However, age groups, such as the teen market, baby boomers, and the mature market, have become increasingly important for marketing strategy. For example, since baby boomers (those born between 1946 and 1962) make up about a third of the U.S. population and soon will account for about half of discretionary spending, many marketers are repositioning products to serve them. Snickers candy bars, for instance, used to be promoted to children as a treat but are now promoted to adults as a wholesome, between-meals snack.

Social Class

While one likes to think of America as a land of equality, a class structure can be observed. Social classes develop on the basis of such things as wealth, skill, and power. The single best indicator of social class is occupation. However, interest at this point is in the influence of social class on the individual's behavior. What is important here is that different social classes tend to have different attitudinal configurations and values, which influence the behavior of individual members. Figure 3–2 presents a social class hierarchy developed specifically for marketing analysis and describes some of these important differences in attitudes and values.

For the marketing manager, social class offers some insights into consumer behavior and is potentially useful as a market segmentation variable. However, there is considerable controversy as to whether social class is superior to income for the purpose of market segmentation.

Reference Groups

Groups that an individual looks to (uses as a reference) when forming attitudes and opinions are described as reference groups.[7] Primary reference groups include family and close friends, while secondary reference groups include fraternal organizations and professional associations. A buyer may also consult a single individual about decisions, and this individual would be considered a reference individual.

A person normally has several reference groups or reference individuals for various subjects or different decisions. For example, a woman may consult one reference group when she is purchasing a car and a

---

[7]See William O. Bearden and Michael J. Etzel, "Reference Group Influence on Product and Brand Purchase Decisions," *Journal of Consumer Research*, September 1982, pp. 183–94; Peter H. Reingen, Brian L. Foster, Jacqueline Johnson Brown, and Stephen B. Seidman, "Brand Congruence in Interpersonal Relations: A Social Network Analysis," *Journal of Consumer Research*, December 1984, pp. 771–83; Jacqueline Johnson Brown and Peter H. Reingen, "Social Ties and Word-of-Mouth Referral Behavior," *Journal of Consumer Research*, December 1987, pp. 350–62.

FIGURE 3–2
Social Class Groups for Marketing Analysis

Upper Americans (14 percent of population). This group consists of the upper-upper, lower-upper, and upper-middle classes. They have common goals and are differentiated mainly by income. This group has many different lifestyles, which might be labeled postpreppy, conventional, intellectual, and political, among others. The class remains the segment of our society in which quality merchandise is most prized, special attention is paid to prestige brands, and the self-image ideal is "spending with good taste." Self-expression is more prized than in previous generations, and neighborhood remains important. Depending on income and priorities, theater, books, investment in art, European travel, household help, club memberships for tennis, golf, and swimming, and prestige schooling for children remain high consumption priorities.

Middle class (32 percent of population). These consumers definitely want to "do the right thing" and buy "what's popular." They have always been concerned with fashion and following recommendations of "experts" in print media. Increased earnings result in better living, which means a "nicer neighborhood on the better side of town with good schools." It also means spending more on "worthwhile experiences" for children, including winter ski trips, college educations, and shopping for better brands of clothes at more expensive stores. Appearance of home is important, because guests may visit and pass judgment. This group emulates upper Americans, which distinguishes it from the working class. It also enjoys trips to Las Vegas and physical activity. Deferred gratification may still be an ideal, but it is not often practiced.

Working class (38 percent of population). Working-class Americans are "family folk" depending heavily on relatives for economic and emotional support (e.g., tips on job opportunities, advice on purchases, help in times of trouble). The emphasis on family ties is only one sign of how much more limited and different working-class horizons are socially, psychologically, and geographically compared to those of the middle class. In almost every respect, a parochial view characterizes this blue-collar world. This group has changed little in values and behaviors in spite of rising incomes in some cases. For them, "keeping up with the times" focuses on the mechanical and recreational, and thus, ease of labor and leisure is what they continue to pursue.

Lower Americans (16 percent of population). The men and women of lower America are no exception to the rule that diversities and uniformities in values and consumption goals are to be found at each social level. Some members of this world, as has been publicized, are prone to every form of instant gratification known to humankind when the money is available. But others are dedicated to resisting worldly temptations as they struggle toward what some believe will be a "heavenly reward" for their earthly sacrifices.

Source: Excerpted from Richard P. Coleman, "The Continuing Significance of Social Class to Marketing," *Journal of Consumer Research*, December 1983, pp. 265–80.

HIGHLIGHT 3–4
Some Common Verbal Tools Used by Reference Groups

Below are a number of verbal tools used by reference groups to influence consumer behavior. If the statements listed below were made to you by a close friend or someone you admired or respected, do you think that they might change your behavior?

Tools	Definitions	Examples
Reporting	Talking about preferences and behaviors.	"All of us drink Budweiser."
Recommendations	Suggesting appropriate behaviors.	"You should get a Schwinn High Sierra."
Invitations	Asking for participation in events.	"Do you want to go to the Lionel Richie concert with us?"
Requests	Asking for behavior performance.	"Would you run down to the corner and get me a newspaper?"
Prompts	Suggesting desired behaviors.	"It sure would be nice if someone would buy us a pizza!"
Commands	Telling someone what to do.	"Get me some Kleenex, and be quick about it!"
Promises	Offering a reward for performing a behavior.	"If you'll go to Penney's with me, I'll take you to lunch later."
Coercion	Threatening to punish for inappropriate behavior.	"If you don't shut up, I'm going to stuff a sock in your mouth!"
Criticism	Saying something negative about a behavior.	"Quit hassling the salesclerk. You're acting like a jerk."
Compliments	Saying something positive about a behavior.	"You really know how to shop. I bet you got every bargain in the store!"
Teasing	Good-natured bantering about behavior or appearance.	"Man, that shirt makes you look like Bozo the clown!"

Source: J. Paul Peter and Jerry C. Olson, *Consumer Behavior and Marketing Strategy,* 2nd ed. (Homewood, Ill.: Richard D. Irwin, 1990), p. 370.

different reference group for lingerie. In other words, the nature of the product and the role the individual is playing during the purchasing process influence which reference group will be consulted. Reference group influence is generally considered to be stronger for products that are "public" or conspicuous—that is, products that other people see the individual using such as clothes or automobiles.

As noted, the family is generally recognized to be an important reference group, and it has been suggested that the household, rather than the individual, is the relevant unit for studying consumer behavior.[8] This is because within a household the purchaser of goods and services is not always the user of these goods and services. Thus, it is important for marketing managers to determine not only who makes the actual purchase but also who makes the decision to purchase. In addition, it has been recognized that the needs, income, assets, debts, and expenditure patterns change over the course of what is called the *family life cycle*. Basic stages in the family life cycle include:

1. Bachelor stage: young, single people not living at home.
2. Newly married couples: young, no children.
3. Full nest I: young married couples with youngest child under six.
4. Full nest II: young married couples with youngest child six or over.
5. Full nest III: older married couples with dependent children.
6. Empty nest I: older married couples, no children living with them, household head(s) in labor force.
7. Empty nest II: older married couples, no children living at home, household head(s) retired.
8. Solitary survivor in labor force.
9. Solitary survivor, retired.

Because the life cycle combines trends in earning power with demands placed on income, it is a useful way of classifying and segmenting individuals and families.[9]

---

[8]See Rosann L. Spiro, "Persuasion in Family Decision Making," *Journal of Consumer Research,* March 1983, pp. 393–402.

[9]See Janet Wagner and Sherman Hanna, "The Effectiveness of Family Life Cycle Variables in Consumer Expenditure Research," *Journal of Consumer Research.* December 1983, pp. 281–91.

PRODUCT CLASS INFLUENCES

The nature of the product class selected by the consumer to satisfy an aroused need plays an important role in the decision-making process. Basically, the nature of the product class and the brands within it determine (1) the amount of information the consumer will require before making a decision, and, consequently (2) the time it takes to move through the buying process. In general, product classes in which there are many alternatives that are expensive, complex, or new will require the consumer to collect more information and take longer to make a purchase decision. As illustration, buying an automobile is probably one of the most difficult purchase decisions most consumers make. An automobile is expensive, complex, and there are many new styles and models to choose from. Such a decision will usually require extensive information search and time before a decision is made.

A second possibility is referred to as limited decision making. For these purchases a lesser amount of information is collected and less time is devoted to shopping. For example, in purchasing a new pair of jeans the consumer may already have considerable experience, and price and complexity are somewhat limited. However, since there are many alternative styles and brands, some information processing and decision making is generally needed.

Finally, some product classes require what is called "routinized decision making." For these product classes, such as candy bars or other food products, the consumer has faced the decision many times before and has found an acceptable alternative. Thus, little or no information is collected, and the consumer purchases in a habitual, automatic manner.

SITUATIONAL INFLUENCES

Situational influences can be defined as "all those factors particular to a time and place of observation which do not follow from a knowledge of personal and stimulus attributes and which have a demonstrable and systematic effect on current behavior."[10] In terms of purchasing situations,

---

[10]Russell W. Belk, "An Exploratory Assessment of Situational Effects in Buyer Behavior," *Journal of Marketing Research*, May 1974, pp. 156–63. Also see Joseph A. Cote, Jr., "Situational Variables in Consumer Research: A Review," working paper (Washington State University, 1985).

five groups of situational influences have been identified.[11] These influences may be perceived either consciously or subconsciously and may have considerable effect on product and brand choice.

1. *Physical surroundings* are the most readily apparent features of a situation. These features include geographical and institutional location, decor, sounds, aromas, lighting, weather, and visible configurations of merchandise or other material surrounding the stimulus object.

2. *Social surroundings* provide additional depth to a description of a situation. Other persons present, their characteristics, their apparent roles and interpersonal interactions are potentially relevant examples.

3. *Temporal perspective* is a dimension of situations that may be specified in units ranging from time of day to season of the year. Time also may be measured relative to some past or future event for the situational participant. This allows such conceptions as time since last purchase, time since or until meals or paydays, and time constraints imposed by prior or standing commitments.

4. *Task definition* features of a situation include an intent or requirement to select, shop for, or obtain information about a general or specific purchase. In addition, task may reflect different buyer and user roles anticipated by the individual. For instance, a person shopping for a small appliance as a wedding gift for a friend is in a different situation than when shopping for a small appliance for personal use.

5. *Antecedent states* make up a final feature that characterizes a situation. These are momentary moods (such as acute anxiety, pleasantness, hostility, and excitation) or momentary conditions (such as cash on hand, fatigue, and illness) rather than chronic

---

[11]Russell W. Belk, "Situational Variables and Consumer Behavior," *Journal of Consumer Research*, December 1975, pp. 156–64. Also see Jacob Hornik, "Situational Effects on the Consumption of Time," *Journal of Marketing*, Fall 1982, pp. 44–55; C. Whan Park, Easwar S. Iyer, and Daniel C. Smith, "The Effects of Situational Factors on In-Store Grocery Shopping Behavior: The Role of Store Environment and Time Available for Shopping," *Journal of Consumer Research*, March 1989, pp. 422–33.

individual traits. These conditions are further stipulated to be immediately antecedent to the current situation to distinguish the states the individual brings to the situation from states of the individual resulting from the situation. For instance, people may select a certain motion picture because they feel depressed (an antecedent state and a part of the choice situation), but the fact that the movie causes them to feel happier is a response to the consumption situation. This altered state then may become antecedent for behavior in the next choice situation encountered, such as passing a street vendor on the way out of the theater.

LESSONS FOR THE MANUFACTURER

Although this chapter discusses a simple model of consumer behavior that highlights a number of influences on purchasing, this should not lead the manufacturer to believe that predicting consumer behavior is an easy task. Consumers often do not know what they need and want until organizations inform them what alternative products are available. Consumer preferences and tastes change over time, and their loyalties to various brands often change. Consumers often do not have the time nor are they willing to take the effort to figure out which products are the best for them. In fact, the recent trend away from national advertising toward consumer and trade promotions has led some analysts to conclude that consumers will increasingly become price oriented and less image oriented. It may also lead to a decrease in brand loyalty among consumers. This has important implications for manufacturers. Becoming the low-cost producer by keeping manufacturing costs low may eventually be the most important competitive advantage because brand names and brand images may no longer allow companies to sell their products at higher prices.

One of the major implications of the study of consumer behavior for organizations is that the more the company knows about its consumers, the better it can design, produce, and market products that satisfy them. Many successful companies constantly monitor consumers and changes in their preferences and product satisfaction in order to stay ahead of competition. A number of leading Japanese firms not only study what product characteristics consumers want and like in various products, but also investigate what price they are willing to pay for a product with desired characteristics. Then, the companies work backwards through design and engineering to build a product that can be sold at the target price and still make a desired level of profit. All of this is done prior to manufacturing. In other words, by studying price levels before manufacturing, these Japanese firms can produce the best product available at a particular price level that consumers are willing to pay rather than waiting until after manufacturing and finding out that the product is priced higher than consumers are willing to pay. This is just one example of how understanding more about consumers can lead to more successful products and strategies.

Finally, some companies now try to more closely connect consumers with the manufacturers who actually build the products. For example, Nissan has a hot line for customer problems that goes directly to the factory. The result is better understanding by manufacturers of how the product is used and the frustrations and problems that consumers have with the product. Changes can then be made in the manufacturing process to reduce these problems and increase customer satisfaction.

ADDITIONAL READINGS

Assael, Henry. *Consumer Behavior and Marketing Action*. 3rd ed. Boston: PWS-Kent Publishing, 1987.

Engel, James F.; Roger D. Blackwell; and Paul W. Miniard. *Consumer Behavior*. 6th ed. Hinsdale, Ill.: Dryden Press, 1990.

Hawkins, Del; Kenneth A. Coney; and Roger Best, Jr. *Consumer Behavior: Implications for Marketing Strategy*. 4th ed. Homewood, Ill.: BPI/Irwin, 1989.

Mowen, John C. *Consumer Behavior*. 2nd ed. New York: Macmillan Publishing, 1990.

Peter, J. Paul, and Jerry C. Olson. *Consumer Behavior and Marketing Strategy*. 2nd ed. Homewood, Ill.: Richard D. Irwin, 1990.

Schiffman, Leon G., and Leslie Kanuck. *Consumer Behavior*. 3rd ed. Englewood Cliffs, N.J.: Prentice Hall, 1987.

Wilkie, William L. *Consumer Behavior*. 2nd ed. New York: John Wiley & Sons, 1990.

APPENDIX: SELECTED CONSUMER BEHAVIOR DATA SOURCES

1. Demographic information:
   U.S. Census of Population.
   Marketing Information Guide.
   A Guide to Consumer Markets.
   State and city governments.
   Media (newspapers, magazines, television, and radio stations) make demographic data about their readers or audiences available.

2. Consumer research findings:

Journal of Consumer Research	*Journal of Advertising Research*
Journal of Marketing	*Journal of Consumer Marketing*
Journal of Marketing Research	*Journal of Applied Psychology*
Journal of Advertising	*Advances in Consumer Research*

3. Marketing applications:

Advertising Age	*Nation's Business*
Marketing Communications	*Fortune*
Sales Management	*Forbes*
Business Week	Industry and trade magazines

CHAPTER 4

ORGANIZATIONAL BUYER BEHAVIOR

Organizational buyers include individuals involved in purchasing products for businesses, government agencies, and other institutions and agencies. Those who purchase for businesses include industrial buyers who purchase goods and services to aid them in producing other goods and services for sale, and resellers who purchase goods and services to resell at a profit. Government agencies purchase products and services to carry out their responsibilities to society, and other institutions and agencies, such as churches and schools, purchase to fulfill their organizational missions.

The purpose of this chapter is to examine the organizational buying process and the factors that influence it. Figure 4–1 provides a model of the organizational buying process that will be used as a framework for discussion in this chapter.

PRODUCT INFLUENCES ON ORGANIZATIONAL BUYING

A major consideration that affects the organizational buying process is the nature of the product itself. Such factors as the price, riskiness, and technical complexity of the product affect the process in three ways. First, they affect how long it will take for the firm to make a purchasing decision. Second, they have an effect on how many individuals will be involved in the purchasing process. Last, these factors may affect whether structural or behavioral influences play the major role in the purchasing process.

FIGURE 4-1
A Model of the Organizational Buying Process

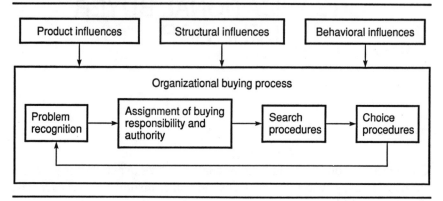

A useful way of examining product class influences is to consider them on the basis of the problems inherent in their adoption.[1] Four basic categories include:

Type I: Routine order products. A Type I product is frequently ordered and used. There is no problem in learning how to use such products, nor is there any question about whether the product will do the job. In short, this type of product is expected to cause no significant problems in use.

Type II: Procedural problem products. For Type II products, the buyer is also confident the product will do the job. However, problems are likely because personnel must be taught how to use the product. A buyer intent on minimizing problems associated with such a product will favor the supplier whose total offering is perceived as likely to reduce to a minimum the time and difficulty required to learn the product's operation.

Type III: Performance problem products. With Type III products, there is doubt whether the product will perform satisfactorily in the application for which it is being considered. Here the problem concerns the technical outcomes of using the product. There is likely to be no firm buying commitment until this problem has been resolved. It is argued that the buyer will favor the supplier who can offer appropriate technical service, providing

[1]Donald R. Lehmann and John O'Shaughnessy, "Difference in Attribute Importance for Different Industrial Products," *Journal of Marketing*, April 1974, pp. 36–42; also see Philip Kotler, *Marketing Management: Analysis, Planning, Implementation, and Control*, 6th ed., Englewood Cliffs, N.J.: Prentice Hall, 1988, chap. 7.

a free trial period, and who appears flexible enough to adjust to the demands of the buyer's company.

Type IV: Political problem products. Type IV products give rise to "political" problems, because there is likely to be difficulty in reaching agreement among those affected if the product is adopted. "Political" problems occur when products necessitate large capital outlays, since there are always allocational rivals for funds. More frequently, political problems arise when the product is an input to several departments whose requirements may not be congruent.

There are two important implications of this classification for marketers. First, in a study of purchasing agents, it was found that different product attributes were rated as relatively more important, depending on the type of product. For example, the most important attributes for Type I products were the reliability of delivery and price; for Type II products, the most important attributes were technical service offered, ease of operation or use, and training offered by supplier; for Type III products, the technical service offered, flexibility of supplier, and product reliability were rated as most important; for Type IV products, the price, reputation of supplier, data on product reliability, reliability of delivery, and flexibility of supplier were rated as most important. Thus, marketing strategy for organizational products should be adapted to variations in buyer perceptions of problems in selection, introduction, and performance.

Second, the type of product may influence whether structural or behavioral factors are relatively more important in the purchasing process. For example, behavioral influences may decrease from Type I to Type IV products while structural influences may increase. A routine order product is most probably the sole responsibility of the purchasing agent. Here organizational influences, such as joint decision making, are minimal, and the purchasing agent may well be more strongly influenced by behavioral influences, such as a personal friendship with the supplier. On the other hand, Type IV product decisions may require considerable joint decision making—such as a purchasing committee—and thus be more influenced by structural factors.

STRUCTURAL INFLUENCES ON ORGANIZATIONAL BUYING

The term *structural influences* refers to the design of the organizational environment and how it affects the purchasing process. Two important

HIGHLIGHT 4–1
Major Differences between Organizational Buyers and Final Consumers

Differences in Purchases
1. Organizational buyers acquire for further production, use in operations, or resale to other consumers. Final consumers acquire only for personal, family, or household use.
2. Organizational buyers commonly purchase installations, raw materials, and semifinished materials. Final consumers rarely purchase these goods.
3. Organizational buyers purchase on the basis of specifications and technical data. Final consumers frequently purchase on the basis of description, fashion, and style.
4. Organizational buyers utilize multiple-buying and team-based decisions more often than final consumers.
5. Organizational buyers are more likely to apply value and vendor analysis.
6. Organizational buyers more commonly lease equipment.
7. Organizational buyers more frequently employ competitive bidding and negotiation.

Differences in the Market
1. The demand of organizational buyers is derived from the demand of final consumers.
2. The demand of organizational buyers is more subject to cyclical fluctuations than final-consumer demand.
3. Organizational buyers are fewer in number and more geographically concentrated than final consumers.
4. Organizational buyers often employ buying specialists.
5. The distribution channel for organizational buyers is shorter than for final consumers.
6. Organizational buyers may require special services.
7. Organizational buyers are more likely than final consumers to be able to make goods and services as alternatives to purchasing them.

Source: Reprinted by permission of Macmillan Publishing Company from *Marketing,* 4th ed., by Joel R. Evans and Barry Berman. Copyright © 1990 by Macmillan Publishing Company, Inc.

structural influences on organizational buying are joint decision making and organization-specific factors.

Joint Decision Making

It is common in organizational buying for more than one department and several persons to be involved in the purchasing process. These people may also play a variety of different roles in arriving at a purchase decision. These roles include:

1. *Users,* or those persons in the organization who actually use the product; for example, a secretary who would use a new word processor.
2. *Influencers,* who affect the buying decision, usually by helping define the specifications for what is bought. For example, an information systems manager would be a key influencer in the purchase of a new mainframe computer.
3. *Buyers,* who have the formal authority and responsibility to select the supplier and negotiate the terms of the contract. For example, in the purchase of a mainframe computer, the purchasing manager would likely perform this role.
4. *Deciders,* who have the formal or informal power to select or approve the supplier that receives the contract. For important technical purchases, deciders may come from R&D, engineering, or quality control.
5. *Gatekeepers,* who control the flow of information in the buying center. Purchasing personnel, technical experts, and secretaries can all keep marketers and their information from reaching people performing the other four roles.[2]

When several persons are involved in the organizational purchase decision, marketers may need to use a variety of means to reach each individual or group. Fortunately, it is often easy to find which individuals in organizations are involved in a purchase because such information is

---

[2]This discussion is taken from Eric N. Berkowitz, Roger A. Kerin, and William Rudelius, *Marketing,* 2nd ed., Homewood, Ill.: Richard D. Irwin, 1989, pp. 124–25.

HIGHLIGHT 4–2
Functional Areas and Their Key Concerns in Purchasing

Functional Area	Key Concerns in Purchase Decision Making
Design and development engineering	Name reputation of vendor; ability of vendors to meet design specifications
Production	Delivery and reliability of purchases such that interruption of production schedules is minimized
Sales/marketing	Impact of purchased items on marketability of the company's products
Maintenance	Degree to which purchased items are compatible with existing facilities and equipment; maintenance services offered by vendor; installation arrangements offered by vendor
Finance/accounting	Effects of purchases on cash flow, balance sheet, and income statement positions; variances in costs of materials over estimates; feasibility of make-or-buy and lease options to purchasing
Purchasing	Obtaining lowest possible price at acceptable quality levels; maintaining good relations with vendors
Quality control	Assurance that purchased items meet prescribed specifications and tolerances, governmental regulations, and customer requirements

---

Source: Michael H. Morris, *Industrial and Organizational Marketing* (Columbus, Ohio: Merrill Publishing, 1988), p. 81.

provided to suppliers. Organizations do this because it makes suppliers more knowledgeable about purchasing practices, thus making the purchasing process more efficient.[3]

---

[3]For research on several influences on the industrial buying process, see John R. Ronchetto, Jr., Michael D. Hutt, and Peter Reingen, "Embedded Influence Patterns in Organizational Buying Systems," *Journal of Marketing,* October 1989, pp. 51–62; Ajay Kohli, "Determinants of Influence in Organizational Buying: A Contingency Approach," *Journal of Marketing,* July 1989, pp. 50–65; Daniel H. McQuiston, "Novelty, Complexity, and Importance as Causal Determinants of Industrial Buyer Behavior," *Journal of Marketing,* April 1989, pp. 66–79.

Organization-Specific Factors

There are three primary organization-specific factors that influence the purchasing process: orientation, size, and degree of centralization. First, in terms of orientation, the dominant function in an organization may control purchasing decisions. For example, if the organization is technology oriented, it is likely to be dominated by engineering personnel, and buying decisions will be made by them. Similarly, if the organization is production oriented, production personnel may dominate buying decisions.

Second, the size of the organization may influence the purchasing process. If the organization is large, it will likely have a high degree of joint decision making for other than routine order products. Smaller organizations are likely to have more autonomous decision making.

Finally, the degree of centralization of an organization influences whether decisions are made individually or jointly with others. Organizations that are highly centralized are less likely to have joint decision making. Thus, a privately owned, small company with technology or production orientations will tend toward autonomous decision making while a large-scale, public corporation with considerable decentralization will tend to have greater joint decision making.[4]

BEHAVIORAL INFLUENCES ON ORGANIZATIONAL BUYING

Organizational buyers are influenced by a variety of psychological and social factors. We will discuss two of these, personal motivations and role perceptions.

Personal Motivations

Organizational buyers are, or course, subject to the same personal motives or motivational forces as other individuals. Although these buyers may emphasize nonpersonal motives in their buying activities, it has been found that organizational buyers often are influenced by such personal

---

[4]Jagdish N. Sheth, "A Model of Industrial Buyer Behavior," *Journal of Marketing,* October 1973, pp. 50–56. Also see Paul F. Anderson and Terry M. Chambers, "A Reward/Measurement Model of Organizational Buying Behavior," *Journal of Marketing,* Spring 1985, pp. 7–23.

factors as friendship, professional pride, fear and uncertainty (risk), and personal ambitions in their buying activities.

For example, professional pride often expresses itself through efforts to attain status in the firm. One way to achieve this might be to initiate or influence the purchase of goods that will demonstrate a buyer's value to the organization. If new materials, equipment, or components result in cost savings or increased profits, the individuals initiating the changes have demonstrated their value at the same time. Fear and uncertainty are strong motivational forces on organizational buyers, and reduction of risk is often important to them. This can have a strong influence on purchase behavior. Marketers should understand the relative strength of personal gain versus risk-reducing motives and emphasize the more important motives when dealing with buyers.[5]

Thus, in examining buyer motivations, it is necessary to consider both personal and nonpersonal motivational forces and to recognize that the relative importance of each is not a fixed quantity. It will vary with the nature of the product, the climate within the organization, and the relative strength of the two forces in the particular buyer.

Role Perception

A final factor that influences organizational buyers is their own perception of their role. The manner in which individuals behave depends on their perception of their role, their commitment to what they believe is expected of their role, the "maturity" of the role type, and the extent to which the institution is committed to the role type.

Different buyers will have different degrees of commitment to their buying role which will cause variations in role behavior from one buyer to the next. By commitment we mean willingness to perform their job in the manner expected by the organization. For example, some buyers seek to take charge in their role as buyer and have little commitment to company expectations. The implication for marketers is that such buyers expect, even demand, that they be kept constantly advised of all new developments to enable them to more effectively shape their own role.

---

[5]See Christopher P. Puto, Wesley E. Patton III, and Ronald H. King, "Risk Handling Strategies in Industrial Vendor Selection Decisions," *Journal of Marketing*, Winter 1985, pp. 89–98.

On the other hand, other buyers may have no interest in prescribing their role activities and accept their role as given to them. Such a buyer is most concerned with merely implementing prescribed company activities and buying policies with sanctioned products. Thus, some buyers will be highly committed to play the role the firm dictates (i.e., the formal organization's perception of their role) while others might be extremely innovative and uncommitted to the expected role performance. Obviously, roles may be heavily influenced by the organizational climate existing in the particular organization.[6]

Organizations can be divided into three groups based on differences in degree of employee commitment. These groups include innovative, adaptive, and lethargic firms. In *innovative* firms, individuals approach their occupational roles with a weak commitment to expected norms of behavior. In an *adaptive* organization, there is a moderate commitment, while in a *lethargic* organization, individuals express a strong commitment to traditionally accepted behavior and behave accordingly. Thus, a buyer in a lethargic firm would probably be less innovative in order to maintain acceptance and status within the organization and would keep conflict within the firm to a minimum.

Buyers' perception of their role may differ from the perception of their role held by others in the organization. This difference can result in variance in perception of the proper and the actual purchase responsibility to be held by the buyer. One study involving purchasing agents revealed that, in every firm included in the study, the purchasing agents believed they had more responsibility and control over certain decisions than the other influential purchase decision makers in the firm perceived them as having. The decisions were (1) design of the product; (2) cost of the product; (3) performance life; (4) naming of the specific supplier; (5) assessing the amount of engineering help available from the supplier; and (6) reduction of rejects. This variance in role perception held true regardless of the size of the firm or the significance of the item purchased to the overall success of the firm. It is important, therefore, that the marketer be aware that such perceptual differences may exist and to determine as accurately as possible the amount of control and responsi-

---

[6]For research on the role of organizational climate in industrial buying, see William J. Qualls and Christopher P. Puto, "Organizational Climate and Decision Framing: An Integrated Approach to Analyzing Industrial Buying Decisions," *Journal of Marketing Research*, May 1989, pp. 179–92.

HIGHLIGHT 4–3
Twenty Potential Decisions Facing Organizational Buyers

1. Is the need or problem pressing enough that it must be acted upon now? If not, how long can action be deferred?
2. What types of products or services could conceivably be used to solve our need or problem?
3. Should we make the item ourselves?
4. Must a new product be designed, or has a vendor already developed an acceptable product?
5. Should a value analysis be performed?
6. What is the highest price we can afford to pay?
7. What trade-offs are we prepared to make between price and other product/vendor attributes?
8. Which information sources will we rely on?
9. How many vendors should be considered?
10. Which attributes will be stressed in evaluating vendors?
11. Should bids be solicited?
12. Should the item be leased or purchased outright?
13. How far can a given vendor be pushed in negotiations? On what issues will that vendor bend the most?
14. How much inventory should a vendor be willing to keep on hand?
15. Should we split our order among several vendors?
16. Is a long-term contract in our interest?
17. What contractual guarantees will we require?
18. How shall we establish our order routine?
19. After the purchase, how will vendor performance be evaluated?
20. How will we deal with inadequate product or vendor performance?

Source: Michael H. Morris, *Industrial and Organizational Marketing* (Columbus, Ohio: Charles E. Merrill Publishing, 1988), p. 87.

bility over purchasing decisions held by each purchase decision influencer in the firm.

STAGES IN THE BUYING PROCESS

As with consumer buying, most organizational purchases are made in response to a particular need or problem faced by the firm. Recognition of the need, however, is only the first step in the organizational buying

HIGHLIGHT 4–4
An Operational View of the Industrial Buying Process

Although there is no single format dictating how industrial companies actually purchase goods and services, a relatively standard process is followed in most cases:

1. A department discovers or anticipates a problem in its operation that it believes can be overcome with the addition of a certain product or service.
2. The department head draws up a requisition form describing the desired specifications he or she believes the product or service must have to solve the problem.
3. The department head sends the requisition form to the firm's purchasing department.
4. Based on the specifications required, the purchasing department conducts a search for qualified sources of supply.
5. Once sources have been located, proposals based on the specifications are solicited, received, and analyzed for price, delivery, service, and so on.
6. Proposals are compared with the cost of producing the product in-house in a make-or-buy decision: if it is decided that the buying firm can produce the product more economically, the buying process for the product in question is terminated; however, if the inverse is true, the process continues.
7. A source or sources of supply is selected from those who have submitted proposals.
8. The order is placed, and copies of the purchase order are sent to the originating department, accounting, credit, and any other interested departments within the company.
9. After the product is shipped, received, and used, a follow-up with the originating department is conducted to determine if the purchased product solved the department's problem.

Although there are many variations of this process in actual operation, this is typical of the process by which industrial goods and services are purchased. It must be understood that in actual practice these steps are combined, not separate.

Source: Robert W. Hass, *Industrial Marketing Management,* 3rd ed. (Boston: Kent Publishing, 1986), p. 96.

process. The following four stages represent one model of the industrial buying process:

1. Problem recognition.
2. Organizational assignment of buying responsibility and authority.
3. Search procedures for identifying product offerings and for establishing selection criteria.
4. Choice procedures for evaluating and selecting among alternatives.

Problem Recognition

As mentioned previously, most organizational purchases are made in response to a particular need or problem. The product purchased is hopefully the means to solve the particular problem. Buyers must be concerned with budgets and profits since the firm cannot put forth a great amount of financial resources if it does not have sufficient funds, regardless of the benefits that might be derived from the purchase. However, as was mentioned, there is more subjective buying and persuasion in the organizational buying process than some earlier writers indicated.

Assignment of Buying Authority

The influence of individuals on the buying decision will be determined in part by their responsibility as defined by the formal organization. An individual's responsibility in a given buying situation will be a function of (1) the technical complexity of the product; (2) the importance of the product to the firm either in dollar terms or in terms of its relationship with the process or system that will use the product; (3) the product-specific technical knowledge that the individual has; (4) the individual's centrality in the process or system that will use the product.

In some organizations the responsibility for the purchasing decision is assigned to a centralized purchasing unit. When centralization of the buying function occurs, it is usually based on the assumption that knowledge of the market and not knowledge of the physical product itself is the major consideration in the buying decision. Therefore, the purchasing agent will concentrate on such market variables as price, delivery, and seller performance, rather than on the technical aspects of the product.

Search Procedures

This stage involves the search procedures for identifying product offerings and for establishing selection criteria.[7] Basically, buyers perform two key tasks related to the collection and analysis of information. First, the criteria against which to evaluate potential sellers have to be developed. These are usually based on a judgment about what is needed compared to what is available. Second, alternative product candidates must be located in the market. The important point here is that buyers seek sellers just as sellers seek buyers.

Choice Procedures

The final stage in the organizational buying process involves establishing choice procedures for evaluating and selecting among alternatives. Once alternative products and alternative suppliers have been identified, the buyer must choose from among the alternatives. The choice process is guided by the use of decision rules and specific criteria for evaluating the product offering. These decision rules evolve from objectives, policies, and procedures established for buying actions by management. Often some type of rating scheme or value index is used.

The above stages in the organizational buying process have particular significance for marketers in their method of approach to potential buyers. This is not to say that these stages are the only activities organizational buyers go through before making a purchase, or that they are even aware that they are going through them. The stages are presented here only as a convenient way to examine the organizational buying process and the importance of certain activities during particular stages.

---

[7]See Rowland T. Moriarty and Robert E. Spekman, *Sources of Information Utilized During the Industrial Buying Process: An Empirical Overview.* Report No. 83–101 (Cambridge, Mass.: Marketing Science Institute, 1983).

LESSONS FOR THE MANUFACTURER

There are several lessons in this chapter for manufacturing companies that sell to organizational buyers. First, manufacturers need to know the degree to which their products create problems for buyers and to devise products and marketing strategies that reduce these problems. Analysis of the buying firm's purchasing processes as well as the uses of the products is clearly important. Process mapping of organizational buyers' uses of products could be a valuable source of insights for this analysis. Selling to organizational buyers often requires both marketing and engineering personnel to call on the buying firm to overcome political and technical problems.

Second, one of the lessons learned by U.S. firms from the Japanese is that close relationships between suppliers and organizational buyers often increase the efficiency of the business process. Relationship marketing, which involves the development of long-term relationships between suppliers and organizational buyers, has been strongly advocated in recent marketing literature. Thus, rather than viewing sales to organizational buyers as one-shot deals, this approach views negotiations and sales as a part of an overall, long-term relationship. Firms selling to organizational buyers are required to carefully analyze the degree to which they offer the levels of product quality, service, delivery, flexibility, financing, and training sought by buyers.

Some companies, such as Xerox, have significantly reduced their vendor base in order to create long-term vendor relationships. These are based on joint problem solving and contact between marketing, engineering, and manufacturing parties in both the vendor and Xerox organizations. Xerox has also developed worldwide benchmarking of manufacturing excellence, which it extends to all of its suppliers in order to develop overall competitive capabilities. Such relationships and benchmarks allow organizational sellers to better satisfy the needs of organizational buyers.

Finally, organizational buyers are more likely than consumer buyers to have done careful cost-benefit analysis for purchasing from one supplier versus another. Thus, organizational sellers need to carefully analyze their offerings to ensure their competitiveness with other suppliers.

ADDITIONAL READINGS

Anderson, Erin; Wujin Chu; and Barton Weitz. "Industrial Purchasing: An Empirical Exploration of the Buyclass Framework." *Journal of Marketing,* July 1987, pp. 71–86.

Frazier, Gary L.; Robert E. Spekman; and Charles R. O'Neal. "Just-In-Time Exchange Relationships in Industrial Markets." *Journal of Marketing,* October 1988, pp. 52–67.

Heide, Jan B., and George John. "Alliances in Industrial Purchasing: The Determinants of Joint Action in Buyer-Seller Relationships." *Journal of Marketing Research,* February 1990, pp. 24–36.

Michaels, Ronald E.; Ralph L. Day; and Erich A. Joachimsthaler. "Role Stress among Industrial Buyers; An Integrative Model." *Journal of Marketing,* April 1987, pp. 28–45.

Morris, Michael H. *Industrial and Organizational Marketing.* Columbus, Ohio: Charles E. Merrill Publishing, 1988.

Reeder, Robert R.; Edward G. Brierty; and Betty H. Reeder. *Industrial Marketing: Analysis, Planning, and Control.* Englewood Cliffs, N.J.: Prentice Hall, 1987.

Robinson, William T. "Sources of Market Pioneer Advantages: The Case of Industrial Goods Industries." *Journal of Marketing Research,* February 1988, pp. 87–94.

CHAPTER 5

MARKET SEGMENTATION

Market segmentation is one of the most important concepts in the marketing literature. In fact, a primary reason for studying consumer and organizational buyer behavior is to provide bases for effective segmentation, and a large portion of marketing research is concerned with segmentation. From a marketing management point of view, selection of the appropriate target market is paramount to developing successful marketing programs.

The logic of market segmentation is quite simple and is based on the idea that a single product item can seldom meet the needs and wants of *all* consumers. Typically, consumers vary as to their needs, wants, and preferences for products and services, and successful marketers adapt their marketing programs to fulfill these preference patterns. For example, even a simple product like chewing gum has multiple flavors, package sizes, sugar contents, calories, consistencies (e.g., liquid centers), and colors to meet the preferences of various consumers. While a single product item cannot meet the needs of all consumers, it can almost always serve more than one consumer. Thus, there are usually *groups of consumers* who can be served well by a single item. If a particular group can be served *profitably* by a firm, it is a viable market segment. In other words, the firm should develop a marketing mix to serve the group or market segment.

In this chapter we consider the process of market segmentation. We define *market segmentation* as the process of dividing a market into groups of similar consumers and selecting the most appropriate group(s) for the firm to serve. We break down the process of market segmentation into six steps, as shown in Figure 5–1. While we recognize that the order of these steps may vary, depending on the firm and situation, there are few if any times when market segmentation analysis can be ignored. In fact, even if the final decision is to "mass market" and not segment at all, this

---

FIGURE 5–1
A Model of the Market Segmentation Process

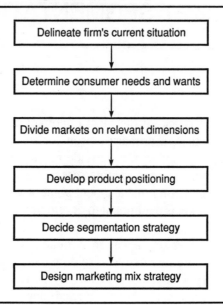

---

decision should be reached only *after* a market segmentation analysis has been conducted. Thus, market segmentation analysis is a cornerstone of sound marketing planning and decision making.

DELINEATE THE FIRM'S CURRENT SITUATION

As emphasized in Chapter 1, a firm must do a complete situational analysis when embarking on a new or modified marketing program. At the marketing planning level, such an analysis aids in determining objectives, opportunities, and constraints to be considered when selecting target markets and developing marketing mixes. In addition, marketing managers must have a clear idea of the amount of financial and other resources that will be available for developing and executing a marketing plan. Thus, the inclusion of this first step in the market segmentation process is intended to be a reminder of tasks to be performed prior to marketing planning.

HIGHLIGHT 5-1
Market Segmentation at Campbell Soup Company

Campbell Soup Company recently cooked up its own version of market segmentation, which it calls "regionalization." Basically, the company divided the United States into 22 regions, each with its own marketing and sales force. Each regional staff studies marketing strategies and media buying and has its own ad and trade-promotion budget. Eventually, up to 50 percent of Campbell's ad budget may be the responsibility of the regional groups, rather than corporate headquarters.

Regional staffs have come up with a number of innovative methods to sell Campbell's products, including:

- In Texas and California, where consumers like their food with a bit of a kick, Campbell's nacho cheese soup is spicier than in other parts of the country.
- In New York, when the Giants were bound for the Super Bowl, a local sales manager used part of her ad budget to arrange a football-related radio promotion for Swanson Frozen dinners.
- In Nevada, Campbell treats skiers at Ski Incline resort to hot samples of its soup of the day.
- In the South, Campbell has experimented with a Creole soup and a red-bean soup for the Hispanic market.

While the company is still ironing out logistical problems, regionalization is a way to deal with the end of the American mass market and perhaps to serve consumers better. Other consumer goods companies are bound to study Campbell's recipe.

DETERMINE CONSUMER NEEDS AND WANTS

As emphasized throughout this text, successful marketing strategies depend on discovering and satisfying consumer needs and wants. In some cases, this idea is quite operational. To illustrate, suppose a firm has a good deal of venture capital and is seeking to diversify its interest into new markets. A firm in this situation may seek to discover a broad variety of unsatisfied needs. However, in most situations, the industry in which the firm operates specifies the boundaries of a firm's need satisfaction activities. For example, a firm in the communication industry may seek more efficient methods for serving consumers' long-distance telephone needs.

As a practical matter, new technology often brings about an investigation of consumer needs and wants for new or modified products and services. In these situations, the firm is seeking the group of consumers whose needs could best be satisfied by the new or modified product. Further, at a strategic level, consumer needs and wants usually are translated into more operational concepts. For instance, consumer attitudes, preferences, and benefits sought, which are determined through marketing research, are commonly used for segmentation purposes.

DIVIDE MARKETS ON RELEVANT DIMENSIONS

In a narrow sense, this step is often considered to be the whole of market segmentation (i.e., consumers are grouped on the basis of one or more similarities and treated as a homogeneous segment of a heterogeneous total market). There are three important questions to be considered here:

1. Should the segmentation be a priori or post hoc?
2. How does one determine the relevant dimensions or bases to use for segmentation?
3. What are some bases for segmenting consumer and industrial buyer markets?

A Priori versus Post Hoc Segmentation

Real-world segmentation has followed one of two general patterns.[1] An *a priori segmentation* approach is one in which the marketing manager has decided on the appropriate basis for segmentation in advance of doing any research on a market. For example, a manager may decide that a market should be divided on the basis of whether people are nonusers, light users, or heavy users of a particular product. Segmentation research is then conducted to determine the size of each of these groups and their demographic or psychographic profiles.

Post hoc segmentation is an approach in which people are grouped into segments on the basis of research findings. For example, people

---

[1]Yoram Wind, "Issues and Advances in Segmentation Research," *Journal of Marketing Research,* August 1978, pp. 317–37. Also see T. P. Bean and D. M. Ennis, "Market Segmentation: A Review," *European Journal of Marketing,* no. 5 (1987), pp. 20–42.

interviewed concerning their attitudes or benefits sought in a particular product category are grouped according to their responses. The size of each of these groups and their demographic and psychographic profiles are then determined.

Both of these approaches are valuable, and the question of which to use depends in part on how well the firm knows the market for a particular product class. If through previous research and experience a marketing manager has successfully isolated a number of key market dimensions, then an a priori approach based on them may provide more useful information. In the case of segmentation for entirely new products, a post hoc approach may be useful for determining key market dimensions. However, even when using a post hoc approach, some consideration must be given to the variables to be included in the research design. Thus, some consideration must be given to the relevant segmentation dimensions regardless of which approach is used.

Relevance of Segmentation Dimensions

Unfortunately, there is no simple solution for determining the relevant dimensions for segmenting markets. Certainly, managerial expertise and experience are needed for selecting the appropriate dimensions or bases on which to segment particular markets. In most cases, however, at least some initial dimensions can be determined from previous research, purchase trends, and managerial judgment. For instance, suppose we wish to segment the market for all-terrain vehicles. Clearly, several dimensions come to mind for initial consideration including sex (male), age (18 to 35 years), lifestyle (outdoorsman), and income level (perhaps $15,000 to $25,000). At a minimum, these variables should be included in subsequent segmentation research. Of course, the most market-oriented approach to segmentation is on the basis of what benefits the potential consumer is seeking. Thus, consideration and research of sought benefits is a strongly recommended approach in the marketing literature. This approach will be considered in some detail in the following section.

Bases for Segmentation

A number of useful bases for segmenting consumer and organizational markets are presented in Figure 5–2. This is by no means a complete list of possible segmentation variables but represents some useful bases

---

FIGURE 5–2
Useful Segmentation Bases for Consumer and Industrial Markets

---

Segmentation Base	Examples of Base Categories

	Consumer Markets
Geographic:	
Region	Pacific, Mountain, West North Central, West South Central, East North Central, East South Central, South Atlantic, Middle Atlantic, New England.
City, county, or SMSA size	Under 5,000; 5,000–19,999; 20,000–49,999; 50,000–99,999; 100,000–249,999; 250,000–499,999; 500,000–999,999; 1,000,000–3,999,999; 4,000,000 or over.
Population density	Urban, suburban, rural.
Climate	Warm, cold.
Demographic:	
Age	Under 6; 6–12; 13–19; 20–29; 30–39; 40–49; 50–59; 60+
Sex	Male, female.
Family size	1–2; 3–4; 5+.
Family life cycle	Young, single; young, married, no children; young, married, youngest child under 6; young, married, youngest child 6 or over; older, married, with children; older, married, no children under 18; older, single; other.
Income	Under $5,000; $5,000–$7,999; $8,000–$9,999; $10,000–$14,999; $15,000–$24,999; $25,000–$34,999; $35,000 or over.
Occupation	Professional and technical; managers, officials, and proprietors; clerical, sales; craftsmen, foremen; operatives; farmers; retired; students; housewives, unemployed.
Education	Grade school or less; some high school; graduated high school; some college; graduated college; some graduate work; graduate degree.
Religion	Catholic, Protestant, Jewish, other.
Race	White, black, oriental, other.
Nationality	American, British, German, Italian, Japanese, other.
Psychographic:	
Social class	Lower-lower, upper-lower, lower-middle, upper-middle, lower-upper, upper-upper.
Lifestyle	Traditionalist, sophisticate, swinger.
Personality	Compliant, aggressive, detached.

FIGURE 5–2   *(concluded)*

Segmentation Base	Examples of Base Categories

Consumer Markets (continued)

Cognitive and behavioral:
Attitudes	Positive, neutral, negative.
Benefits sought	Convenience, economy, prestige.
Readiness stage	Unaware, aware, informed, interested, desirous, intention to purchase.
Perceived risk	High, moderate, low.
Innovativeness	Innovator, early adopter, early majority, late majority, laggard.
Involvement	Low, high.
Loyalty status	None, some, total.
Usage rate	None, light, medium, heavy.
User status	Nonuser, ex-user, potential user, current user.

Industrial Buyer Markets

Source loyalty	Purchase from one, two, three, four, or more suppliers.
Size of company	Small, medium, large relative to industry.
Average size of purchase	Small, medium, large.
Usage rate	Light, medium, heavy.
Product application	Maintenance, production, final product component, administration.
Type of business	Manufacturer, wholesaler, retailer; SIC categories.
Location	North, East, South, West; sales territories.
Purchase status	New customer, occasional purchaser, frequent purchaser, nonpurchaser.
Attribute importance	Reliability of supply, price, service, durability, convenience, reputation of supplier.

---

and categories. Two commonly used approaches for segmenting markets include benefit segmentation and psychographic segmentation. We will discuss these two in some detail.

Benefit Segmentation

The belief underlying this segmentation approach is that the benefits people are seeking in consuming a given product are the basic reasons for the existence of true market segments.[2] Thus, this approach attempts to measure consumer value systems and consumer perceptions of various brands in a product class. To illustrate, the classic example of a benefit segmentation was provided by Russell Haley and concerned the toothpaste market. Haley identified five basic segments, which are presented in Figure 5–3. Haley argued that this segmentation could be very useful for selecting advertising copy, media, commercial length, packaging, and new product design. For example, colorful packages might be appropriate for the Sensory Segment, perhaps aqua (to indicate fluoride) for the Worrier Group, and gleaming white for the Social Segment because of this segment's interest in white teeth.

Calantone and Sawyer also used a benefit segmentation approach to segment the market for bank services.[3] Their research was concerned with the question of whether benefit segments remain stable across time. While they found some stability in segments, there were some differences in attribute importance, size, and demographics at different times. Thus, they argue for ongoing benefit segmentation research to keep track of any changes in a market that might affect marketing strategy.

Benefit segmentation is clearly a market-oriented approach to segmentation that seeks to identify consumer needs and wants and to satisfy them by providing products and services with the desired benefits. It is clearly very consistent with the approach to marketing suggested by the marketing concept.

Psychographic Segmentation

Whereas benefit segmentation focuses on the benefits sought by the consumer, psychographic segmentation focuses on the personal attributes of the consumer. The psychographic or lifestyle approach typically follows a post hoc model of segmentation. Generally, a large number of questions

---

[2]Russell I. Haley, "Benefit Segmentation: A Decision-Oriented Research Tool," *Journal of Marketing,* July 1968, pp. 30–35; Russell I. Haley, "Benefit Segmentation—20 Years Later," *Journal of Consumer Marketing,* no. 2 (1983), pp. 5–13; Russell I. Haley, "Benefit Segments: Backwards and Forwards," *Journal of Advertising Research,* February–March 1984, pp. 19–25.

[3]Roger J. Calantone and Alan G. Sawyer, "The Stability of Benefit Segments," *Journal of Marketing Research,* August 1978, pp. 395–404; also see James R. Merrill and William A. Weeks, "Predicting and Identifying Benefit Segments in the Elderly Market," in *AMA Educator's Proceedings,* ed. Patrick Murphy et al. (Chicago: American Marketing Association, 1983), pp. 399–403; Wagner A. Kamakura, "A Least Squares Procedure for Benefit Segmentation with Conjoint Experiments," *Journal of Marketing Research,* May 1988, pp. 157–67.

FIGURE 5–3
Toothpaste Market Benefit Segments

	Sensory Segment	Sociable Segment	Worrier Segment	Independent Segment
Principal benefit sought	Flavor and product appearance.	Brightness of teeth.	Decay prevention.	Price.
Demographic strengths	Children.	Teens, young people.	Large families.	Men.
Special behavioral characteristics	Users of spearmint-flavored toothpaste.	Smokers.	Heavy users.	Heavy users.
Brands disproportionately favored	Colgate.	Macleans, Ultra Brite.	Crest.	Cheapest brand.
Lifestyle characteristics	Hedonistic.	Active.	Conservative.	Value oriented.

Source: Adapted from Russell I. Haley, "Benefit Segmentation: A Decision-Oriented Research Tool," *Journal of Marketing*, July 1968, pp. 30–35. Reprinted by permission of the American Marketing Association.

are asked concerning consumers' activities, interests, and opinions, and then consumers are grouped together empirically based on their responses. Although questions have been raised about the validity of this segmentation approach, it provides much useful information about markets.[4]

A well-known psychographic segmentation was developed at SRI International in California. The original segmentation divided consumers in the United States into nine groups and was called VALS™, which stands for "values and lifestyles." However, while this segmentation was commercially successful, it tended to place the majority of consumers into only one or two groups, and SRI felt it needed to be updated to reflect changes in society. Thus, SRI developed a new typology called VALS 2.[5]

---

[4]John L. Lastovicka, John P. Murry Jr., and Erich Joachimsthaler, "Evaluating the Measurement Validity of Lifestyle Typologies with Qualitative Measures and Multiplicative Factoring," *Journal of Marketing Research*, February 1990, pp. 11–23.

[5]This discussion is taken from J. Paul Peter and Jerry C. Olson, *Consumer Behavior and Marketing Strategy*, 2nd ed. (Homewood, Ill.: Richard D. Irwin, 1990), p. 411.

HIGHLIGHT 5–2
An Operational Approach to Person-Situation Benefit Segmentation

Peter Dickson argues that market segmentation has focused too narrowly on customer characteristics and needs to include the usage situation in segmentation research. Not only do different types of people purchase different types of products, but they also purchase them for use in different situations. For example, different types of camping gear are needed for cold weather versus hot weather versus mountain-climbing situations. Below is an operational approach for segmenting markets on the basis of both person and situational factors.

Step 1: Use observational studies, focus group discussions, and secondary data to discover whether different usage situations exist and whether they are determinant, in the sense that they appear to affect the importance of various product characteristics.

Step 2: If step 1 produces promising results, undertake a benefit, product perception, and reported market behavior segmentation survey of consumers. Measure benefits and perceptions by usage situation as well as by individual difference characteristics. Assess situation usage frequency by recall estimates or by usage situation diaries.

Step 3: Construct a person-situation segmentation matrix. The rows are the major usage situations; the columns are groups of users identified by a single characteristic or a combination of characteristics.

Step 4: Rank the cells in the matrix in terms of their submarket sales volume. The situation-person combination that results in the greatest consumption of the generic product would be ranked first.

Step 5: State the major benefits sought, the important product dimensions, and the unique market behavior for each nonempty cell of the matrix (some person types will never consume the product in certain usage situations).

Step 6: Position your competitor's offerings within the matrix. The person-situation segments they currently serve can be determined by the product feature they promote and their marketing strategy.

Step 7: Position your offering within the matrix on the same criteria.

Step 8: Assess how well your current offering and marketing strategy meet the needs of the submarkets, compared to the competition.

Step 9: Identify market opportunities based on submarket size, needs, and competitive advantage.

Source: Peter R. Dickson, "Person-Situation: Segmentation's Missing Link," *Journal of Marketing,* Fall 1982, p. 61. Reprinted by permission of the American Marketing Association.

HIGHLIGHT 5–3
Examples of Items Used in Psychographic Segmentation Research

1. I often watch the newspaper advertisements for announcements of department store sales.
2. I like to watch or listen to baseball or football games.
3. I often try new stores before my friends and neighbors do.
4. I like to work on community projects.
5. My children are the most important thing in my life.
6. I will probably have more money to spend next year than I have now.
7. I often seek out the advice of my friends regarding which store to buy from.
8. I think I have more self-confidence than most people.
9. I enjoy going to symphony concerts.
10. It is good to have charge accounts.

(These items are scored on a "agree strongly" to "disagree strongly" scale.)

VALS 2 is based on two national surveys of 2,500 consumers who responded to 43 lifestyle questions. The first survey developed the segmentation, and the second validated it and linked it to buying and media behavior. The questionnaire asked consumers to respond to whether they agreed or disagreed with statements such as "My idea of fun at a national park would be to stay at an expensive lodge and dress up for dinner" and "I could stand to skin a dead animal." Consumers were then clustered into the eight groups shown and described in Figure 5–4.

The VALS 2 groups are arranged in a rectangle and are based on two dimensions. The vertical dimension represents resources, which include income, education, self-confidence, health, eagerness to buy, intelligence, and energy level. The horizontal dimension represents self-orientations, and includes three different types. *Principle-oriented consumers* are guided by their views of how the world is or should be; *status-oriented consumers* by the action and opinions of others; and *action-oriented consumers* by a desire for social or physical activity, variety, and risk taking.

Each of the VALS 2 groups represents from 9 to 17 percent of the U.S. adult population. Marketers can buy VALS 2 information for a variety of products and can have it tied to a number of other consumer databases.

FIGURE 5–4
VALS 2™ Eight American Lifestyles

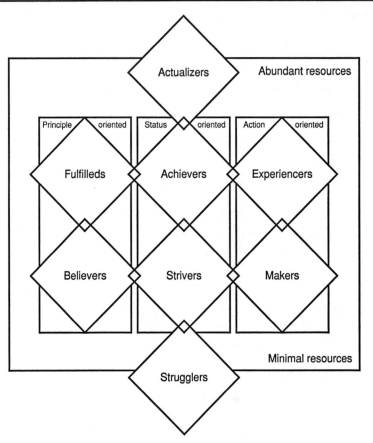

Actualizers. These consumers have the highest incomes and such high self-esteem and abundant resources that they can indulge in any or all self-orientations. They are located above the rectangle. Image is important to them as an expression of their taste, independence, and character. Their consumer choices are directed toward the finer things in life.

Fulfilleds. These consumers are the high-resource group of those who are principle-oriented. They are mature, responsible, well-educated professionals. Their leisure activities center on their homes, but they are well-informed about what goes on in the world, and they are open to new ideas and social change. They have high incomes but are practical consumers.

FIGURE 5–4 *(concluded)*

Believers. These consumers are the low-resource group of those who are principle-oriented. They are conservative and predictable consumers who favor American products and established brands. Their lives are centered on family, church, community, and the nation. They have modest incomes.

Achievers. These consumers are the high-resource group of those who are status-oriented. They are successful, work-oriented people who get their satisfaction from their jobs and families. They are politically conservative and respect authority and the status quo. They favor established products and services that show off their success to their peers.

Strivers. These consumers are the low-resource group of those who are status-oriented. They have values very similar to Achievers but have fewer economic, social, and psychological resources. Style is extremely important to them as they strive to emulate people they admire and wish to be like.

Experiencers. These consumers are the high-resource group of those who are action-oriented. They are the youngest of all the segments with a median age of 25. They have a lot of energy, which they pour into physical exercise and social activities. They are avid consumers, spending heavily on clothing, fast foods, music, and other youthful favorites—with particular emphasis on new products and services.

Makers. These consumers are the low-resource group of those who are action-oriented. They are practical people who value self-sufficiency. They are focused on the familiar—family, work, and physical recreation—and have little interest in the broader world. As consumers, they appreciate practical and functional products.

Strugglers. These consumers have the lowest incomes. They have too few resources to be included in any consumer self-orientation and are thus located below the rectangle. They are the oldest of all the segments with a median age of 61. Within their limited means, they tend to be brand-loyal consumers.

Source: Martha Farnsworth Riche, "Psychographics for the 1990s," *American Demographics,* July 1989, pp. 24–26ff. Adapted with permission © American Demographics.

DEVELOP PRODUCT POSITIONING

By this time the firm should have a good idea of the basic segments of the market that could potentially be satisfied with its product. The current step is concerned with positioning the product in the minds of consumers relative to competing products. Undoubtedly, the classic example of positioning is the 7UP "Uncola" campaign. Prior to this campaign, 7UP had difficulty convincing consumers that the product could be enjoyed

---

HIGHLIGHT 5–4
Positioning Your Product

A variety of positioning strategies is available to the advertiser. An object can be positioned:

1. By attributes—Crest is a cavity fighter.
2. By price/quality—Sears is a "value" store.
3. By competitor—Avis positions itself with Hertz.
4. By application—Gatorade is for flu attacks.
5. By product user—Miller is for the blue-collar, heavy beer drinker.
6. By product class—Carnation Instant Breakfast is a breakfast food.

The selection of a positioning strategy involves identifying competitors, relevant attributes, competitor positions, and market segments. Research-based approaches can help in each of these steps by providing conceptualization even if the subjective judgments of managers are used to provide the actual input information to the positioning decision.

Source: David A. Aaker and J. Gary Shansby, "Positioning Your Product." Reprinted from *Business Horizons*, May–June 1982, p. 62. Copyright 1982 by the Foundation for the School of Business at Indiana University. Used with permission.

as a soft drink and not just as a mixer. Consumers believed that colas were soft drinks but apparently did not perceive 7UP in this way. However, by positioning 7UP as the "Uncola" the company was capable of positioning the product (1) as a soft drink that could be consumed in the same situations as colas and (2) as an alternative to colas. This positioning was very successful.

In determining the appropriate positioning of the product, the firm must consider its offering relative to competition. Some experts argue that different positioning strategies should be used, depending on whether the firm is the market leader or a follower, and that followers usually should not attempt positioning directly against the industry leader.[6] While there are many sophisticated research tools available for investigating positioning, they are beyond the scope of this text. The main point here is that, in segmenting markets, some segments otherwise

---

[6]See Al Ries and Jack Trout, *Positioning: The Battle for Your Mind* (New York: Warner Books, 1981); Al Ries and Jack Trout, *Marketing Warfare* (New York: McGraw-Hill, 1986).

appearing to be approachable might be forgone, since competitive products may already dominate that segment in sales and in the minds of consumers. Product positioning studies also are useful for giving the marketing manager a clearer idea of consumer perceptions of market offerings.

DECIDE SEGMENTATION STRATEGY

The firm is now ready to select its segmentation strategy. There are four basic alternatives. First, the firm may decide not to enter the market. For example, analysis to this stage may reveal there is no viable market niche for the firm's offering. Second, the firm may decide not to segment but to be a mass marketer. There are at least three situations when this may be the appropriate decision for the firm:

1. The market is so small that marketing to a portion of it is not profitable.
2. Heavy users make up such a large proportion of the sales volume that they are the only relevant target.
3. The brand is the dominant brand in the market, and targeting to a few segments would not benefit sales and profits.[7]

Third, the firm may decide to market to one segment. And fourth, the firm may decide to market to more than one segment and design a separate marketing mix for each. In any case, the firm must have some criteria on which to base its segmentation strategy decisions. Three important criteria on which to base such decisions are that a viable segment must be (1) measurable, (2) meaningful, and (3) marketable.

1. *Measurable.* For a segment to be selected, the firm must be capable of measuring its size and characteristics. For instance, one of the difficulties with segmenting on the basis of social class is that the concept and its divisions are not clearly defined and measured. Alternatively, income is a much easier concept to measure.

---

[7]Shirley Young, Leland Ott, and Barbara Feigin, "Some Practical Considerations in Market Segmentation," *Journal of Marketing Research,* August 1978, p. 405.

HIGHLIGHT 5–5
Segmentation Bases for Particular Marketing Decision Areas

For General Understanding of the Market:
Benefits sought.
Product purchase and usage patterns.
Needs.
Brand loyalty and switching patterns.
A hybrid of the variables above.

For Positioning Studies:
Product Usage.
Product preference.
Benefits sought.
A hybrid of the variables above.

For New Product Concepts (and New Product Introduction):
Reaction to new concepts (intention to buy, preference over current brand, and so on).
Benefits sought.

For Pricing Decisions:
Price sensitivity.
Deal proneness.
Price sensitivity by purchase/usage patterns.

For Advertising Decisions:
Benefits sought.
Media usage.
Psychographic/lifestyle.
A hybrid (of the variables above or purchase/usage pattern, or both).

For Distribution Decisions:
Store loyalty and patronage.
Benefits sought in store selection.

Source: Yoram Wind, "Issues and Advances in Segmentation Research," *Journal of Marketing Research,* August 1978, p. 320. Reprinted by permission of the American Marketing Association.

2. *Meaningful.* A meaningful segment is one that is large enough to have sufficient sales potential and growth potential to offer long-run profits for the firm.
3. *Marketable.* A marketable segment is one that can be reached and served by the firm in an efficient manner.

HIGHLIGHT 5–6
Differences in Marketing Strategy for Three Segmentation Alternatives

Strategy Elements	Mass Marketing	Single Market Segmentation	Multiple Market Segmentation
Market definition	Broad range of consumers.	One well-defined consumer group.	Two or more well-defined consumer groups.
Product strategy	Limited number of products under one brand for many types of consumers.	One brand tailored to one consumer group.	Distinct brand for each consumer group.
Pricing strategy	One "popular" price range.	One price range tailored to the consumer group.	Distinct price range for each consumer group.
Distribution strategy	All possible outlets.	All suitable outlets.	All suitable outlets—differs by segment.
Promotion strategy	Mass media.	All suitable media.	All suitable media—differs by segment.
Strategy emphasis	Appeal to various types of consumers through a uniform, broad-based marketing program.	Appeal to one specific consumer group through a highly specialized, but uniform, marketing program.	Appeal to two or more distinct market segments through different marketing plans catering to each segment.

Source: Reprinted with the permission of MacMillan Publishing Company from *Marketing*, 4th ed., by Joel R. Evans and Barry Berman. Copyright © 1990 by MacMillan Publishing Company, Inc.

Segments that meet these criteria are viable markets for the firm's offering. The firm must now give further attention to completing its marketing mix offering.

DESIGN MARKETING MIX STRATEGY

The firm is now in a position to complete its marketing plan by finalizing the marketing mix or mixes to be used for each segment. Clearly, selection of the target market and designing the marketing mix go hand in hand, and thus many marketing mix decisions should have already been carefully considered. To illustrate, the target market selected may be price sensitive, so some consideration has already been given to price levels, and clearly product positioning has many implications for promotion and channel decisions. Thus, while we place marketing mix design at the end of the model, many of these decisions are clearly made in *conjunction* with target market selection. In the next six chapters of this text, marketing mix decisions will be discussed in detail.

LESSONS FOR THE MANUFACTURER

Market segmentation is not only an important marketing concept, but also a key for the success of many manufacturing organizations. For example, consider automobile manufacturers. The reason that each major carmaker has a variety of models is that it is attempting to appeal to different market segments. There are segments of consumers who want sports cars, luxury cars, station wagons, sedans, economy cars, and minivans. Also, each of the major U.S. carmakers offers a variety of brands to choose from, such as GM's Chevrolet, Pontiac, Oldsmobile, Buick, Cadillac, and Saturn. Of interest here for manufacturers is that the manufacturing process for many of these brands is identical. In fact, while some cars have different names, they are nearly identical in terms of construction and often come off the same assembly lines. This is highly efficient manufacturing when the same product can be given slight variations and different names and still appeal to different target markets.

The need for marketing and manufacturing personnel to work closely together is particularly evident when a firm chooses a multiple market segmentation strategy. As noted, this strategy involves offering a variety of different products to a variety of different markets. In order for this strategy to be successful, firms often need cleverly designed products that facilitate fast changeovers in manufacturing, JIT manufacturing for non-repetitive products, and a manufacturing system that is flexible enough to meet the needs of the distribution channel and final consumers.

Finally, it is important to recognize that it is only in recent times that manufacturers have had detailed data on various markets and the ability to segment consumers individually. Due to the increase in the use of scanner cable methods, manufacturers today often have data on hundreds of thousands of consumers, including demographic information and detailed purchasing data for supermarket and other products. For example, one manufacturer of tobacco products is reported to have the names, addresses, and purchasing data for over 30 million smokers. Thus, manufacturers can expect to become more effective at targeting various products and product alterations at specific markets. Such detailed data and the ability to use them effectively is a major competitive advantage for many manufacturing companies and may become more important in the future.

ADDITIONAL READINGS

Dickson, Peter R., and James L. Ginter. "Market Segmentation, Product Differentiation, and Marketing Strategy." *Journal of Marketing*, April 1987, pp. 1–10.

Dröge, Cornelia, and René Y. Darmon. "Associative Positioning Strategies through Comparative Advertising: Attribute versus Overall Similarity Approaches." *Journal of Marketing Research*, November 1987, pp. 377–88.

Grover, Rajiv, and V. Srinivasan. "A Simultaneous Approach to Market Segmentation and Market Structuring." *Journal of Marketing Research*, May 1987, pp. 139–53.

Kahn, Barbara E.; Monohar U. Kalwani; and Donald G. Morrison. "Niching versus Change-of-Pace Brands: Using Purchase Frequencies and Penetration Rates to Infer Brand Positionings." *Journal of Marketing Research*, November 1988, pp. 384–90.

Kamakura, Wagner A., and Gary J. Russell. "A Probabilistic Choice Model for Market Segmentation and Elasticity Structure." *Journal of Marketing Research*, November 1989, pp. 379–90.

Shostack, Lynn G. "Service Positioning through Structural Change." *Journal of Marketing*, January 1987, pp. 34–43.

Sujen, Mita, and James R. Bettman. "The Effects of Brand Positioning Strategies on Consumers' Brand and Category Perceptions: Some Insights from Schema Research." *Journal of Marketing Research*, November 1989, pp. 454–67.

Zeithaml, Valarie A. "The New Demographics and Market Fragmentation." *Journal of Marketing*, Summer 1985, pp. 64–75.

PART 3

DEVELOPING THE MARKETING MIX

CHAPTER 6

PRODUCT STRATEGY

Product strategy is a critical element of marketing and business strategy, since it is through the sale of products and services that companies survive and grow. This chapter discusses four important areas of concern in developing product strategies. First, some basic issues are discussed including product definition, product classification, product mix and product line, and packaging and branding. Second, the product life cycle and its implications for product strategy are explained. Third, the product audit is reviewed, and finally, five ways to organize for product management are overviewed. These include the marketing manager system, product (brand) manager system, product planning committee, new product manager system, and venture team approaches.

BASIC ISSUES IN PRODUCT MANAGEMENT

Successful marketing depends on understanding the nature of products and basic decision areas in product management. In this section, we discuss the definition and classification of products and the nature of a product mix and product lines. Also considered is the role of packaging and branding.

Product Definition

The way in which the product variable is defined can have important implications for the survival, profitability, and long-run growth of the firm. For example, the same product can be viewed at least three different ways. First, it can be viewed in terms of the tangible product—the physical entity or service that is offered to the buyer. Second, it can be viewed in terms of the extended product—the tangible product along with the whole cluster of services that accompany it. For example, a

---

HIGHLIGHT 6–1
Elements of Product Strategy

1. An audit of the firm's actual and potential resources.
   a. Financial strength.
   b. Access to raw materials.
   c. Plant and equipment.
   d. Operating personnel.
   e. Management.
   f. Engineering and technical skills
   g. Patents and licenses.
2. Approaches to current markets.
   a. More of the same products.
   b. Variations of present products in terms of grades, sizes, and packages.
   c. New products to replace or supplement current lines.
   d. Product deletions.
3. Approaches to new or potential markets.
   a. Geographical expansion of domestic sales.
   b. New socioeconomic or ethnic groups.
   c. Overseas markets.
   d. New uses of present products.
   e. Complementary goods.
   f. Mergers and acquisitions.
4. State of competition.
   a. New entries into the industry.
   b. Product imitation.
   c. Competitive mergers or acquisitions.

---

manufacturer of computer software may offer a 24-hour hotline to answer questions users may have, free or reduced-cost software updates, free replacement of damaged software, and a subscription to a newsletter that documents new applications of the software. Third, it can be viewed in terms of the generic product—the essential benefits the buyer expects to receive from the product. For example, many personal care products bring to the purchaser feelings of self-enhancement and security in addition to the tangible benefits they offer.

From the standpoint of the marketing manager, to define the product solely in terms of the tangible product is to fall into the error of "marketing myopia." Executives who are guilty of committing this error define their company's product too narrowly, since overemphasis is placed on the physical object itself. The classic example of this mistake can be found

in railroad passenger service. Although no amount of product improvement could have staved off its decline, if the industry had defined itself
as being in the transportation business, rather than the railroad business,
it might still be profitable today. On the positive side, toothpaste manufacturers have been willing to exercise flexibility in defining their product. For years toothpaste was an oral hygiene product where emphasis
was placed solely on fighting tooth decay and bad breath (e.g., Crest
with fluoride). More recently, many manufacturers have recognized the
need to market toothpaste as a cosmetic item (to clean teeth of stains),
as a defense against gum disease (to reduce the buildup of tartar above
the gumline), as an aid for denture wearers, and as a breath freshener.
As a result, special purpose brands have been designed to serve these
particular needs, such as Ultra Brite, Close-Up, Aqua-fresh, Aim, Fresh
'n Brite, and the wide variety of tartar-control formula and gel toothpastes
offered under existing brand names.

   In line with the marketing concept philosophy, a reasonable definition of product is that it is *the sum of the physical, psychological, and
sociological satisfactions the buyer derives from purchase, ownership,
and consumption.* From this standpoint, products are consumer-satisfying
objects that include such things as accessories, packaging, and service.

Product Classification

A product classification scheme can be useful to the marketing manager
as an analytical device to assist in planning marketing strategy and programs. A basic assumption underlying such classifications is that products
with common attributes can be marketed in a similar fashion. In general,
products are classed according to two basic criteria: (1) end use or market;
and (2) degree of processing or physical transformation.

1. *Agricultural products and raw materials.* These are goods grown
   or extracted from the land or sea, such as iron ore, wheat, sand.
   In general these products are fairly homogenous, sold in large
   volume, and have low value per unit or bulk weight.
2. *Industrial goods.* Such products are purchased by business firms
   for the purpose of producing other goods or for running the
   business. This category includes the following:
   a. Raw materials and semifinished goods.
   b. Major and minor equipment, such as basic machinery, tools,
   and other processing facilities.

      c. Parts or components, which become an integral element of some other finished good.

      d. Supplies or items used to operate the business but that do not become part of the final product.

3. *Consumer goods.* Consumer goods can be divided into three classes:

      a. Convenience goods, such as food, which are purchased frequently with minimum effort. Impulse goods would also fall into this category.

      b. Shopping goods, such as appliances, which are purchased after some time and energy are spent comparing the various offerings.

      c. Specialty goods, which are unique in some way so the consumer will make a special purchase effort to obtain them.

In general, the buying motive, buying habits, and character of the market are different for industrial goods vis-à-vis consumer goods. A primary purchasing motive for industrial goods is, of course, profit. As mentioned in a previous chapter, industrial goods are usually purchased as means to an end, and not as an end in themselves. This is another way of saying that the demand for industrial goods is a derived demand. Industrial goods are often purchased directly from the original source with few middlemen, because many of these goods can be bought in large quantities; they have high unit value; technical advice on installation and use is required; and the product is ordered according to the user's specifications. Many industrial goods are subject to multiple-purchase influence and a long period of negotiation is often required.

    The market for industrial goods has certain attributes that distinguish it from the consumer goods market. Much of the market is concentrated geographically, as in the case of steel, auto, or shoe manufacturing. For certain products there are a limited number of buyers; this is known as a *vertical market,* which means that *(a)* it is narrow, because customers are restricted to a few industries; and *(b)* it is deep, in that a large percentage of the producers in the market use the product. Some products, such as office supplies, have a *horizontal market,* which means that the goods are purchased by all types of firms in many different industries. In general, buyers of industrial goods are reasonably well informed. As noted previously, heavy reliance is often placed on price, quality control, and reliability of supply source.

In terms of consumer products, many marketing scholars have found the convenience, shopping, and specialty classification inadequate and have attempted to either refine it or to derive an entirely new typology. None of these attempts appear to have met with complete success.[1] Perhaps there is no "best" way to deal with this problem. From the standpoint of the marketing manager, product classification is useful to the extent that it assists in providing guidelines for developing an appropriate marketing mix. For example, convenience goods generally require broadcast promotion and long channels of distribution as opposed to shopping goods, which generally require more targeted promotion and somewhat shorter channels of distribution.

Product Mix and Product Line

The *product mix* is the composite products offered for sale by the firm; *product line* refers to a group of products that are closely related, either because they satisfy a class of need, are used together, are sold to the same customer groups, are marketed through the same types of outlets, or fall within given price ranges. There are three primary dimensions of a firm's product mix: (1) width of the product mix, which refers to the number of product lines the firm handles; (2) depth of the product mix, which refers to the average number of products in each line; (3) consistency of the product mix, which refers to the similarity of product lines. Thus, McDonald's hamburgers represent a product item in its line of sandwiches; whereas hot cakes or Egg McMuffins represent items in a different line, namely, breakfast foods.

Development of a plan for the existing product line has been called the most critical element of a company's product planning activity.[2] In designing such plans, management needs accurate information on the current and anticipated performance of its products, which should encompass:

1. Consumer evaluation of the company's products, particularly their strengths and weaknesses vis-à-vis competition (i.e., product positioning by market segment information).

---

[1] For a review and suggestions for product classification, see Patrick E. Murphy and Ben M. Enis, "Classifying Products Strategically," *Journal of Marketing,* July 1986, pp. 24–42.

[2] Yoram Wind and Henry J. Claycamp, "Planning Product Line Strategy: A Matrix Approach," *Journal of Marketing,* January 1976, p. 2.

HIGHLIGHT 6–2
A. Classes of Consumer Goods—Some Characteristics and Marketing Considerations

Characteristics and Marketing Considerations	Type of Product		
	Convenience	Shopping	Specialty
Characteristics			
1. Time and effort devoted by consumer to shopping.	Very little.	Considerable.	Cannot generalize; consumer may go to nearby store and buy with minimum effort or may have to go to distant store and spend much time and effort.
2. Time spent planning the purchase.	Very little.	Considerable.	Considerable.
3. How soon want is satisfied after it arises.	Immediately.	Relatively long time.	Relatively long time.
4. Are price and quality compared?	No.	Yes.	No.
5. Price.	Low.	High.	High.
6. Frequency of purchase.	Usually frequent.	Infrequent.	Infrequent.
7. Importance.	Unimportant.	Often very important.	Cannot generalize.
Marketing Considerations			
1. Length of channel.	Long.	Short.	Short to very short.
2. Importance of retailer.	Any single store is relatively unimportant.	Important.	Very important.
3. Number of outlets.	As many as possible.	Few.	Few; often only one in a market.
4. Stock turnover.	High.	Lower.	Lower.
5. Gross margin.	Low.	High.	High.
6. Responsibility for advertising.	Manufacturer's.	Retailer's.	Joint responsibility.
7. Importance of point-of-purchase display.	Very important.	Less important.	Less important.
8. Advertising used.	Manufacturer's.	Retailer's.	Both.
9. Brand or store name important.	Brand name.	Store name.	Both.
10. Importance of packaging.	Very important.	Less important.	Less important.

B. Classes of Industrial Products—Some Characteristics and Marketing Considerations

Characteristics and Marketing Considerations	Type of Product				
	Raw Materials	Fabricating Parts and Materials	Installations	Accessory Equipment	Operating Supplies
Example:	Iron ore.	Engine blocks.	Blast furnaces.	Storage racks.	Paper clips.
Characteristics					
1. Unit price.	Very low.	Low.	Very high.	Medium.	Low.
2. Length of life.	Very short.	Depends on final product.	Very long.	Long.	Short.
3. Quantities purchased.	Large.	Large.	Very small.	Small.	Small.
4. Frequency of purchase.	Frequent delivery; long-term purchase contract.	Infrequent purchase, but frequent delivery.	Very infrequent.	Medium frequency.	Frequent.
5. Standardization of competitive products.	Very much; grading is important.	Very much.	Very little; custom-made.	Little.	Much.
6. Limits on supply.	Limited; supply increases slowly or not at all.	Usually no problem.	No problem.	Usually no problem.	Usually no problem.
Marketing Considerations					
1. Nature of channel.	Short; no middlemen.	Short; middlemen for small buyers.	Short; no middlemen.	Middlemen used.	Middlemen used.
2. Negotiation period.	Hard to generalize.	Medium.	Long.	Medium.	Short.
3. Price competition.	Important.	Important.	Not important.	Not main factor.	Important.
4. Presale/postsale service.	Not important.	Important.	Very important.	Important.	Very little.
5. Demand stimulation.	Very little.	Moderate.	Sales people very important.	Important.	Not too important.
6. Brand preference.	None.	Generally low.	High.	High.	Low.
7. Advance buying contract.	Important; long-term contracts used.	Important; long-term contracts used.	Not usually used.	Not usually used.	Not usually used.

Source: William J. Stanton and Charles Futrell, *Fundamentals of Marketing*, 8th ed., pp. 195, 198, © 1987 by McGraw-Hill, Inc. Reprinted by permission of the publisher.

2. Objective information on actual and anticipated product performance on relevant criteria, such as sales, profits, and market share.[3]

Packaging and Branding

Distinctive or unique packaging is one method of differentiating a relatively homogeneous product. To illustrate, shelf-stable microwave dinners, pumps rather than tubes of toothpaste or bars of soap, and different sizes and designs of tissue packages are attempts to differentiate a product through packaging and to satisfy consumer needs at the same time.

In making packaging decisions, the marketing manager must again consider both the consumer and costs. On one hand, the package must be capable of protecting the product through the channel of distribution to the consumer. In addition, it is desirable for packages to be convenient size and easy to open for the consumer. For example, single-serving soups and zip-lock packaging in cereal boxes are attempts by manufacturers to serve consumers better. Hopefully, the package is also attractive and capable of being used as an in-store promotional tool. However, maximizing these objectives may increase the cost of the product to such an extent that consumers are no longer willing to purchase it. Thus, the marketing manager must determine the optimal protection, convenience, and promotional strengths of packages, subject to cost constraints.

As a product strategy, many firms produce and market their own products under a so-called private label. For example, A&P uses the Ann Page label, among others, and Sears uses the Kenmore label, among others. Such a strategy is highly important in industries where the middleman has gained control over distribution to the consumer. The advent of large chain stores, such as K mart, has accelerated the growth of private brands. If a manufacturer refuses to supply certain middlemen with private branded merchandise, the alternative is for these middlemen to go into the manufacturing business, as in the case of Kroger.

As a general rule, private brands are lower priced than national brands because there are some cost savings involved, and this has been the strongest appeal of private brand merchandisers. If a manufacturer is

---

[3]Yoram Wind and Henry J. Claycamp, "Planning Product Line Strategy: A Matrix Approach," *Journal of Marketing,* January 1976, p. 2.

HIGHLIGHT 6–3
Tips for Developing Effective Packages

1. Ultimate authority and responsibility must lie in the marketing department.
2. A team or systems approach should be utilized including personnel from other areas such as production and engineering.
3. A sequential approach should be followed.
4. Work on new product packages should begin early in the product development process.
5. Needs of both consumers and dealers should be considered.
6. The final package should take into consideration the packages of competitors and any legal or regulatory requirements.
7. The most important objective should be profitability.
8. Packages should not be changed for the sake of change.
9. Consumers and dealers should provide input during the development process.
10. The package should be test-marketed.
11. Package changes should be introduced all at once, not gradually.

Source: Adapted from Richard T. Hise and James U. McNeal, "Effective Package Management," *Business Horizons,* January–February 1988 and reported in Steven J. Skinner, *Marketing* (Boston: Houghton Mifflin Co, 1990), p. 262.

selling its national branded products to middlemen under a private label, then the Robinson-Patman Act requires that any price differential reflect *(a)* genuine differences in grade and quality; or *(b)* cost savings in manufacturing or distribution. One of the reasons why manufacturers will supply resellers with private branded merchandise is to utilize their production capacity more fully. Similarly, generic brands use excess capacity and offer manufacturers an alternative for selling their products.

Many companies use branding strategies in order to increase the strength of the product image. Factors that serve to increase the brand image strength include:[4] (1) product quality where products do what they do very well (e.g., Windex and Easy-off); (2) consistent advertising and other marketing communications in which brands tell their story often

---

[4]James Lowry, "Survey Finds Most Powerful Brands," *Advertising Age,* July 11, 1988, p. 31.

and well (e.g., McDonald's and Pepsi); and (3) brand personality where the brand stands for something (e.g., Disney and Marlboro). The brand name is perhaps the single most important element on the package. It is the brand name that serves to identify and differentiate the product from all others. A good brand name can evoke feelings of trust, confidence, security, strength, and many other desirable associations.[5] To illustrate, consider the case of Bayer aspirin. Bayer can be sold at up to two times the price of generic aspirins due to the strength of its brand image.

In addition, many companies also make use of branding in carrying out market and product development strategies. Line extension is an approach whereby a brand name is used to facilitate entry into a new market segment (e.g., Diet Coke and Liquid Tide). An alternative to line extension is brand extension. In brand extension, a current brand name is used to enter a completely different product class (e.g., Jello pudding pops, Ivory shampoo).[6] A final form of branding commonly used is franchise extension whereby a company attaches the corporate name to a product either to enter a new market segment or different product class (e.g., Honda lawnmower, Toyota Lexus). Each of the above three approaches is an attempt by companies to gain a competitive advantage by making use of an established reputation.

PRODUCT LIFE CYCLE

A firm's product strategy must take into account the fact that products have a life cycle. Figure 6–1 illustrates this life-cycle concept. Products are introduced, grow, mature, and decline. This cycle varies according to industry, product, technology, and market. Marketing executives need to be aware of the life-cycle concept because it can be a valuable aid in developing marketing strategies.

During the introduction phase of the cycle, there are usually high production and marketing costs, and, since sales are only beginning to materialize, profits are low or nonexistent. Profits increase and are pos-

---

[5]Terance Shimp, *Promotion Management and Marketing Communications*, 2nd ed. (Hinsdale, Ill.: Dryden Press, 1990), p. 67.

[6]David A. Aaker and Kevin Lane Keller, "Consumer Evaluations of Brand Extensions", *Journal of Marketing*, January 1990, pp. 27–41.

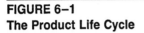

FIGURE 6–1
The Product Life Cycle

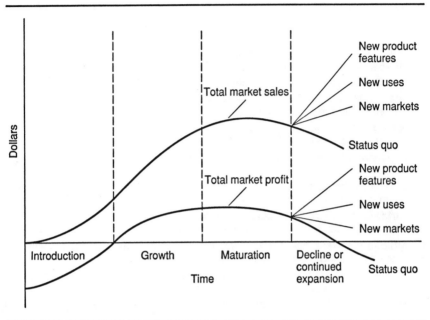

itively correlated with sales during the growth stage as the market begins trying and adopting the product. As the product matures, profits for the initiating firm do not keep pace with sales because of competition. Here the seller may be forced to "remarket" the product, which may involve making price concessions, increasing product quality, or expanding outlays on advertising and sales promotion just to maintain market share. At some time sales decline, and the seller must decide whether to *(a)* drop the product; *(b)* alter the product; *(c)* seek new uses for the product; *(d)* seek new markets; or *(e)* continue with more of the same.[7]

The usefulness of the product life-cycle concept is primarily that it forces management to take a long-range view of marketing planning. In doing so, it should become clear that shifts in phases of the life cycle

---

[7]Note that the labeling of the new product features, new uses, and new markets curves is arbitrary. In other words, any of the three may result in the highest sales and profits depending on the product and situation.

HIGHLIGHT 6–4
Marketing Milestones of the Decade

Hits

IBM PC. Big Blue claimed the power to set industry standards.

Microwave food. It's changing our definition of good food.

Diet Coke. Brilliant brand extension.

Lean Cuisine. Pricey diet entrees launched at the height of the recession. Caught the fit-but-fast wave.

Macintosh computer. Apple Computer's new design changed the way people use these machines.

Superpremium ice cream. Häagen-Dazs, Ben & Jerry's, DoveBar, the perfect end to low-calorie meals.

Chrysler minivans. These station wagons of the 80s created a new category of cars.

Tartar Control Crest. P&G's efforts to teach consumers about nasty tooth deposits helped restore its toothpaste market share.

Athletic footwear. After stumbling in 1986, Nike slamdunked rival Reebok by winning the favor of big-city kids.

USA Today. The colorful national daily is still mired in red ink, but it's changed the way many newpapers look and act.

Swatch watches. A new look at an old product made watches into hot fashion accessories.

Nintendo video games. Games like Super Mario Brothers continue so strong they're zapping the rest of the toy business.

SPF suncreens. Do you need SPF 5 or SPF 15? High-tech sunscreens sell well to aging baby boomers.

Flashes

Oat bran. With oat bran snacks and oat bran beer on the market, this one's got to be peaking.

Corona beer. Competition from wine coolers and a decline in beer consumption have hurt this product.

Cabbage Patch Kids. They're still around, although sales have crashed. Maker Coleco wasn't so lucky.

Miniskirts. They're in. They're out. Or are they?

Granola bars. In the mid-1980s, nearly a score of companies battled to be "health" snack king, while consumers snuck back to salty favorites.

Dry beer. Why is it called "dry" again?

Wine coolers. They're sweet as ever, but sales have cooled.

Misses

New Coke. Fixed what wasn't broken; customers immediately clamored for the original.

HIGHLIGHT 6–4 *concluded*

Premier cigarette. "Smokeless" cigarette couldn't be lit with matches.

IBM PC Jr. A problematic keyboard contributed to its demise.

Yugo. Yugoslavian minicar was billed as cheapest new car in America, and it showed.

LA Beer. Despite the new sobriety, the market for reduced-alcohol beer has little fizz.

Home banking. Consumers weren't ready for this complicated "service."

Pontiac Fiero. Looked great, but was discontinued after problems with engine fires.

Disk camera. Kodak's Edsel.

RCA's SelectaVision. Bad timing for the videodisc player once lauded as RCA's premier product of the 80s.

Generic products. An 80s flop, if not an 80s innovation; consumers felt queasy about their quality.

Fab 1 Shot. Colgate-Palmolive Co.'s premeasured laundry detergent means consumers can't use just enough for a small load.

Holly Farms roasted chickens. Consumers liked these fully cooked birds, but retailers balked at their short shelf life.

Source: *The Wall Street Journal,* November 28, 1989, p. B1.

correspond to changes in the market situation, competition, and demand. Thus, the astute marketing manager should recognize the necessity of altering the marketing mix to meet these changing conditions. It is possible for managers to undertake strategies which, in effect, can lead to a revitalized product life cycle. For example, past advancements in technology led to the replacement of rotary dial telephones by touch-tone, push-button phones. Today, newer technology is allowing the cordless and cellular phone to replace the traditional touch-tone, push-button phone. When applied with sound judgment, the life-cycle concept can aid in forecasting, pricing, advertising, product planning, and other aspects of marketing management.[8] However, the marketing manager must also

---

[8]For an overview of issues concerning the product life cycle, see George Day, "The Product Life Cycle: Analysis and Application Issues," *Journal of Marketing,* Fall 1981, pp. 60–67. This is the introductory article to a special section dealing with the product life cycle.

recognize that the length and slope of the product life cycle varies across products. Thus, while the product life cycle is useful for recognizing the stages a product will go through, it is difficult to forecast the exact time periods for these stages.

THE PRODUCT AUDIT

The product audit is a marketing management technique whereby the company's current product offerings are reviewed to ascertain whether each product should be continued as is, improved, or modified, or be deleted. The audit is a task that should be carried out at regular intervals as a matter of policy. Product audits are the responsibility of the product manager unless specifically delegated to someone else.

Deletions

It can be argued that the major purpose of the product audit is to detect "sick" products and then bury them. Criteria must be developed for deciding whether a product is a candidate for deletion. Some of the more obvious factors to be considered are:

- *Sales trends*. How have sales moved over time? What has happened to market share? Why have sales declined? What changes in sales have occurred in competitive products both in our line and in those of other manufacturers?
- *Profit contribution*. What has been the profit contribution of this product to the company? If profits have declined, how are these tied to price? Have selling, promotion, and distribution costs risen out of proportion to sales? Does the product require excessive management time and effort?
- *Product life cycle*. Has the product reached a level of maturity and saturation in the market? Has new technology been developed that poses a threat to the product? Are there more effective substitutes on the market? Has the product outgrown its usefulness? Can the resources used on this product be put to better use?

The above factors should be used as guidelines for making the final decision to delete a product. Deletion decisions are very difficult to make

HIGHLIGHT 6–5
Marketing Strategy Implications of the Product Life Cycle

Effects/ Responses	Introduction	Growth	Maturity	Decline
			Stages of the Product Life Cycle	
Competition	None of importance.	Some emulators.	Many rivals competing for a small piece of the pie.	Few in number, with a rapid shakeout of weak members.
Overall strategy	Market establishment; persuade early adopters to try the product.	Market penetration; persuade mass market to prefer the brand.	Defense of brand position; check the inroads of competition.	Preparations for removal; milk the brand dry of all possible benefits.
Profits	Negligible because of high production and marketing costs.	Reach peak levels as a result of high prices and growing demand.	Increasing competition cuts into profit margins and ultimately into total profits.	Declining volume pushes costs up to levels that eliminate profits entirely.
Retail prices	High, to recover some of the excessive costs of launching.	High, to take advantage of heavy consumer demand.	What the traffic will bear; need to avoid price wars.	Low enough to permit quick liquidation of inventory.
Distribution	Selective, as distribution is slowly built up.	Intensive; employ small trade discounts since dealers are eager to store.	Intensive; heavy trade allowances to retain shelf space.	Selective; unprofitable outlets slowly phased out.
Advertising strategy	Aim at the needs of early adopters.	Make the mass market aware of brand benefits.	Use advertising as a vehicle for differentiation among otherwise similar brands.	Emphasize low price to reduce stock.
Advertising emphasis	High, to generate awareness and interest among early adopters and persuade dealers to stock the brand.	Moderate, to let sales rise on the sheer momentum of word-of-mouth recommendations.	Moderate, since most buyers are aware of brand characteristics.	Minimum expenditures required to phase out the product.
Consumer sales and promotion expenditures	Heavy, to entice target groups with samples, coupons, and other inducements to try the brand.	Moderate, to create brand preference (advertising is better suited to do this job).	Heavy, to encourage brand switching, hoping to convert some buyers into loyal users.	Minimal, to let the brand coast by itself.

Source: William Zikmund and Michael D'Amico, *Marketing*, 3rd ed., p. 243. Copyright © 1989 by John Wiley & Sons. Reprinted by permission of John Wiley & Sons, Inc.

because of their potential impact on customers and the firm. For example, eliminating a product may force a company to lay off some employees. There are other factors to consider, such as keeping consumers supplied with replacement parts and repair service and maintaining the good will of distributors who have an inventory of the product. The deletion plan should provide for the clearing out of stock in question.[9]

Product Improvement

One of the other important objectives of the audit is to ascertain whether to alter the product in some way or to leave things as they are. Altering the product means changing one or more of the product's attributes or marketing dimensions. Attributes refer mainly to product features, design, package, and so forth. Marketing dimensions refer to such things as price, promotion strategy, and channels of distribution.

It is possible to look at the product audit as a management device for controlling the product strategy. Here, control means feedback on product performance and corrective action in the form of product improvement. Product improvement is a top-level management decision, but the information needed to make the improvement decision may come from the consumer or the middlemen. Suggestions are often made by advertising agencies or consultants. Reports by the sales force should be structured in a way to provide management with certain types of product information; in fact, these reports can be the firm's most valuable product improvement tool. Implementing a product improvement decision will often require the coordinated efforts of several specialists, plus some research. For example, product design improvement decisions involve engineering, manufacturing, accounting, and marketing. When a firm becomes aware that a product's design can be improved, it is not always clear as to how consumers will react to the various alterations. To illustrate, in blind taste tests, the Coca-Cola Company found that consumers overwhelmingly preferred the taste of a reformulated sweeter new Coke over old Coke. However, when placed on the market in labeled containers,

---

[9]For further discussion of product deletion decisions, see George J. Avlonitis, "Product Elimination Decision Making: Does Formality Matter?" *Journal of Marketing*, Winter 1985, pp. 41–52.

HIGHLIGHT 6–6
A 10-Point Vitality Test for Older Products, or How to Get That Sales Curve to Slope Upward Again

1. Does the product have new or extended uses? Sales of Arm & Hammer baking soda increased considerably after the product was promoted as a refrigerator deodorant.
2. Is the product a generic item that can be branded? Sunkist puts its name on oranges and lemons, thus giving a brand identity to a formerly generic item.
3. Is the product category "underadvertised?" Tampons were in this category until International Playtex and Johnson & Johnson started spending large advertising appropriations, particularly on television ads.
4. Is there a broader target market? Procter & Gamble increased the sales of Ivory soap by promoting it for adults, instead of just for babies.
5. Can you turn disadvantages into advantages? The manufacturer of Smucker's jams and jellies advertised: "With a name like Smucker's, it has to be good."
6. Can you build volume and profit by cutting the price? Sales of Tylenol increased considerably after Johnson & Johnson cut Tylenol's price to meet the lower price set by Bristol-Myers' Datril brand.
7. Can you market unused by-products? Lumber companies market sawdust as a form of kitty litter.
8. Can you sell the product in a more compelling way? Procter & Gamble's Pampers disposable diapers were only a moderate success in the market when they were sold as a convenience item for mothers. Sales increased, however, after the advertising theme was changed to say that Pampers kept babies dry and happy.
9. Is there a social trend to exploit? Dannon increased its sales of yogurt tremendously by linking this product to consumers' interest in health foods.
10. Can you expand distribution channels? Hanes Hosiery Company increased its sales of L'eggs panty hose by distributing this product through supermarkets.

Source: William J. Stanton and Charles Futrell, *Fundamentals of Marketing,* 8th ed., p. 224. © 1987 by McGraw-Hill, Inc. Reprinted by permission of the publisher.

new Coke turned out to be a failure due to consumers' emotional attachments to the classic Coke. Consequently, it is advisable to conduct some market tests in realistic settings.

ORGANIZING FOR PRODUCT MANAGEMENT

A firm can organize for managing its products in a variety of ways.[10] Figure 6–2 describes five methods and the types of companies for which they are most useful. Under a *marketing-manager system,* all the functional areas of marketing report to one manager. These include sales, advertising, sales promotion, and product planning. Such companies as PepsiCo, Purex, Eastman Kodak, and Levi Strauss use some form of the marketing-manager system.

With the *product (brand) manager system* there is a middle manager in the organization who focuses on a single product or a small group of new or existing products. Typically, this manager is responsible for everything from marketing research to package design to advertising. This method of organizing is sometimes criticized because product managers often do not have authority commensurate with their responsibilities. However, such companies as General Mills, Pillsbury, and Proctor & Gamble have successfully used this method.

A *product-planning committee* is staffed by executives from functional areas, including marketing, production, engineering, finance, and R&D. The committee handles product approval, evaluation, and development on a part-time basis and typically disbands after a product is introduced. The product then becomes the responsibility of a product manager.

A *new product manager system* uses separate managers for new and existing products. After a new product is introduced, the new product manager turns it over to a product manager. This system can be expensive and can cause discontinuity when the product is introduced. However, such firms as General Foods, NCR, and General Electric have used this system successfully.

A *venture team* is a small, independent department consisting of a broad range of specialists who manage a new product's entire development process. The team disbands when the product is introduced. While it can be an expensive method, Xerox, IBM, and Westinghouse use a venture team approach.

Which method to use depends on the diversity of a firm's offerings, the number of new products introduced, the level of innovation, company

---

[10]This section is based on Joel R. Evans and Barry Berman, *Marketing,* 4th ed. (New York: Macmillan, 1990), pp. 273–75.

FIGURE 6–2
Five Methods of Organizing for Product Management

	Characteristics		
Organization	*Staffing*	*Ideal Use*	*Permanency*
Marketing-manager system	All functional areas of marketing report to one manager.	A company makes one product line or has a dominant line.	The system is ongoing.
Product (brand) manager system	A middle manager focuses on a single product or group of products.	A company makes many distinct products, each requiring expertise.	The system is ongoing.
Product-planning committee	Executives from various functional areas participate.	The committee should supplement another product organization.	The committee meets irregularly.
New product manager system	Separate managers direct new products and existing products.	A company makes several existing products, and substantial time, resources, and expertise are needed to develop new products.	The system is ongoing, but new products are shifted to product managers after production.
Venture team	An independent group of specialists guides all phases of a new product's development.	A company wants to create vastly different products than those currently made, and it needs an autonomous structure to aid development.	The team disbands after a new product is introduced, turning responsibility over to a product manager.

Source: Reprinted with the permission of Macmillan Publishing Company from *Marketing*, 4th ed., by Joel R. Evans and Barry Berman. Copyright © 1990 by Macmillan Publishing Company, Inc.

resources, and management expertise. A combination of product management methods also can be used and many firms find this desirable.

LESSONS FOR THE MANUFACTURER

One of the more important concepts for manufacturers in this chapter is the product life cycle. Although the life cycle concept is limited because the exact time it takes for products to complete various stages is unknown until after a product has run its course, the life cycle does have heuristic value. For example, the fact that most products today are in the mature stage of the product life cycle has important implications for judging competitive intensity. In the mature stage, market growth is small or nonexistent, and thus companies must compete for market share in order to grow. In fact, some analysts argue that most industries are market-share driven. This is one reason why product quality has become a more essential element in organizational strategies in the last decade.

Product life cycles are generally considered to be shorter nowadays than they were in the past. Thus, companies who can bring quality products to the market ahead of competition can get first-mover advantages that may spell the difference between survival and failure of the firm. Naturally, shorter product life cycles require firms to be more efficient in design, engineering, and production in order to beat competition to the market and to keep costs at a level where the firm can make reasonable margins. The use of cross-functional teams facilitates coordination in these efforts.

Another important lesson in the chapter concerns the role that marketing personnel play in managing existing products. Marketing personnel play different roles in product management depending on how this function is organized in the company. However, in some companies, product managers trained in marketing have profit responsibility for the products and brands that they manage and must interact effectively with managers in all of the other functional areas. From marketing research information, salespeople's reports, and analysis of competitive products, product managers may propose various changes to existing products, including alterations in the product, alterations in the packaging of the product, changes in channels, and changes in promotion messages and media. Manufacturing personnel might also have recommendations for changes in products or packaging. Of course, any changes in the product or packaging would require the inputs of design, engineering, and manufacturing before a recommendation would be made to higher levels of management. Also, if trade or consumer deals were to be offered, product managers need to coordinate with manufacturing personnel to ensure that adequate supplies of products can be made available to meet increased demand.

Finally, it should be clear that product audits benefit greatly from joint efforts of both marketing and manufacturing personnel. Recommendations from such audits to improve existing products clearly need to include consumer needs and wants as well as manufacturing constraints and abilities.

ADDITIONAL READINGS

Dowdy, William L., and Julien Nikolchev. "Can Industries De-Mature?—Applying New Technologies to Mature Industries." *Long Range Planning* 19, no. 2 (1986), pp. 38–49.

Gupta, Ashok K.; S. P. Raj; and David Wilemon. "A Model for Studying R&D—Marketing Interface in the Product Innovation Process." *Journal of Marketing*, April 1986, pp. 7–17.

Park, C. Whan; Bernard J. Jaworski; and Deborah J. Macinnis. "Strategic Brand Concept-Image Management." *Journal of Marketing*, October 1986, pp. 135–45.

Pessemier, Edgar E. *Product Management*. 2nd ed. New York: John Wiley & Sons, 1981.

Quelch, John A. "Why Not Exploit Dual Marketing?" *Harvard Business Review*, January–February 1987, pp. 52–60.

Varadarajan, P. Rajan. "Product Diversity and Firm Performance: An Empirical Investigation." *Journal of Marketing*, July 1986, pp. 43–57.

Wind, Yoram. *Product Policy: Concepts, Methods, and Strategy*. Reading, Mass.: Addison-Wesley Publishing, 1982.

CHAPTER 7

NEW PRODUCT PLANNING AND DEVELOPMENT

New products are a vital part of a firm's competitive growth strategy. Most manufacturers cannot live without new products. It is commonplace for major companies to have 50 percent or more of their current sales in products introduced within the past 10 years. For example, the 3M Corporation insists that 25 percent of each division's annual sales come from products developed within the past five years.

Some additional facts about new products are:

1. Many new products are failures. Estimates of new-product failure range from 33 percent to 90 percent.
2. Companies vary widely in the effectiveness of their new-product programs.
3. Common elements tend to appear in the management practices that generally distinguish the relative degree of efficiency and success between companies.
4. About four out of five hours devoted by scientists and engineers to technical development of new products are spent on projects that do not reach commercial success.[1]

In one recent year, almost 10,000 supermarket items were introduced into the market. Less than 20 percent met sales goals. The cost of introducing a new brand in some consumer markets has been estimated to range from $50 million to the hundreds of millions of dollars.[2] To

---

[1]Also see Robert Hisrich and Michael Peters, *Marketing Decisions for New and Mature Products* (Columbus, Ohio: Charles E. Merrill Publishing Co, 1984), chap. 1.

[2]Paul Brown, "New? Improved?" *Business Week*, October 21, 1985, pp. 108–12 and Edward M. Tauber, "Brand Leverage: Strategy for Growth in a Cost-Controlled World," *Journal of Advertising Research*, August/September 1988, pp. 26–30.

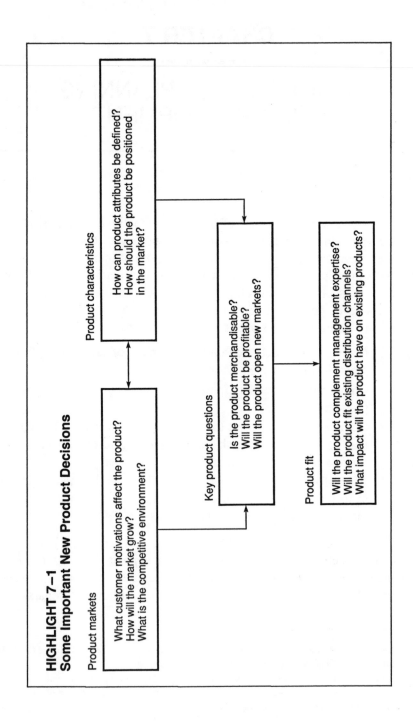

HIGHLIGHT 7–1
Some Important New Product Decisions

Product markets

What customer motivations affect the product?
How will the market grow?
What is the competitive environment?

Product characteristics

How can product attributes be defined?
How should the product be positioned
in the market?

Key product questions

Is the product merchandisable?
Will the product be profitable?
Will the product open new markets?

Product fit

Will the product complement management expertise?
Will the product fit existing distribution channels?
What impact will the product have on existing products?

illustrate, Alpo Petfoods spent over $70 million on advertising and promotion alone in launching their new line of cat food. The Gillette Co. spent over $300 million on R&D and promotion costs in introducing the Sensor razor.[3] In addition to the outlay cost of new product failures, there are also opportunity costs. These opportunity costs refer not only to the alternative uses of funds spent on product failures but also to the time spent in unprofitable product development. Product development can take many years. For example, Hills Brothers spent 22 years in developing its instant coffee, while it took General Foods 10 years to develop Maxim, its concentrated instant coffee.

Good management, with heavy emphasis on planning, organization, and interaction among the various functional units (e.g, marketing, manufacturing, engineering, R&D), seems to be the key factor contributing to a firm's success in launching new products. The primary reason found for new product failure is an inability on the part of the selling company to match up its offerings to the needs of the customer. This inability to satisfy customer needs can be attributed to three main sources: inadequacy of upfront intelligence efforts, failure on the part of the company to stick close to what the company does best, and the inability to provide better value than competing products and technologies.

NEW PRODUCT POLICY

In developing new product policies, the first question a marketing manager must ask is: "In how many ways can a product be new?" There are at least nine different ways:

1. A product performing an entirely *new function,* such as television, which for the first time permitted the transmission of audiovisual signals.
2. A product that offers *improved performance of an existing function,* such as a wristwatch whose balance wheel has been replaced by a tuning fork.
3. A product that is a *new application of an existing product.* For

---

[3]"The $300 Million Shave," *Business Week,* January 29, 1990, pp. 62–64.

HIGHLIGHT 7–2
Ten Steps in the Development of a New Product Policy

1. Prepare a long-range industry forecast for existing product lines.
2. Prepare a long-range profit plan for the company, using existing product lines.
3. Review the long-range profit plan.
4. Determine what role new products will play in the company's future.
5. Prepare an inventory of company capabilities.
6. Determine market areas for new products.
7. Prepare a statement of new product objectives.
8. Prepare a long-range profit plan, incorporating new products.
9. Assign new product responsibility.
10. Provide for evaluation of new product performance.

---

example, the aerosol bomb, which was first developed for insecticides, was later applied in paints.

4. A product that offers *additional functions*. The cordless telephone, for instance, does what the earlier telephone did, plus more.

5. An existing product offered to a *new market*. This may be done, for example, by repositioning or by taking a regional brand into other regions. For example, Coors Beer used to be sold only in the states surrounding Colorado.

6. A product that through *lower cost* is able to reach more buyers. Hand calculators are an example.

7. An upgraded product defined as an *existing product integrated into another existing product*. The clock-radio is an example.

8. A *downgraded product*. For example, a manufacturer switches from buying a component to producing a cheaper component in-house and marketing it.

9. A *restyled product*. Annual auto and clothing changes are examples.[4]

---

[4]C. Merle Crawford, *New Product Management,* 2nd ed. (Homewood, Ill.: Richard D. Irwin, 1987), p. 18.

Another approach to the *new* product question has been developed by H. Igor Ansoff in the form of *growth vectors*.[5] This is the matrix first introduced in Chapter 1 that indicates the direction in which the organization is moving with respect to its current products and markets. It is shown again in Figure 7–1.

Market penetration denotes a growth direction through the increase in market share for present product-markets. *Market development* refers to finding new customers for present products. *Product development* refers to creating new products to replace existing ones. *Diversification* refers to developing new products and cultivating new markets.

In Figure 7–1, market penetration and market development are product line strategies where the focus is upon altering the breadth and depth of the firm's existing product offerings. Product development and diversification can be characterized as product mix strategies. New products, as defined in the growth vector matrix, usually require the firm to make significant investments in research and development and may require major changes in its organizational structure.

It has already been stated that new products are the lifeblood of successful business firms. Thus, the critical product policy question is not whether to develop new products but in what direction to move. One way of dealing with this problem is to formulate standards or norms that new products must meet if they are to be considered candidates for launching. In other words, as part of its new product policy, management must ask itself the basic question: "What is the potential contribution of each anticipated new product to the company?"

Each company must answer this question in accordance with its long-term goals, corporate mission, resources, and so forth. Unfortunately, some of the reasons commonly given to justify the launching of new products are so general that they become meaningless. Phrases such as *additional profits* or *increased growth* or *cyclical stability* must be translated into more specific objectives. For example, one objective may be to reduce manufacturing overhead costs by utilizing plant capacity better. This may be accomplished by using the new product as an offseason filler. Naturally, the new product proposal would also have to include production and accounting data to back up this cost argument.

---

[5]H. Igor Ansoff, *Corporate Strategy* (New York: McGraw-Hill, 1965), pp. 109–10.

FIGURE 7–1
Growth Vector Components

	Products	
	---	---
Markets	Present	New

| Present | Market penetration | Product development |
| New | Market development | Diversification |

In every new product proposal some attention must be given to the ultimate economic contribution of each new product candidate. If the argument is that a certain type of product is needed to "keep up with competition" or "to establish leadership in the market," it is fair to ask, "Why?" To put the question another way, top management can ask: "What will be the effect on the firm's long-run profit picture if we do not develop and launch this or that new product?" Policymaking criteria on new products should specify *(a)* a working definition of the profit concept acceptable to top management; *(b)* a minimum level or floor of profits; *(c)* the availability and cost of capital to develop a new product; and *(d)* a specified time period in which the new product must recoup its operating costs and begin contributing to profits.

NEW PRODUCT PLANNING AND DEVELOPMENT PROCESS

Ideally, products that generate a maximum dollar profit with a minimum amount of risk should be developed and marketed. However, it is very difficult for planners to implement this idea because of the number and nature of the variables involved. What is needed is a systematic, formalized process for new product planning. Although such a process does not provide management with any magic answers, it can increase the probability of new product success. Initially, the firm must establish some new product policy guidelines that include: the product fields of primary interest, organizational responsibilities for managing the various stages in new-product development, and criteria for making go-ahead decisions. After these guidelines are established, a process such as the one shown in Figure 7–2 should be useful in new-product development.

FIGURE 7–2
The New Product Development Process

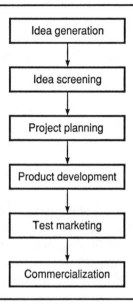

Idea Generation

Every product starts as an idea. But all new product ideas do not have equal merit or potential for economic or commercial success. Some estimates indicate that as many as 60 or 70 ideas are necessary to yield one successful product. This is an average figure, but it serves to illustrate the fact that new product ideas have a high mortality rate. In terms of money, of all the dollars of new product expense, almost three fourths go to unsuccessful products.

The problem at this stage is to ensure that all new product ideas available to the company at least have a chance to be heard and evaluated. This includes recognizing available sources of new product ideas and funneling these ideas to appropriate decision makers for screening.

Top management support is critical to providing an atmosphere that stimulates new product activity. A top management structure that is unwilling to take risks will avoid new product and other innovation activities and instead concentrate on minor areas of product improvement such as simple style changes. In order to facilitate top management support, it is essential that new product development be focused on meeting market needs.

Both technology push and market pull research activities play an important role in new product ideas and development. By taking a broad view of customer wants and needs, basic research can lead to ideas that will yield profits to the firm. Marketing, on the other hand, is more responsible for gathering and disseminating information gained from customer and competitor contact. This information relates mainly to specific features and functions of the product that can be improved upon or market needs that current products are not satisfying. Both approaches are essential to the generation of new product ideas.

Idea Screening

The primary function of the screening stage is twofold: first, to eliminate ideas for new products that could not be profitably marketed by the firm and, second, to expand viable ideas into a full product concept. New product ideas may be eliminated either because they are outside the fields of the firm's interest or because the firm does not have the necessary resources or technology to produce the product at a profit. However, organizations should not act too hastily in discounting new product ideas due solely to a lack of resources or expertise. Instead, firms should consider forming joint or strategic alliances with other firms. Potential benefits to be gained from alliances include: (1) increased access to technology, funding, and information; (2) market expansion and greater penetration of current markets; and (3) de-escalated competitive rivalries. Motorola is a company that has prospered by forming numerous joint ventures with both American and foreign companies.[6]

Ideas that appear to have adequate profit potential and offer the firm a competitive advantage in the market should be accepted for further study.

---

[6]For a more complete discussion on the advantages and disadvantages of strategic alliances see, Godfrey Devlin and Mark Bleackley, "Strategic Alliances—Guidelines for Success," *Long Range Planning* 21, no. 5, (1988) pp. 18–23; Charles W. Joiner, "Harvesting American Technology—Lessons from the Japanese Garden," *Sloan Management Review*, Summer 1989, pp. 61–68; Richard P. Neilson, "Cooperative Strategies in Marketing," *Harvard Business Review*, July–August 1987, pp. 61–68; and Pedro Nueno and Jan Oosterveld, "Managing Technology Alliances," *Long Range Planning* 21, no. 3, (1988), pp. 11–17.

HIGHLIGHT 7–3
Some Sources of New Product Ideas

1. *Sales force.*
   a. Knowledge of customers' needs.
   b. Inquiries from customers or prospects.
   c. Knowledge of the industry and competition.
2. *Research and engineering.*
   a. Application of basic research.
   b. Original or creative thinking.
   c. Testing existing products and performance records.
   d. Accidental discoveries.
3. *Other company sources.*
   a. Suggestions from employees.
   b. Utilization of by-products or scrap.
   c. Specific market surveys.
4. *Outside sources.*
   a. Inventors.
   b. Stockholders.
   c. Suppliers or vendors.
   d. Middlemen.
   e. Ad agencies.
   f. Customer suggestions.

Project Planning

This stage of the process involves several steps. It is here that the product proposal is evaluated further and responsibility for the project is assigned to a project team. The proposal is analyzed in terms of production, marketing, financial, and competitive factors. A development budget is established, and some preliminary marketing and technical research is undertaken. The product is actually designed in a rough form. Alternative product features and component specifications are outlined. Finally, a project plan is written up, which includes estimates of future development, production, and marketing costs along with capital requirements and manpower needs. A schedule or timetable is also included. Finally, the project proposal is given to top management for a go or no-go decision.

Various alternatives exist for creating and managing the project teams. Two of the better-known methods are the establishment of a skunk-works whereby a project team can work in relative privacy away from

---

HIGHLIGHT 7–4
How Much Should You Spend on New Product Development?

Based on a study of 203 new products (123 successes and 80 failures), the researchers concluded that the successful companies:

1. Spend twice as much money and three times as much time for preliminary market assessment.
2. Spend twice as much money for marketing research.
3. Spend twice as much time and twice as much money on preliminary technical assessment.
4. Spend 50 percent more money and 35 percent more time on product development.
5. Spend twice as much money and 50 percent more time on in-house tests.

Source: Based on research conducted by R. G. Cooper and E. J. Kleinschmidt, "Resources Allocation in the New Product Process," *Industrial Marketing Management*, August 1988, pp. 249–62.

the rest of the organization and a rugby or relay approach whereby groups in different areas of the company are simultaneously working on the project.[7] The common tie that binds these and other successful approaches together is the degree of interaction that develops between the marketing, engineering, production, and other research staff.

Product Development

At this juncture the product idea has been evaluated from the standpoint of engineering, manufacturing, finance, and marketing. If it has met all expectations, it is considered a candidate for further research and testing. In the laboratory, the product is converted into a finished good and tested. A development report to management is prepared that spells out in fine detail: *(a)* the results of the studies by the engineering department; *(b)* required plan design; *(c)* production facilities design; *(d)* tooling

---

[7]James Quinn, "Managing Innovation: Controlled Chaos," *Harvard Business Review*, May–June 1985, pp. 73–84 and Hirotaka Takeuchi and Ikujiro Nonaka, "The New New Product Development Game," *Harvard Business Review*, January–February 1986, pp. 137–46.

HIGHLIGHT 7–5
Six Ss for New Product Success

Below is a list of product attributes that have been found to have a significant effect on new product purchase and acceptance by consumers:

1. *Superiority.* The degree to which the new product has a clear differential or relative advantage over previous products.
2. *Sociability.* The degree to which the new product is compatible or consistent with consumers' existing beliefs, values, and lifestyles.
3. *Satisfaction.* The degree to which the new product satisfies consumers' felt needs.
4. *Simplicity.* The degree to which the new product is easy for consumers to understand and use and for marketers to promote and make available.
5. *Separability.* The degree to which the new product can be tested on a trial basis with limited investment by consumers.
6. *Speed.* The degree to which the benefits of the product are experienced immediately, rather than at a later time.

---

requirements; *(e)* marketing test plan; *(f)* financial program survey; and *(g)* an estimated release date.

Test Marketing

Up until now the product has been a company secret. Now management goes outside the company and submits the product candidate for customer approval. Test market programs are conducted in lines with the general plans for launching the product. Several of the more commonly utilized forms of test marketing are:[8]

1. *Pseudo sales.* Potential buyers are asked to answer survey questions or pick items off a shelf in a make-believe store. The key factor is that no spending or risk for the consumer takes place.
2. *Cash sales.* Here, the buyer must actually make a purchase. The test may be informal, controlled, or in a full-scale test market.

---

[8]The material on test marketing was excerpted from C. Merle Crawford, *New Products Management,* 2nd ed. (Homewood, Ill.: Richard D. Irwin, 1987), pp. 284–98.

However, it is still research, and no release of the product has been made.

3. *Limited marketing.* In this case, the firm decides to market the product gradually. This method allows for continual learning before the product reaches national availability.

4. *National launch.* Here the firm just launches the product on a national scale and makes adjustments as needed.

The main goal of a test market is to evaluate and adjust as necessary the general marketing strategy to be used and the appropriate marketing mix. Test findings are analyzed, forecasts of volume are developed, the product design is frozen into production, and a marketing plan is finalized.

Commercialization

This is the launching step. During this stage, heavy emphasis is placed on the organization structure and management talent needed to implement the marketing strategy. Emphasis is also given to following up such things as bugs in the design, production costs, quality control, and inventory requirements, Procedures and responsibility for evaluating the success of the new product by comparison with projections are also finalized.

The Importance of Time

A company that can bring out new products faster than its competitors enjoys a huge advantage.[9] Today in many industries, Japanese manufacturers are successfully following such a strategy. In projection television, Japanese producers can develop a new television in one third the time required by U.S. manufacturers. Successful time-based innovation can be attributed to the use of short production runs whereby products are improved upon on an incremental basis, the use of cross-functional project teams, decentralized work scheduling and monitoring, and a responsive system for gathering and analyzing customer feedback.

Several U.S. companies, including Procter & Gamble have taken steps to speed up the new product development cycle by giving managers,

---

[9]George Stalk, Jr., "Time—The Next Source of Competitive Advantage," *Harvard Business Review*, July–August 1988, pp. 41–51.

at the product class and brand family level, more decision-making power. Increasingly, companies are bypassing time-consuming regional test markets in favor of national launches. It is becoming, more than ever, important that firms do a successful job of developing the new product right the first time.

CAUSES OF NEW PRODUCT FAILURE

Many new products with satisfactory potential have failed to make the grade. Many of the reasons for new product failure relate to execution and control problems. Below is a brief list of some of the more important causes of new product failures after they have been carefully screened, developed, and marketed.

1. Faulty estimates of market potential.
2. Unexpected reactions from competitors.
3. Poor timing in the introduction of the product.
4. Rapid change in the market (economy) after the product was approved.
5. Inadequate quality control.
6. Faulty estimates in production costs.
7. Inadequate expenditures on initial promotion.
8. Faulty market testing.
9. Improper channel of distribution.

Some of the above problems are beyond the control of management; but it is clear that successful new product planning requires large amounts of reliable information in diverse areas. Each department assigned functional responsibility for product development automatically becomes an input to the information system needed by the new product decision maker. For example, when a firm is developing a new product, it is wise for both engineers and marketers to consider both the kind of market to be entered (e.g., consumer, industrial, defense, or export) and specific target segments. These decisions will be of paramount influence on the design and cost of the finished good, which will, of course, directly influence price, sales, and profits.

HIGHLIGHT 7–6
Examples of Misfires in Test Marketing

1. When Campbell Soup first test-marketed Prego spaghetti sauce, Campbell marketers say they noticed a flurry of new Ragu ads and cents-off deals that they feel were designed to induce shoppers to load up on Ragu and to skew Prego's test results. They also claim that Ragu copied Prego when it developed Ragu Homestyle spaghetti sauce, which was thick, red, flecked with oregano and basil, and which Ragu moved into national distribution before Prego.
2. P&G claims that competitors stole its patented process for Duncan Hines chocolate chip cookies when they saw how successful the product was in test markets.
3. A health and beauty aids firm developed a deodorant containing baking soda. A competitor spotted the product in a test market, rolled out its own version of the deodorant nationally before the first firm completed its testing, and later successfully sued the product originator for copyright infringement when it launched its deodorant nationally.
4. Whe P&G introduced its Always brand sanitary napkin in test marketing in Minnesota, Kimberly Clark Corporation and Johnson & Johnson countered with free products, lots of coupons, and big dealer discounts, which caused Always not to do as well as expected.
5. A few years ago, Snell (Booz Allen's design and development division, which does product development work under contract) developed a nonliquid temporary hair coloring that consumers use by inserting a block of solid hair dye into a special comb. "It went to market, and it was a bust," the company's Mr. Schoenholz recalls. On hot days when people perspired, any hair dye excessively applied ran down their necks and foreheads. "It just didn't occur to us to look at this under conditions where people perspire," he says.

Source: G. Churchill, *Basic Marketing Research* (Hinsdale, Ill: Dryden Press, 1988), p. 14.

Need for Research

In many respects it can be argued that the keystone activity of any new product planning system is research—not just marketing research but technical research as well. Regardless of the way in which the new product planning function is organized in the company, new product development decisions by top management require data that provide a base for making more intelligent choices. New product project reports ought to be more than a collection of "expert" opinions. Top management has a responsibility to ask certain questions, and the new product planning team has an obligation to generate answers to these questions based on research that provides marketing, economic, engineering, and production information. This need will be more clearly understood if some of the specific questions commonly raised in evaluating product ideas are examined:

1. What is the anticipated market demand over time? Are the potential applications for the product restricted?
2. Can the item be patented? Are there any antitrust problems?
3. Can the product be sold through present channels and sales force? What will be the number of new salespersons needed? What additional sales training will be required?
4. At different volume levels, what will be the unit manufacturing costs?
5. What is the most appropriate package to use in terms of color, material, design, and so forth?
6. What is the estimated return on investment?
7. What is the appropriate pricing strategy?

While this list is not intended to be exhaustive, it serves to illustrate the serious need for reliable information. Note, also, that some of the essential facts required to answer these questions can only be obtained through timeconsuming and expensive marketing research studies. Other data can be generated in the engineering laboratories or pulled from accounting records. Certain types of information must be based on assumptions, which may or may not hold true, and on expectations about what will happen in the future, as in the case of "anticipated competitive reaction" or the projected level of sales.

Another complication is that many different types of information must be gathered and formulated into a meaningful program for decision making. To illustrate, in trying to answer questions about return on investment of a particular project, the analyst must know something about (1) the pricing strategy to be used and (2) the investment outlay. Regardless of the formula used to measure the investment worth of a new product, different types of information are required. Using one of the simplest approaches—the payback method (the ratio of investment outlay to annual cash flow)—one needs to estimate the magnitude of the product investment outlay and the annual cash flow. The investment outlay requires estimates of such things as production equipment, R&D costs, and nonrecurring introductory marketing expenditures; the annual cash flow requires a forecast of unit demand and price. These data must be collected or generated from many different departments and processed into a form that will be meaningful to the decision maker.

LESSONS FOR THE MANUFACTURER

The designing, manufacturing, and marketing of successful new products obviously requires input from a variety of functional areas. New product ideas might come from R&D or from marketing research or other sources. However, the process of transforming a product idea into a successful market entry involves a variety of steps and may be done differently in different firms. However, the model offered in this chapter of new product development is consistent with the way marketing personnel are taught to think about the process.

It is also important to consider the factors that lead to the success of new products. Surely, while there are many factors, the degree to which the product offers a clear differential advantage over competitive products is crucial. The main differential advantage created by marketing is likely to be image related in the sense that the product is considered by consumers to have meaning to them because of its brand name. Successful brand names allow companies to sell more products, often at higher prices and margins than competitive offerings. Manufacturing differential advantages are likely to be the development of superior product quality or at least equal quality to competitors at lower manufacturing cost.

ADDITIONAL READINGS

Crawford, C. Merle. *New Products Management*. 2nd ed. Homewood, Ill.: Richard D. Irwin, 1987.

Hauser, John R., and Don Clausing. "The House of Quality," *Harvard Business Review*, May–June 1988, pp. 63–73.

Johne, F. Axel, and Patricia A. Snelson. "Product Development in Established Firms," *Industrial Marketing Management* 18 (1989), pp. 113–24.

Narasimhan, Chakravarthi, and Subrata K. Sen. "New Product Models for Test Market Data." *Journal of Marketing,* Winter 1983, pp. 11–24.

Robertson, Thomas S., and Hubert Gatignon. "Competitive Effects on Technology Diffusion." *Journal of Marketing,* July 1986, pp. 1–12.

von Hippel, Eric. *The Sources of Innovation.* New York: Oxford University Press, 1988.

CHAPTER 8

PROMOTION STRATEGY: ADVERTISING AND SALES PROMOTION

To simplify the discussion of the general subject of promotion, the topic has been divided into two basic categories, personal selling and nonpersonal selling. Personal selling will be discussed in detail in the next chapter, and this chapter will be devoted to nonpersonal selling.

Nonpersonal selling includes all demand creation and demand maintenance activities of the firm, other than personal selling. It is mass selling. In more specific terms, nonpersonal selling includes *(a)* advertising, *(b)* sales promotion, and *(c)* publicity. For purposes of this text, primary emphasis will be placed on advertising and sales promotion. Publicity is a special form of promotion that amounts to "free advertising," such as a writeup about the firm's products in a newspaper article. It will not be dealt with in detail in this text.

THE PROMOTION MIX

The promotion mix concept refers to *the combination and types of promotional effort the firm puts forth during a specified time period.* Most business concerns make use of more than one form of promotion, but some firms rely on a single technique. An example of a company using only one promotional device would be a manufacturer of novelties who markets its products exclusively by means of mail order.

In devising its promotion mix the firm should take into account three basic factors: (1) the role of promotion in the overall marketing mix; (2) the nature of the product; and (3) the nature of the market. Also, it must be recognized that a firm's promotion mix is likely to change over time to reflect changes in the market, competition, the product's life cycle,

HIGHLIGHT 8–1
Some Advantages and Disadvantages of Major Promotion Methods

Advertising

Advantages

Can reach many consumers simultaneously.

Relatively low cost per exposure.

Excellent for creating brand images.

High degree of flexibility and variety of media to choose from; can accomplish many different types of promotion objectives.

Disadvantages

Many consumers reached are not potential buyers (waste of promotion dollars).

High visibility makes advertising a major target of marketing critics.

Advertisement exposure time is usually brief.

Advertisements are often quickly and easily screened out by consumers.

Personal Selling

Advantages

Can be the most persuasive promotion tool; salespeople can directly influence purchase behaviors.

Allows two-way communication.

Often necessary for technically complex products.

Allows direct one-on-one targeting of promotional effort.

Disadvantages

High cost per contact.

Sales training and motivation can be expensive and difficult.

Personal selling often has a poor image, making salesforce recruitment difficult.

Poorly done sales presentations can hurt sales as well as company, product, and brand images.

Sales Promotion

Advantages

Excellent approach for short-term price reductions for stimulating demand.

A large variety of sales promotion tools to choose from.

Can be effective for changing a variety of consumer behaviors.

Can be easily tied in with other promotion tools.

Disadvantages

May influence primarily brand-loyal customers to stock up at lower price but attract few new customers.

May have only short-term impact.

Overuse of price-related sales promotion tools may hurt brand image and profits.

Effective sales promotions are easily copied by competitors.

Source: J. Paul Peter and Jerry C. Olson, *Consumer Behavior and Marketing Strategy*, 2nd ed. (Homewood, Ill: Richard D. Irwin, 1990), p. 459.

and the adoption of new strategies. The following example illustrates how one firm developed its promotion mix along these lines.

When IBM began to market its magnetic character sensing equipment for banks, the company defined the 500 largest banks as its likeliest market and a research firm was commissioned to study the marketing problems. They selected a representative sample of 185 banks and interviewed the officer designated by each bank as the person who would be most influential in deciding whether or not to purchase the equipment. Researchers sought to establish which of the following stages each banker had reached in the sales process: (1) *awareness* of the new product; (2) *comprehension* of what it offered; (3) *conviction* that it would be a good investment; or (4) the *ordering* stage. They also tried to isolate the promotional factors that had brought the bankers to each stage. IBM's promotional mix consisted of personal selling, advertising, education (IBM schools and in-bank seminars), and publicity (through news releases). Figure 8–1 illustrates the process.

The findings were a revelation to IBM. In the marketing of such equipment IBM had consistently taken the position that advertising had a very minor role to play; that nothing could replace the sales call. IBM found it could cut back on personal selling in the early stages of the selling process, thereby freeing salespeople to concentrate on the vital phase of the process—the actual closing of the sale. While these results may not hold true for all products, they are an excellent example of the concept of the promotion mix and the effectiveness of different combinations of promotion tools for achieving various objectives.

ADVERTISING: PLANNING AND STRATEGY

Advertising seeks to promote the seller's product by means of printed and electronic media. This is justified on the grounds that messages can reach large numbers of people and inform, persuade, and remind them about the firm's offerings. The traditional way of defining advertising is as follows: It is any paid form of nonpersonal presentation of ideas, goods, or services by an identified sponsor.[1]

---

[1]Peter D. Bennett, ed., *Dictionary of Marketing Terms* (Chicago: American Marketing Association, 1988), p. 4.

FIGURE 8–1

An Example of the Role of Various Promotion Tools in the Selling Process

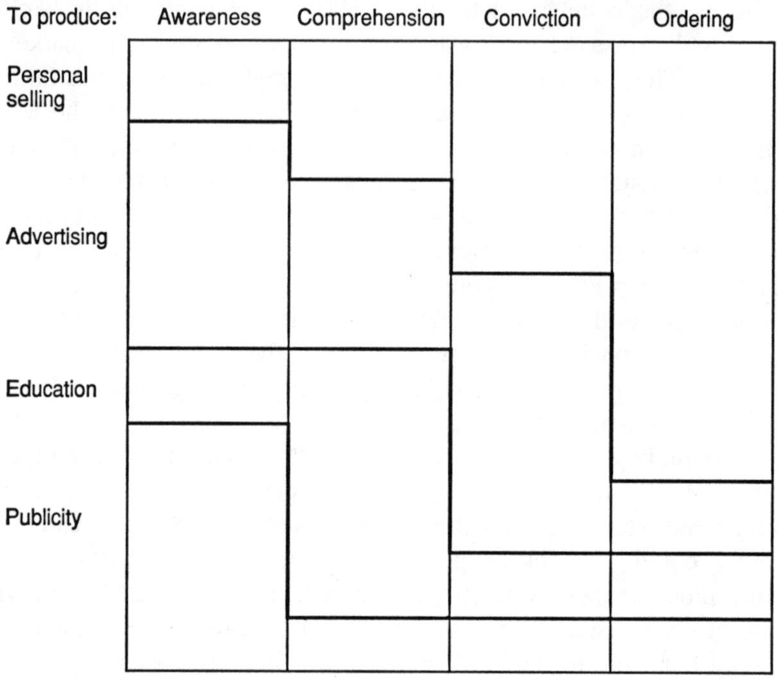

To produce:	Awareness	Comprehension	Conviction	Ordering
Personal selling				
Advertising				
Education				
Publicity				

From a management viewpoint, advertising is a strategic device for gaining or maintaining a competitive advantage in the marketplace. For example, in 1988, advertising expenditures went over the $118 billion mark. The top 100 leading national advertisers spent over $27 billion in advertising.[2] Based on past growth patterns, it is expected advertising expenditures will reach $150 billion before 1993. For manufacturers and resellers alike, advertising budgets represent a large and growing element in the cost of marketing goods and services. As part of the seller's promotion mix, advertising dollars must be appropriated and budgeted according to a marketing plan that takes into account such factors as:

---

[2]*Advertising Age*, September 27, 1989, p. 1.

HIGHLIGHT 8–2
Preparing the Advertising Campaign: The Eight-M Formula

Effective advertising should follow a plan. There is no one best way to go about planning an advertising campaign, but, in general, marketers should have good answers to the following eight questions:

1. *The management question:* Who will manage the advertising program?
2. *The money question:* How much should be spent on advertising as opposed to other forms of selling?
3. *The market question:* To whom should the advertising be directed?
4. *The message question:* What should the ads say about the product?
5. *The media question:* What types and combinations of media should be used?
6. *The macroscheduling question:* How long should the advertising campaign be in effect before changing ads or themes?
7. *The microscheduling question:* At what times and dates would it be best for ads to appear during the course of the campaign?
8. *The measurement question:* How will the effectiveness of the advertising campaign be measured and how will the campaign be evaluated and controlled?

---

1. Nature of the product, including life cycle.
2. Competition.
3. Government regulations.
4. Nature and scope of the market.
5. Channels of distribution.
6. Pricing strategy.
7. Availability of media.
8. Availability of funds.
9. Outlays for other forms of promotion.

Objectives of Advertising

In the long run, and often in the short run, advertising is justified on the basis of the revenues it produces. Revenues in this case may refer either to sales or profits. Economic theory assumes that firms are profit maximizers, and that advertising outlays should be increased in every market and medium up to the point where the additional cost of getting more business just equals the incremental profits. Since most business firms do not have the data required to use the marginal analysis of economic theory, they usually employ a less sophisticated decision-making model. There is also evidence to show that many executives advertise to maximize sales on the assumption that higher sales mean more profits (which may or may not be true).

The point to be made here is that the ultimate goal of the business advertiser is sales and profits. To achieve this goal an approach to advertising is needed that provides guidelines for intelligent decision making. This approach must recognize the need for measuring the results of advertising, and these measurements must be as valid and reliable as possible. Marketing managers must also be aware of the fact that advertising not only complements other forms of selling but is subject to the law of diminishing returns. This means that for any advertised product it can be assumed a point is eventually reached at which additional advertising produces little or no additional sales.

Specific Tasks of Advertising

In attempting to evaluate the contribution of advertising to the economic health of the firm, there are at least three different viewpoints on the subject. The generalist viewpoint is primarily concerned with sales, profits, return on investment, and so forth. At the other extreme, the specialist viewpoint is represented by advertising experts who are primarily concerned with measuring the effects of specific ads or campaigns; here primary attention is given to such matters as the Nielsen Index, Starch Reports, Arbitron Index, Simmons Reports, copy appeal, and so forth. A middle view, one that might be classified as more of a marketing management approach, understands and appreciates the other two viewpoints but, in addition, views advertising as a competitive weapon. Emphasis in this approach is given to the strategic aspects of the advertising problem. Following are some of the marketing tasks generally assigned to the advertising function as part of the overall marketing mix:

1. Maintaining dealer cooperation.
2. Familiarizing the consumer with the use of the product.
3. Emphasizing a trademark or brand.
4. Obtaining a list of prospects.
5. Creating goodwill for the product, brand, or company.

HIGHLIGHT 8–3
An Advertising Process Model

Consumer Psychosocial State	Marketing Situation
1. Ignorance	Consumer has no knowledge of the product.
2. Indifference	Consumer is conscious of product's existence by means of advertising.
3. Awareness	Advertising messages generate an awareness of a need for the product or reinforce a need once generated.
4. Interest	Consumer begins seeking more product-brand information by paying closer attention to various ads.
5. Comprehension	Consumer knows main features of product and various brands after intense ad exposure.
6. Conviction	Consumer is receptive to purchase and ready to act.
7. Action	Consumer shops for the product often as a result of the "act now" advertisements or special sales.

---

   6. Stressing unique features of the product.

   7. Introducing new products.

   8. Generating store traffic.

   9. Informing customers of sales prices.

   10. Building customer or brand loyalty.

   11. Establishing a relationship between the producer and distributor.

   The above list is representative but not exhaustive, and it should be noted that some of the points pertain more to middlemen than to producers. For example, the first point is a "channel task," where advertising and other forms of sales promotion are employed to facilitate the flow of the producer's goods through distributors to the ultimate consumer; "cooperative advertising" programs are specifically designed to meet this objective. This is where a channel member, such as a retailer, will receive a certain percentage of gross sales as an advertising allowance. Some manufacturers also provide advertising copy, illustrations, and so forth.

ADVERTISING DECISIONS

In line with what has just been said, the marketing manager must make two key decisions. The first decision deals with determining the size of the advertising budget, and the second deals with how the advertising budget should be allocated. Although these decisions are highly inter-related, we deal with them separately to achieve a better understanding of the problems involved.

The Expenditure Question

Most firms determine how much to spend on advertising by one of the following methods:

Percent of Sales. This is one of the most popular rule-of-thumb methods, and its appeal is found in its simplicity. The firm simply takes a percentage figure and applies it to either past or future sales. For example, suppose next year's sales are estimated to be $1 million. Using a 2-percent-of-sales criterion, the ad budget would be $20,000. This approach is usually justified by its advocates in terms of the following argument: *(a)* advertising is needed to generate sales; *(b)* a number of cents, that is, the percentage used, out of each dollar of sales should be devoted to advertising in order to generate needed sales; and *(c)* the percentage is easily adjusted and can be readily understood by other executives. The percent-of-sales approach is popular in retailing.

Per-Unit Expenditure. Closely related to the above technique is one in which a fixed monetary amount is spent on advertising for each unit of the product expected to be sold. This method is popular with higher priced merchandise, such as automobiles or appliances. For instance, if a company is marketing color televisions priced at $500, it may decide that it should spend $30 per set on advertising. Since this $30 is a fixed amount for each unit, this method amounts to the same thing as the percent-of-sales method. The big difference is in the rationale used to justify each of the methods. The per-unit expenditure method attempts to determine the retail price by using production costs as a base. Here the seller realizes that a reasonably competitive price must be established for the product in question and attempts to cost out the gross margin. All this means is that, if the suggested retail price is to be $500 and manufacturing costs are $250, there is a gross margin of $250 available to cover certain expenses, such as transportation, personal selling, advertising, and dealer profit. Some of these expense items are flexible, such as advertising, while others are nearly fixed, as in the case of transportation. The basic problem with this method and the percent-of-sales method is that they view advertising as a function of sales, rather than sales as a function of advertising.

All You Can Afford.   Here the advertising budget is established as a predetermined share of profits or financial resources. The availability of current revenues sets the upper limit of the ad budget. The only advantage to this approach is that it sets reasonable limits on the expenditures for advertising. However, from the standpoint of sound marketing practice, this method is undesirable because there is no necessary connection between liquidity and advertising opportunity. Any firm that limits its advertising outlays to the amount of available funds will probably miss opportunities for increasing sales and profits.

Competitive Parity.   This approach is often used in conjunction with other approaches, such as the percent-of-sales method. The basic philosophy underlying this approach is that advertising is defensive. Advertising budgets are based on those of competitors or other members of the industry. From a strategy standpoint, this is a "followership" technique and assumes that the other firms in the industry know what they are doing and have similar goals. Competitive parity is not a preferred method, although some executives feel it is a "safe" approach. This may or may not be true depending in part on the relative market share of competing firms and their growth objectives.

The Research Approach.   Here the advertising budget is argued for and presented on the basis of research findings. Advertising media are studied in terms of their productivity by the use of media reports (such as the Starch Reports) and research studies. Costs are also estimated and compared with study results. A typical experiment is one in which three or more test markets are selected. The first test market is used as a control, either with no advertising or with normal levels of advertising. Advertising with various levels of intensity are used in the other markets, and comparisions are made to see what effect different levels of intensity have. The advertising manager then evaluates the costs and benefits of

HIGHLIGHT 8–4
Some Relative Merits of Major Advertising Media

Newspapers

Advantages	Disadvantages
1. Flexible and timely.	1. Short life.
2. Intense coverge of local markets.	2. Read hastily.
3. Broad acceptance and use.	3. Small "pass-along" audience.
4. High believability of printed word.	

Television

Advantages	Disadvantages
1. Combination of sight, sound, and motion.	1. Nonselectivity of audience.
2. Appeals to senses.	2. Fleeting impressions.
3. Mass audience coverage.	3. Short life.
4. Psychology of attention.	4. Expensive.

Radio

Advantages	Disadvantages
1. Mass use (over 25 million radios sold annually).	1. Audio presentation only.
2. Audience selectivity via station format.	2. Less attention than TV.
3. Low cost (per unit of time.)	3. Chaotic buying (nonstandardized rate structures).
4. Geographic flexibility.	4. Short life.

Magazines

Advantages	Disadvantages
1. High geographic and demographic selectivity.	1. Long closing periods (6 to 8 weeks prior to publication).
2. Psychology of attention.	2. Some waste circulation.
3. Quality of reproduction.	3. No guarantee of position (unless premium is paid).
4. Pass-along readership.	

Outdoor

Advantages	Disadvantages
1. Flexible.	1. Creative limitations.
2. Relative absence of competing advertisements.	2. Many distractions for viewer.
3. Repeat exposure.	3. Public attack (ecological implications).
4. Relatively inexpensive.	4. No selectivity of audience.

HIGHLIGHT 8–4 *concluded*

Direct Mail

Advantages	**Disadvantages**
1. Audience selectivity.	1. Relatively high cost.
2. Flexible.	2. Consumers often pay little
3. No competition from competing	attention and throw it away.
advertisements.	
4. Personalized.	

---

the different approaches and intensity levels to determine the overall budget. Although the research approach is generally more expensive than some other models, it is a more rational approach to the expenditure decision.

The Task Approach. Well-planned advertising programs usually make use of the task approach, which initially formulates the advertising goals and defines the tasks to accomplish these goals. Once this is done, management determines how much it will cost to accomplish each task and adds up the total. This approach is often used in conjunction with the research approach. A variation of the task approach is referred to as the *marketing-program approach*. Here all promotional or selling programs are budgeted in relation to each other, and, given a set of objectives, the goal is to find the optimum promotional mix. It should be clear that, in the task or marketing-program approach, the expenditure and allocation decisions are inseparable.

The Allocation Question

This question deals with the problem of deciding on the most effective way of spending advertising dollars. A general answer to the question is that management's choice of strategies and objectives determines the media and appeals to be used. In other words, the firm's or product division's overall marketing plan will function as a general guideline for answering the allocation question.

From a practical standpoint, however, the allocation question can be framed in terms of message and media decisions. A successful ad campaign has two related tasks: (1) say the right things in the ads them- selves and (2) use the appropriate media in the right amounts at the right time to reach the target market.

Message Strategy. The advertising process involves creating mes- sages with words, ideas, sounds, and other forms of audiovisual stimuli that are designed to affect consumer (or distributor) behavior. It follows that much of advertising is a communication process. To be effective, the advertising message should meet two general criteria: (1) it should take into account the basic principles of communication, and (2) it should be predicated upon a good theory of consumer motivation and behavior.[3]

The basic communication process involves three elements: (1) the sender or source of the communication; (2) the communication or mes- sage; and (3) the receiver or audience. Advertising agencies are considered experts in the communications field and are employed by most large firms to create meaningful messages and assist in their dissemination. Trans- lating the product idea or marketing message into an effective ad is termed *encoding*. In advertising, the goal of encoding is to generate ads that are understood by the audience. For this to occur, the audience must be able to decode the message in the ad so that the perceived content of the message is the same as the intended content of the message. From a practical standpoint, all this means is that advertising messages must be sent to consumers in an understandable and meaningful way.

Advertising messages, of course, must be transmitted and carried by particular communication channels commonly known as advertising media. These media or channels vary in efficiency, selectivity, and cost. Some channels are preferred to others because they have less "noise," and thus messages are more easily received and understood. For example, a particular newspaper ad must compete with other ads, pictures, or stories on the same page. In the case of radio or TV, while only one firm's message is usually broadcast at a time, there are other distractions (noise) that can hamper clear communications, such as driving while listening to the radio.

The relationship between advertising and consumer behavior is quite obvious. For many products and services, advertising is an influence that

---

[3]For a full discussion of message strategy, see James F. Engel, Martin R. Warshaw, and Thomas C. Kinnear, *Promotional Strategy,* 6th ed. (Homewood, Ill.: Richard D. Irwin, 1987).

may affect the consumer's decision to purchase a particular product or brand. It is clear that consumers are subjected to many selling influences, and the question arises about how important advertising is or can be. Here is where the advertising expert must operate on some theory of consumer behavior. The reader will recall from the discussion of consumer behavior that the buyer was viewed as progressing through various stages from an unsatisfied need through and beyond a purchase decision. The relevance of this discussion is illustrated in Figure 8–2, which compares the role of advertising in various stages of the buying process.

The planning of an advertising campaign and the creation of persuasive messages requires a mixture of marketing skill and creative know-how. Relative to the dimension of marketing skills, there are some important pieces of marketing information needed before launching an ad campaign. Most of this information must be generated by the firm and kept up to date. Listed below are some of the critical types of information an advertiser should have:

1. *Who* the firm's customers and potential customers are; their demographic, economic, and psychological characteristics; and any other factors affecting their likelihood of buying.
2. *How many* such customers there are.

FIGURE 8–2
Advertising and the Buying Process

Stage in the Buying Process	Possible Advertising Objective	Examples
1. Unsatisfied need.	Awareness.	"The reciprocating engine is inefficient." "Dishwashing roughens hands."
2. Alternative search and evaluation.	Comprehension.	"The Wankel engine is efficient." "Palmolive is mild."
3. Purchase decision.	Conviction-ordering.	"Come in and see for yourself." "Buy some today."
4. Postpurchase feelings.	Reassurance.	"Thousands of satisfied owners." "Compare with any other brand."

Source: Adapted for the purposes of this text from Ben M. Enis, *Marketing Principles: The Management Process* (Santa Monica, Calif.: Goodyear Publishing, 1980), p. 466.

3. *How much* of the firm's type and brand of product they are currently buying and can reasonably be expected to buy in the short-term and long-term future.
4. *What* individuals, other than customers, and potential customers, *influence* purchasing decisions.
5. *Where* they *buy* the firm's brand of product.
6. *When* they buy, and frequency of purchase.
7. *What* competitive brands they buy and frequency of purchase.
8. *How* they *use* the product.
9. *Why* they buy particular *types* and *brands* of products.

Media Mix. Media selection is no easy task. To start with, there are numerous types and combinations of media to choose from. Below is a general outline of some of the more common advertising media.

A. *Printed media.*
  1. National.
     a. Magazines.
     b. Newspapers.
     c. Direct mail.
  2. Local.
     a. Newspapers.
     b. Magazines.
     c. Direct mail.
     d. Handbills or flyers.
     e. Yellow Pages.
B. *Electronic media.*
  1. National (network).
     a. Radio.
     b. Television.
  2. Local.
     a. Radio (AM–FM).
     b. Television.
  3. Individual.
     a. Videocassette.
     b. Floppy disk.
C. *Other.*
  1. Outdoor (example: billboards).
  2. Transit.

3. Specialty (giveaways).
4. Point-of-purchase.
5. Telemarketing (telephone selling).

Of course, each of the above media categories can be further refined. For example, magazines can be broken down into more detailed classes, such as mass monthlies *(Reader's Digest)*, news weeklies *(Time)*, men's magazines *(Playboy)*, women's fashion magazines *(Vogue)*, sports magazines *(Sports Illustrated)*, business magazines *(Forbes)*, and so forth. Clearly, one dimension of this advertising management problem involves having an overabundance of media to select from. With only four media to choose from, there are 16 possible go or no-go decisions. With 10 media, there would be approximately 1,000 combinations.

Although the number of media and media combinations available for advertising is overwhelming at first glance, four interrelated factors limit the number of practical alternatives. First, *the nature of the product* limits the number of practical and efficient alternatives. For instance, a radically new and highly complex product could not be properly promoted using billboard advertisements. Second, *the nature and size of the target market* also limits appropriate advertising media. For example, it is generally inefficient to advertise industrial goods in mass media publications. Third, *the advertising budget* may restrict the use of expensive media, such as television. And fourth, *the availability* of some media may be limited in particular geographic areas. Although these factors reduce media alternatives to a more manageable number, specific media must still be selected. A primary consideration at this point is media effectiveness or efficiency.

In the advertising industry, a common measure of efficiency or productivity of media is "cost per thousand." This figure generally refers to the dollar cost of reaching 1,000 prospects, and its chief advantage is in making media comparisons. Generally, such measures as circulation, audience size, and sets in use per commercial minute are used in the calculation. Of course, different relative rankings of media can occur, depending on the measure used. Another problem deals with what is meant by "reaching" the prospect, and at least five levels of reaching are possible:

1. *Distribution.* This level refers to circulation or physical distribution of the vehicle into households or other decision-making

units. In only some of these households or decision-making units are there genuine prospects for the product.

2. *Exposure*. This level refers to actual exposure of prospects to the message. If the TV set is on, distribution is taking place; but only if the program is being watched can exposure occur.

3. *Awareness*. This level refers to the prospect becoming alert to the message in the sense of being conscious of the ad. Actual information processing starts at this point.

4. *Communication*. This level goes one step beyond awareness— to the point where the prospect becomes affected by the message. Here the effect is to generate some sort of change in the prospect's knowledge, attitude, or desire concerning the product.

5. *Response*. This level represents the overt action that results because of the ad. Response can mean many things, such as a simple telephone or mail inquiry, a shopping trip, or a purchase.

The advertiser has to decide at what level to evaluate the performance of a medium, and this is a particularly difficult problem. Ideally, the advertiser would like to know exactly how many dollars of sales are generated by ads in a particular medium. However, this is very difficult to measure since so many other factors are simultaneously at work that could be producing sales. On the other hand, the distribution of a medium is much easier to measure but distribution figures are much less meaningful. For example, a newspaper may have a distribution (circulation) of 100,000 people, yet none of these people may be prospects for the particular product being advertised. Thus, if this media were evaluated in terms of distribution, it might be viewed as quite effective even though it may be totally ineffective in terms of producing sales. This problem further illustrates the importance of insuring that the media selected are those used by the target market.

From what has been said so far, it should be clear that advertising decisions involve a great deal of complexity and a myriad of variables. Not surprising, therefore, is that application of quantitative techniques have become quite popular in the area. Linear programming, dynamic programming, heuristic programming, and simulation have been applied to the problem of selecting media schedules, and more comprehensive models of advertising decisions have also been developed. Although these

---

HIGHLIGHT 8–5
Procedures for Evaluating Advertising Programs and Some Services Using the Procedures

Procedures for Evaluating Specific Advertisements

1. *Recognition tests:* Estimate the percentage of people claiming to have read a magazine who recognize the ad when it is shown to them (e.g., Starch Message Report Service).
2. *Recall tests:* Estimate the percentage of people claiming to have read a magazine who can (unaided) recall the ad and its contents (e.g., Gallup and Robinson Impact Service, various services for TV ads as well).
3. *Opinion tests:* Potential audience members are asked to rank alternative advertisements as most interesting, most believable, best liked.
4. *Theater tests:* Theater audience is asked for brand preferences before and after an ad is shown in context of a TV show (e.g., Schwerin TV Testing Service).

Procedures for Evaluating Specific Advertising Objectives

1. *Awareness:* Potential buyers are asked to indicate brands that come to mind in a product category. A message used in an ad campaign is given and buyers are asked to identify the brand that was advertised using that message.
2. *Attitude:* Potential buyers are asked to rate competing or individual brands on determinant attributes, benefits, characterizations using rating scales.

Procedures for Evaluating Motivational Impact

1. *Intention to buy:* Potential buyers are asked to indicate the likelihood they will buy a brand (on a scale from "definitely will not" to "definitely will").
2. *Market test:* Sales changes in different markets are monitored to compare the effects of different messages, budget levels.

Source: Joseph Guiltinan and Gordon Paul, *Marketing Management,* 2nd ed., p. 263, © 1988 by McGraw-Hill, Inc. Reprinted by permission of the publisher.

models can be extremely useful as an aid in advertising decision making, they must be viewed as tools and not as replacement for sound managerial decisions and judgment.

HIGHLIGHT 8–6
Some Objectives of Sales Promotion

When Directed at Consumers:
1. To obtain the trial of a product.
2. To introduce a new or improved product.
3. To encourage repeat or greater usage by current users.
4. To bring more customers into retail stores.
5. To increase the total number of users of an established product.

When Directed at Salespersons:
1. To motivate the sales force.
2. To educate the sales force about product improvements.
3. To stabilize a fluctuating sales pattern.

When Directed at Resellers:
1. To increase reseller inventories.
2. To obtain displays and other support for products.
3. To improve product distribution.
4. To obtain more and better shelf space.

Source: Adapted from Steven J. Skinner, *Marketing* (Boston: Houghton Mifflin Co., 1990), p. 542.

SALES PROMOTION

In marketing, the word *promotion* is used in many ways. For instance, it is sometimes used to refer to a specific activity, such as advertising or publicity. In the general sense, promotion has been defined as "any identifiable effort on the part of the seller to persuade buyers to accept the seller's information and store it in retrievable form." However, the term *sales promotion* has a more restricted and technical meaning and has been defined by the American Marketing Association as follows:

> Media and nonmedia marketing pressure applied for a predetermined, limited period of time at the level of consumer, retailer, or wholesaler in order

to stimulate trial, increase consumer demand, or improve product availability.[4]

The popularity of sales and other promotions has been increasing. In the 10-year period between 1977 and 1987, the promotion-to-advertising expenditure ratio increased from a 58 percent to 42 percent split to a 65 percent to 35 percent level.[5] Current estimates show a similar pattern. Reasons for this growth of sales promotion include a shifting emphasis from pull to push marketing strategies by many firms, a widening of the focus of advertising agencies to include promotional services to firms, an emphasis on the part of management towards short-term results, and the emergence of new technology. For example, supermarket cash registers can now be equipped with a device that will dispense coupons to a customer at the point of purchase. The type, variety, and cash amount of the coupon will vary from customer to customer based on their purchases. In essence, it is now possible for the Coca-Cola Company to dispense coupons to only those customers who purchase Pepsi thus avoiding wasting promotional dollars on already loyal Coke drinkers.

Push versus Pull Marketing

Push and pull marketing strategies comprise the two options available to firms interested in getting their product into customers' hands. Push strategies include all activities aimed at getting products into the dealer pipeline and accelerating sales by offering inducements to dealers, retailers, and salespeople. Inducements might include introductory price allowances, distribution allowances, and advertising-dollar allowances.[6] A pull strategy, on the other hand, is one whereby a manufacturer relies mainly on product advertising or consumer sales promotions. These activities

---

[4]Peter D. Bennett, ed., *Dictionary of Marketing Terms* (Chicago: American Marketing Association, 1988), p. 179.

[5]Nathaniel Frey, "Ninth Annual Advertising and Sales Promotion Report," *Marketing Communications,* August 1988, p. 11.

[6]Definition of push marketing and its activities is from Courtland L. Bovee and William F. Arens, *Contemporary Advertising,* 3rd ed. (Homewood, Ill.: Richard D. Irwin, 1989), p. G–16.

are aimed at motivating the consumer to pull the product through the channel.

Several forces and developments have contributed to the increasing use of push marketing strategies by many manufacturers.[7]

1. *Changes in the balance of power between manufacturers and retailers.* Due to the decreasing importance of network television and the increasing use of optical scanning equipment, retailers no longer have to depend on manufacturers for facts. This leads to more power on the part of retailers.

2. *Growth and consolidation of retail package goods businesses.* The growth of regional and national grocery chains such as Safeway and Kroger have led to increasing clout for the retailer. For example, many supermarkets now charge manufacturers a slotting allowance on new products. A slotting allowance is a fee manufacturers pay retailers to allocate shelf space to new products.

3. *Reduced product differentiation and brand loyalty.* Due to the similarity of many brands and the growing use of sales promotions, consumers are no longer as brand loyal as they once were. Therefore, more and more sales promotions are needed as an incentive to get the consumer to buy a particular brand. To illustrate, consider the case of domestic car manufacturers. Advertising can no longer be used as a stand-alone promotional strategy to induce consumer automobile purchases. Instead the manufacturer must also offer additional incentives to the consumer through the dealer including rebates, special option packages, and extended warranties.

Trade Sales Promotions

Trade promotions are those promotions aimed at distributors and retailers of products who make up the distribution channel. The major objectives of trade promotions are to: (1) convince retailers to carry the

---

[7]For a fuller explanation of the rise in push marketing strategies, see Terence A. Shimp, *Promotion Management and Marketing Communications,* 2nd ed. (Hinsdale, Ill.: Dryden Press, 1990), pp. 517–20 and Alvin Achenbaum and F. Kent Mitchel, "Pulling Away from Push Marketing," *Harvard Business Review,* May–June 1987, pp. 38–40.

manufacturer's products; (2) reduce the manufacturer's and increase the distributor's or retailer's inventories; (3) support advertising and consumer sales promotions; (4) encourage retailers to either give the product more favorable shelf space or place more emphasis on selling the product; and (5) serve as a reward for past sales efforts.

Types of dealer sales promotions vary. The most common types are:[8]

1. Point-of-purchase displays including special racks, banners, signs, price cards, and other mechanical product dispensers. For example, an end-of-the-aisle display for Chips Ahoy cookies would be provided to the retailer by Nabisco.
2. Contests in which organizations and individual sales people are rewarded for sales efforts.
3. Trade shows that are regularly scheduled events where manufacturers display products, provide information, and display products.
4. Sales meetings at which information and support materials are presented to dealers.
5. Push money, which is a form of extra payment given to resellers for meeting specified sales goals.
6. Dealer loaders, which are premiums in the form of either merchandise, gifts, or displays given to the reseller for purchasing large quantities of the product.
7. Trade deals, which are price discounts given for meeting certain purchase requirements.
8. Advertising allowances whereby the manufacturer helps to support retailer advertising efforts in which the manufacturer's product is displayed.

Consumer Promotions

Consumer promotions can fulfill several distinct objectives for the manufacturer. Some of the more commonly sought-after objectives include: (1) inducing the consumer to try the product; (2) rewarding the consumer

---

[8]For a fuller discussion of trade and consumer sales promotion activities, see John Burnett, *Promotion Management,* 2nd ed. (St. Paul, Minn.: West Publishing, 1988), chaps. 13 and 14.

for brand loyalty; (3) encouraging the consumer to trade up or purchase larger sizes of a product; (4) stimulating the consumer to make repeat purchases of the product; (5) reacting to competitor efforts; and (6) reinforcing and serving as a complement to advertising and personal selling efforts.

Listed below are brief descriptions of some of the most commonly utilized forms of consumer promotion activities.

1. *Sampling*. Consumers are offered regular or trial sizes of the product either free or at a nominal price. For example, Hershey Foods Corp. handed out 750,000 candy bars on 170 college campuses as a means of gaining trial.[9]

2. *Price deals*. Consumers are given discounts from the product's regular price. For example, Coke and Pepsi are frequently available at discounted prices.

3. *Bonus packs*. Bonus packs consist of additional amounts of the product that a company gives to buyers of the product. For example, manufacturers of disposable razors frequently add additional razors to their packages at no additional charge.

4. *Rebates and refunds*. Consumers, either on the spot or through the mail are given cash reimbursements for purchasing products. For example, consumers are offered a $3 mail-in-rebate for purchasing a Norelco coffee maker.

5. *Sweepstakes and contests*. Consumers can win cash and/or prizes either through chance selection or games of skill. For example, Marriott Hotels teamed up with Hertz Rent-A-Car in a scratch card sweepstakes that offered over $90 million in prizes.

6. *Premiums*. A premium is a reward or gift that comes from purchasing a product. For example, Coca-Cola gave away an estimated 20 million pairs of 3-D glasses to enable Super Bowl watchers to see their 3-D commercial. AT&T gave away fax and voice-paging machines to purchasers of their small business systems.

7. *Coupons*. Probably the most familiar and widely used of all consumer promotions, coupons are cents-off or added value

---

[9]*Advertising Age*, September 27, 1989, p. 3.

incentives. Due to the high incidence of coupon fraud, manufacturers including Royal Crown Cola and General Mills are now experimenting with the use of personalized checks as an alternative to coupons. An added advantage of this alternative is a quicker redemption for retailers. As mentioned previously, point-of-purchase coupons are becoming an increasingly efficient way for marketers to target their promotional efforts at specific consumers.

What Sales Promotion Can and Can't Do

Advocates of sales promotion often point to its growing popularity as a justification for the argument that we don't need advertising; sales promotion itself will suffice. Marketers should bear in mind that sales promotion is only one part of a well-constructed overall promotional plan. While proven to be extremely effective in achieving the objectives listed in the previous sections, there are several compelling reasons why sales promotion should not be utilized as the sole promotional tool. These reasons include sales promotion's inability to: (1) generate long-term buyer commitment to a brand; (2) change, except on a temporary basis, declining sales of a product; (3) convince buyers to purchase an otherwise unacceptable product; and (4) make up for a lack of advertising or sales support for a product. To illustrate, General Foods cut back the yearly advertising expenditures on Maxwell House coffee by $60 million in the mid-80s and reallocated the funds to sales promotion activities. Within a year, Folger's coffee dislodged Maxwell House as the largest selling brand. It took three years for Maxwell House to finally regain the top spot. In the process, General Foods ended up restoring the advertising budget to an even higher level than it was prior to Maxwell House's fall from grace.

LESSONS FOR THE MANUFACTURER

Advertising and sales promotion decisions are more likely to be made by marketing executives than other functional area managers. However, budget approval for advertising and sales promotion is usually obtained from business level or corporate level managers. Marketing personnel have greater involvement because these decisions are more directly related to reaching target markets and generating demand for products, both of which are primarily marketing tasks.

Although the nature of the product and its functional advantages over competitive products may be built into the product through design, engineering, and manufacturing, the job of communicating with target markets is usually done by marketing. Marketing personnel also are the most likely to work closely with ad agencies and outside marketing research firms in the design of promotion messages and media strategies. However, excellence in manufacturing can be the basis for advertising strategies. For example, companies such as Motorola and Federal Express often advertise the fact that they have won a Baldrige Award as a way of telling consumers that they provide quality products and services.

ADDITONAL READINGS

Aaker, David A., and Donald E. Bruzzone. "Causes of Irritation in Advertising." *Journal of Marketing,* Spring 1985, pp. 47–57.

Bovee, Courtland L., and William F. Arens. *Contemporary Advertising.* 3rd ed. Homewood, Ill.: Richard D. Irwin, 1989.

Burnett, John. *Promotion Management.* 2nd ed. St. Paul, Minn.:West Publishing, 1988.

Engel, James F.; Martin R. Warshaw; and Thomas C. Kinnear. *Promotional Strategy: Managing the Marketing Communications Process.* 6th ed. Homewood, Ill.: Richard D. Irwin, 1987.

Healy, John S., and Harold H. Kassarjian. "Advertising Substantiation and Advertiser Response: A Content Analysis of Magazine Advertisements." *Journal of Marketing,* Winter 1983, pp. 107–17.

Heath, Robert L., and Richard A. Nelson. "Image and Issue Advertising: A Corporate and Public Policy Perspective." *Journal of Marketing,* Spring 1985, pp. 58–68.

Pollay, Richard W. "The Subsiding Sizzle: A Descriptive History of Print Advertising, 1900–1980." *Journal of Marketing,* Summer 1985, pp. 24–37.

——— "The Distorted Mirror: Reflections on the Unintended Consequences of Advertising." *Journal of Marketing,* April 1986, pp. 18–36.

Rothschild, Michael L. *Advertising.* Lexington, Mass.: D. C. Heath and Co., 1987.

Sandage, C. H.; V. Fryburger; and K. R. Rotzell. *Advertising Theory and Practice.* 11th ed. Homewood, Ill.: Richard D. Irwin, 1983.

Sewall, M. A., and D. Sarel. "Characteristics of Radio Commercials and Their Recall Effectiveness." *Journal of Marketing,* January 1986, pp. 52–60.

Shimp, Terence A. *Promotion Management and Marketing Communications.* 2nd ed. Hinsdale, Ill.: Dryden Press, 1990.

APPENDIX: MAJOR FEDERAL AGENCIES INVOLVED IN CONTROL OF ADVERTISING

Agency	*Function*
Federal Trade Commission	Regulates commerce between states; controls unfair business practices; takes action on false and deceptive advertising; most important agency in regulation of advertising and promotion.
Food and Drug Administration	Regulatory division of the Department of Health, Education, and Welfare; controls marketing of food, drugs, cosmetics, medical devices, and potentially hazardous consumer products.
Federal Communications Commission	Regulates advertising indirectly, primarily through the power to grant or withdraw broadcasting licenses.
Postal Service	Regulates material that goes through the mails, primarily in areas of obscenity, lottery, and fraud.
Alcohol and Tobacco Tax Division	Part of the Treasury Department; has broad powers to regulate deceptive and misleading advertising of liquor and tobacco.
Grain Division	Unit of the Department of Agriculture responsible for policing seed advertising.
Securities and Exchange Commission	Regulates advertising of securities.

Information Source	*Description*
Patent Office	Regulates registration of trademarks.
Library of Congress	Controls protection of copyrights.
Department of Justice	Enforces all federal laws through prosecuting cases referred to it by other government agencies.

CHAPTER 9

PROMOTION STRATEGY: PERSONAL SELLING

Personal selling, unlike advertising or sales promotion, involves direct face-to-face relationships between the seller and the prospect or customer. The behavioral scientist would probably characterize personal selling as a type of personal influence. Operationally, it is a complex communication process, one not completely understood by marketing scholars.

IMPORTANCE OF PERSONAL SELLING

Most business firms find it impossible to market their products without some form of personal selling. To illustrate, some years ago vending machines became quite popular. The question may be raised about whether or not these machines replaced the salesperson. The answer is both yes and no. In a narrow sense of the word, the vending machine has replaced some retail sales clerks who, for most convenience goods, merely dispensed the product and collected money. On the other hand, vending machines and their contents must be "sold" to the vending machine operators, and personal selling effort must be exerted to secure profitable locations for the machines.

The policies of self-service and self-selection have done much to eliminate the need for personal selling in some types of retail stores. However, the successful deployment of these policies have required manufacturers to do two things: *(a)* presell the consumer by means of larger advertising and sales promotion outlays; and *(b)* design packages for their products that would "sell" themselves, so to speak.

The importance of the personal selling function depends partially on the nature of the product. As a general rule, goods that are new, technically complex, and/or expensive require more personal selling effort. The

---

HIGHLIGHT 9–1
The Typical American Salesperson

Age: 33.
Male: 70 percent.
Female: 30 percent.
Some college or degree: 82 percent.
Graduate degree: 92 percent.
Most likely to leave after: 4.3 years.
Average length of service: 6.3 years.
Usual pay: salary, 20 percent; commission, 30 percent; combination, 50 percent.
Earnings per years: trainee, $25,000; experienced salesperson, $40,000.
Cost to train: $18,000.
Length of training: 3 months.
Cost per sales call: $95 to $350.
Sales calls per day: 6.5.
Number of calls to close: 5.
Cost of field expenses: $20,000.
Value of benefits: $14,000.
Average sales volume: $1 million.
Hours per week in selling activities within the territory: 41.
Hours per week in nonselling activities, such as paperwork and planning sales calls: 10.
Turnover rate: 20 percent.

Source: Charles Futrell, *Fundamentals of Selling,* 3rd ed. (Homewood, Ill.: Richard D. Irwin, 1990), p. 8.

salesperson plays a key role in providing the consumer with information about such products to reduce the risks involved in purchase and use. Insurance, for example, is a complex and technical product that often needs significant amounts of personal selling. In addition, many industrial goods cannot be presold, and the salesperson (or sales team) has a key role to play in finalizing the sale. However, most national branded convenience goods are purchased by the consumer without any significant assistance from store clerks.

The importance of personal selling also is determined to a large extent by the needs of the consumer. In the case of pure competition (a large number of small buyers with complete market knowledge of a homogeneous product), there is little need for personal selling. A close approximation to this situation is found at auctions for agricultural products, such as tobacco or wheat. At the other extreme, when a product is highly differentiated, such as housing, and marketed to consumers with imperfect knowledge of product offerings, then personal selling becomes a key factor in the promotion mix. In fact, in some cases, the consumer may not even be seeking the product; for instance, life insurance is often categorized as an unsought good. Finally, sellers who differentiate their products at the point of sale will usually make heavy use of personal selling in their promotion mix. For example, automobile buyers are given the opportunity to purchase various extras or options at the time of purchase.

It is important to remember that, for many companies, the salesperson represents the customer's main link to the firm. In fact, to some, the salesperson is the company. Therefore, it is imperative that the company take advantage of this unique link. Through the efforts of the successful salesperson, a company can build relationships with customers that continue long beyond the initial sale. It is the salesperson who serves as the conduit through which information regarding product flaws, improvements, applications, and/or new uses can pass from the customer to the marketing department. To illustrate the importance of using salespeople as an information resource, consider this fact. In some industries, customer information serves as the source for up to 90 percent of new product and process ideas.[1] Along with techniques described in the previous chapter, personal selling provides the push needed to get middlemen to carry new products, increase their amount of purchasing, and devote more effort in merchandising a product or brand.[2]

THE SALES PROCESS

Personal selling is as much an art as it is a science. The word *art* is used to describe that portion of the selling process that is highly creative in nature and difficult to explain. This does not mean there is little control

---

[1]Eric von Hipple, "The Sources of Innovation," *The McKinsey Quarterly,* Winter 1988, pp. 72–79.

[2]Terance A. Shimp, *Promotion Management and Marketing Communications,* 2nd ed. (Hinsdale: Dryden Press, 1990), p. 602.

FIGURE 9–1
A Model of the Selling Process

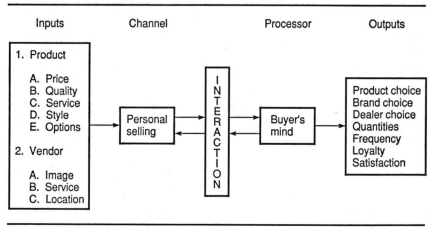

Inputs	Channel	Processor	Outputs

over the personal selling element in the promotion mix. It does imply that, all other things equal, the trained salesperson can outsell the untrained one.

Before management selects and trains salespeople, it should have an understanding of the sales process. Obviously, the sales process will differ according to the size of the company, the nature of the product, the market, and so forth, but there are some elements common to almost all selling situations that should be understood. For the purposes of this text, the term *sales process* refers to two basic factors: (1) the sequence of stages or steps the salesperson should follow in trying to sell goods and services; and (2) a set of basic principles that, if adhered to, will increase the likelihood of a sale being made.

The traditional approach to personal selling involves a formula or step-by-step procedure. It is known as the AIDAS formula and has five steps: (1) get the prospect's *attention;* (2) arouse the prospect's *interest;* (3) stimulate the prospect's *desire* for the product; (4) get buying *action;* and (5) build *satisfaction* into the transaction. This approach to selling implies two things. First, the prospect or potential buyer goes through these five steps. Second, the salesperson can influence the behavior of the prospect if this process is managed skillfully. Although this model represents a logical approach to explaining the sales process, it emphasizes a how-to approach to selling, rather than attempting to explain why sales are made, or conversely, why purchases are made.

An explanation of the selling process in terms of why individuals purchase would require a full understanding of consumer behavior. Obviously, as we saw in Chapter 3, this is a difficult task, because so many variables are difficult to measure or control. However, a useful framework for a better understanding of the selling process is illustrated in Figure 9–1.

This approach views the selling process as an input-output system: the inputs are marketing stimuli, such as price, quality, service, and style. Personal selling is viewed as one of the channels by which knowledge about these marketing stimuli are transmitted to the buyer. In this model, the buyer's mind is a processor of the various stimuli, and, since the workings of the mind are only partially understood, it can be considered a "black box." The explanation of what goes on in this black box depends on which approach or theory of behavior is employed.[3] The outputs for the model represent purchasing responses, such as brand choice, dealer choice, and the like. Here the sales process is viewed as a social situation involving two persons. The interaction of the two persons depends on the economic, social, physical, and personality characteristics of both the seller and the buyer.[4] A successful sale is situationally determined by these factors and can be considered social behavior as well as individual behavior. The prospect's perception of the salesperson is a key factor in determining the salesperson's effectiveness and role expectations.[5] The salesperson's confidence and ability to "play the role" of a salesperson is crucial in determining behavior and is influenced by personality, knowledge, training, and previous experience.[6]

Selling Fundamentals

From what has been said so far, the only reasonable conclusion that can be drawn is that there is no one clear-cut theory of personal selling nor

---

[3]For a review, see J. Paul Peter and Jerry C. Olson, *Consumer Behavior and Marketing Strategy,* 2nd ed. (Homewood, Ill.: Richard D. Irwin, 1990).

[4]Kaylene C. Williams and Rosann L. Spiro, "Communication Style in the Salesperson-Customer Dyad," *Journal of Marketing Research,* November 1985, pp. 434–43.

[5]Barton A. Weitz, Harish Sujen, and Mita Sujen, "Knowledge, Motivation, and Adaptive Behavior: A Framework for Improving Selling Effectiveness," *Journal of Marketing,* October 1986, pp. 174–91.

[6]Alan J. Dubinsky, Roy D. Howell, Thomas N. Ingram, and Danny N. Bellenger, "Salesforce Socialization," *Journal of Marketing,* October 1986, pp. 192–207.

HIGHLIGHT 9–2
Qualities Most Valued, Disliked, and Hated in Salespersons by Purchasing Agents

Most Valued

Reliability/credibility	98.6%
Professionalism/integrity	93.7
Product knowledge	90.7
Innovativeness in problem solving	80.5
Presentation/preparation	69.7

And in the purchasing agents' own words:

Qualities Liked

"Honesty."
"Loses a sale graciously."
"Admits mistakes."
"Problem-solving capabilities."
"Friendly but professional."
"Dependable."
"Adaptability."
"Knows my business."
"Well prepared."
"Patience."

Qualities Disliked

"No follow-up."
"Walking in without an appointment."
"Begins call by talking sports."
"Puts down competitor's products."
"Poor listening skills."
"Too many phone calls."
"Lousy presentation."
"Fails to ask about needs."
"Lacks product knowledge."
"Wastes my time."

Qualities Hated

"Wise-ass attitude."
"Calls me 'dear' or 'sweetheart' (I am female)."
"Gets personal."
"Doesn't give purchasing people credit for any brains."
"Whiners."
"Bullshooters."
"Wines and dines me."
"Plays one company against another."
"Pushy."
"Smokes in my office."

Source: Reprinted by permission of *Sales and Marketing Management*, Copyright: November 11, 1985, "PAs Examine the People Who Sell to Them."

one single technique that can be applied universally. Most sales training programs attempt to provide the trainee with the fundamentals of selling, placing emphasis on the "how" and "what" and leaving the "why" questions to the theorists.

A primary objective of any sales training program is to impart knowledge and techniques to the participants. An analysis of numerous training manuals reveals subjects or topics common to many programs. Following are brief descriptions of some fundamentals well-trained salespeople should know.

1. They should have thorough knowledge of the company they represent, including its past history. This includes the philosophy of management as well as the firm's basic operating policies.
2. They should have thorough technical and commercial knowledge of their products or product lines. This is particularly true when selling industrial goods. When selling very technical products, many firms require their salespeople to have training as engineers.
3. They should have good working knowledge of competitor's products. This is a vital requirement because the successful salesperson will have to know the strengths and weaknesses of those products that are in competition for market share.
4. They should have in-depth knowledge of the market for their merchandise. The market here refers not only to a particular sales territory but also to the general market, including the economic factors that affect the demand for their goods.
5. They should have a thorough understanding of the importance of prospecting and the methods used to effectively locate and qualify prospects (the decision-making unit). General issues to be evaluated are the prospective buyer's needs, financial resources, and willingness to be approached.
6. They should have accurate knowledge of the buyer or the prospect to whom they are selling. Under the marketing concept, knowledge of the customer is a vital requirement. Areas of desirable knowledge salespeople should possess include customer applications of the product and customer requirements as they relate to product quality, durability, cost, design, and service. Knowledgeable salespeople should be able to quantify, as well as describe, product benefits to the buyer. Effective selling requires

HIGHLIGHT 9–3
A Comparison of Order Takers, Order Generators, and Sales Support Personnel

	Order Takers	Order Generators	Sales Support Personnel
Typical position	Retail sales clerk.	IBM mainframe computer salesperson.	Pharmaceutical detailer.
Purpose	Process routine orders or reorders.	Identify new sales opportunities.	Promote new products or services.
Types of sales transaction	Simple rebuy.	New product sales or a modified rebuy situation.	Stimulate interest in either a routine rebuy or a new product opportunity.
Product line	Well-known, simple products.	Complex or customized products.	Typically responsible for both simple and complex product lines.
Training	Minimum and limited to order processing.	Technical skills in addition to extensive skills training.	Technical skills and interpersonal communication skills.
Compensation	Primarily salary.	Either straight commission or combination of salary and a commission.	Primarily salary.
Source of sales	Existing customers.	New customers.	Both existing customers and targeted new customers.

Source: J. Barry Mason and Hazel F. Ezell, *Marketing: Principles and Strategy* (Homewood, Ill.: Richard D. Irwin Business Publications, Inc., 1987), p. 635.

salespeople to understand the unique characteristics of each account.

There are no magic secrets of successful selling. The difference between good salespeople and mediocre ones is often the result of training plus experience. Training is no substitute for experience; the two complement each other. The difficulty with trying to discuss the selling job in terms of basic principles is that experienced, successful salespeople will always be able to find exceptions to these principles. Often successful selling seems to defy logic and, sometimes, common sense. Trying to program salespeople to follow definite rules or principles in every situation can stifle their originality and creativity.[7]

MANAGING THE SALES PROCESS

Every personal sale can be divided into two parts: the part done by the salespeople and the part done for the salespeople by the company. For example, from the standpoint of the product, the company should provide the salesperson with a product skillfully designed, thoroughly tested, attractively packaged, adequately advertised, and priced to compare favorably with competitive products. Salespeople have the responsibility of being thoroughly acquainted with the product, its selling features, points of superiority, and a sincere belief in the value of the product. From a sales management standpoint, the company's part of the sale involves the following:

1. Efficient and effective sales tools, including continuous sales training, promotional literature, samples, trade shows, product information, and adequate advertising.

2. An efficient delivery and reorder system to ensure that customers will receive the merchandise as promised.

3. An equitable compensation plan that rewards performance, motivates the salesperson, and promotes company loyalty. It should

---

[7]For a review of research findings regarding factors that are predictive of salespeople's performance, see Gilbert A. Churchill, Jr., Neil M. Ford, Steven W. Hartley, and Orville C. Walker, Jr., "The Determinants of Salesperson Performance: A Meta-Analysis," *Journal of Marketing Research*, May 1985, pp. 87–93.

also reimburse the salesperson for all reasonable expenses incurred while doing the job.

4. Adequate supervision and evaluation of performance as a means of helping salespeople do a better job, not only for the company but for themselves as well.

The Sales Management Task

Since the advent of the marketing concept, a clear-cut distinction has been made between marketing management and sales management. Marketing management refers to all activities in the firm that have to do with satisfying demand. Sales management is a narrower concept dealing with those functions directly related to personal selling. Generally speaking, sales managers are in middle management and report directly to the vice president of marketing. Their basic responsibilities can be broken down into at least seven major areas: (1) developing an effective sales organization for the company; (2) formulating short-range and long-range sales programs; (3) recruiting, training, and supervising the sales force; (4) formulating sales budgets and controlling selling expenses, (5) coordinating the personal selling effort with other forms of promotional activities; (6) maintaining lines of communication between the sales force, customers, and other relevant parts of the business, such as advertising, production, and logistics; and in some firms, (7) developing sales forecasts and other types of relevant marketing studies to be used in sales planning and control.

Sales managers are line officers whose primary responsibility is establishing and maintaining an active sales organization. In terms of authority, they usually have equivalent rank to that of other marketing executives who manage aspects of the marketing program, such as advertising, product planning, or physical distribution. The sales organization may have separate departments and department heads to perform specialized tasks, such as training, personnel, promotion, and forecasting. Figure 9–2 is an example of such a sales organization.

In other cases, a general marketing manager may have product managers, or directors, reporting to them. This is common in cases where the firm sells numerous products and each product or product line is handled by a separate manager. Another common arrangement is to have sales managers assigned to specific geographic regions or customer groups. This type of specialization enables the sales force to operate more

FIGURE 9–2
An Example of a Sales Organization

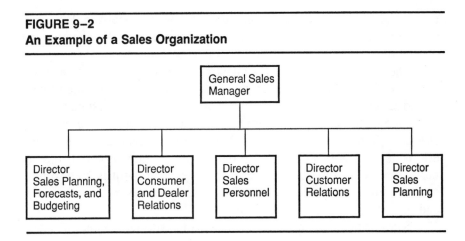

efficiently by avoiding overlaps. Regardless of the method used, the sales force should be structured to meet the unique needs of the consumer, the company, and its management.

Controlling the Sales Force

There are two obvious reasons why it is critical that the sales force be properly controlled. First, personal selling can be the largest marketing expense component in the final price of the product. Second, unless the sales force is somehow directed, motivated, and audited on a continual basis, it is likely to be less efficient than it is capable of being. Controlling the sales force involves four key functions: (1) forecasting sales; (2) establishing sales territories and quotas; (3) analyzing expenses; and (4) motivating and compensating performance.

Forecasting Sales. Sales planning begins with a forecast of sales for some future period or periods. From a practical standpoint, these forecasts are made on a short-term basis of a year or less, although long-range forecasts of one to five years are made for purposes other than managing the sales force, such as financing, production, and development. Generally speaking, forecasting is the marketing manager's responsibility. In large firms, because of the complexity of the task, it is usually delegated to a specialized unit, such as the marketing research department. Forecast data should be integrated into the firm's marketing decision support system for use by sales managers and other corporate executives. For many companies the sales forecast is the key instrument in the planning and control of operations.[8]

The sales forecast is an estimate of how much of the company's output, either in dollars or in units, can be sold during a specified future period under a proposed marketing plan and under an assumed set of economic conditions. A sales forecast has several important uses: (1) it is used to establish sales quotas; (2) it is used to plan personal selling efforts as well as other types of promotional activities in the marketing mix; (3) it is used to budget selling expenses; and (4) it is used to plan and coordinate production, physical distribution, inventories, personnel, and so forth.

Sales forecasting has become very sophisticated in recent years, especially with the increased availability of computer hardware and software. It should be mentioned, however, that a forecast is never a substitute for sound business judgment. At the present time there is no single method of sales forecasting known that gives uniformly accurate results with infallible precision. Outlined below are some commonly used sales forecasting methods.[9]

1. *Jury of executive opinion method.* This combines and averages the views of top management representing marketing, production, finance, purchasing, and administration.

2. *Sales force composite method.* This is similar to the first method in that it obtains the combined views of the sales force about the future outlook for sales. In some companies all salespeople, or district managers, submit estimates of the future sales in their territory or district.

3. *Customer expectations method.* This approach involves asking customers or product users about the quantity they expect to purchase.

---

[8]For additional discussion on the use of technological systems in sales management, see "Selling Meets the Technological Age," *Sales and Marketing Management* (special section on the "Computer in Marketing"), December 6, 1982, pp. 45–54; and Brad Hamman, "Rebirth of a Salesman: Willy Loman Goes Electronic," *Business Week,* February 27, 1984, p. 103.

[9]Based on a survey by the National Industrial Conference Board: "Forecasting Sales," *Studies in Business Policy,* No. 106.

4. *Time series analyses.* This approach involves analyzing past sales data and the impact of factors that influence sales (long-term growth trends, cyclical fluctuations, seasonal variations).

5. *Correlation analysis.* This involves measuring the relationship between the dependent variable, sales, and one or more independent variables that can explain increases or decreases in sales volumes.

6. *Other quantitative techniques.* Numerous statistical and mathematical techniques can be used to predict or estimate future sales. Two of the more important techniques are *(a)* growth functions, which are mathematical expressions specifying the relationship between demand and time; and *(b)* simulation models, where a statistical model of the industry is developed and programmed to develop values for the key parameters of the model.

Establishing Sales Territories and Quotas.   The establishment of sales territories and sales quotas represents management's need to match personal selling effort with sales potential (or opportunity). Sales territories are usually specified geographic areas assigned to individual salespeople. These areas represent an attempt to make the selling task more efficient.[10] The underlying rationale is that the control of sales operations will be facilitated by breaking down the total market into smaller and more manageable units. Implied here is the notion that there are some distinct economic advantages to dividing the total market into smaller segments. These segments should represent clusters of customers, or prospects, within some degree of physical proximity. Of course, there are criteria other than geography for establishing territories. One important criterion is that of product specialization. In this case, salespeople are specialists relative to particular product or customer situations.

From a marketing management point of view, there are many advantages to establishing sales territories. First, it facilitates the process of sales planning by making it easier to coordinate personal selling, transportation, storage, and other forms of promotion. Second, it promotes better customer relations because salespeople will be more familiar

---

[10]For a complete discussion of establishing territories and quotas, see William J. Stanton and Richard H. Buskirk, *Management of the Sales Force,* 7th ed. (Homewood, Ill.: Richard D. Irwin, 1987).

with the accounts they service. Third, it is an effective way of making sure that each market is well covered. Fourth, it aids management in the evaluation and control of selling costs. And fifth, it helps in the evaluation of performance.[11]

The question of managing sales territories cannot be discussed meaningfully without saying something about quotas. *Sales quotas* represent specific sales goals assigned to each territory or sales unit over a designated time period. Quotas are primarily a planning and control device, because they provide management with measurable, quantitative standards of performance. The most common method of establishing quotas for territories is to relate sales to forecasted sales potential. For example, if the Ajax Drug Company's territory M has an estimated industry sales potential for a particular product of $400,000 for the year, the quota might be set at 25 percent of that potential, or $100,000. The 25 percent figure represents the market share Ajax estimates to be a reasonable target. This $100,000 quota may represent an increase of $20,000 in sales over last year (assuming constant prices) that is expected from new business.

In establishing sales quotas for its individual territories or sales personnel, management needs to take into account three key factors. First, all territories will not have equal potential and, therefore, compensation must be adjusted accordingly. Second, all salespeople will not have equal ability, and assignments may have to be made accordingly. Third, the sales task in each territory may differ from time period to time period. For instance, the nature of some territories may require that salespeople spend more time seeking new accounts, rather than servicing established accounts, especially in the case of so-called new territories. The point to be made here is that quotas can vary, not only by territory but also by assigned tasks. The effective sales manager should assign quotas not only for dollar sales but also for each major selling function. Figure 9–3 is an example of how this is done for the Ajax Drug Company, where each activity is assigned a quota and a weight reflecting its relative importance.

Analyzing Expenses. Sales forecasts should include a sales expense budget. In some companies sales expense budgets are developed

---

[11]For additional discussion, consult Andris Zoltners and P. Sinha, "Sales Territory Alignment: A Review and Model," *Management Science,* November 1983, pp. 1237–56.

FIGURE 9–3
Ajax Drug Company Sales Activity Evaluation

Territory: M
Salesperson: Smith

Functions	(1) Quota	(2) Actual	(3) Percent (2 ÷ 1)	(4) Weight	(5) Score (3 × 4)
Sales volume:					
A. Old business	$380,000	$300,000	79	0.7	55.7
B. New business	$ 20,000	$ 20,000	100	0.5	50.0
Calls on prospects:					
A. Doctors	20	15	75	0.2	15.0
B. Druggists	80	60	75	0.2	15.0
C. Wholesalers	15	15	100	0.2	20.0
D. Hospitals	10	10	100	0.2	20.0
				2.0	175.7

Performance Index = 175.7

---

from the bottom up. Each territorial or district manager submits estimates of expenses and forecasted sales quotas. These estimates are usually prepared for a period of a year and then broken down into quarters and months. The chief sales executive then reviews the budget requests from the field offices and from staff departments. Expenses may be classified as fixed, semivariable or variable, and direct or indirect. Certain items, such as rent or administrative salaries, are fixed. In field offices, employee compensation is the principal expense, and it may be fixed or semivariable, depending on the plan. Other items, such as travel, samples, or other promotional material, are variable in nature. Some expenses are directly traceable to the sale of specific products, such as samples or displays, while other expenses are indirect, as in the case of administrative salaries and rent. Sales commissions and shipping expenses tend to vary in direct proportion to sales, while travel expense and entertainment may not be tied to sales volume in any direct proportion.

It should be understood that selling costs are budgeted much in the same way as manufacturing costs. Selling costs are usually broken down by product lines, sales region, customers, salespersons, or some other unit. Proper budgeting requires a reasonable cost accounting system. From

---

HIGHLIGHT 9–4
Effort- and Results-Oriented Measures for Evaluating Salespersons

Effort-Oriented Measures

1. Number of sales calls made.
2. Number of complaints handled.
3. Number of checks on reseller stocks.
4. Uncontrollable lost job time.
5. Number of inquiries followed up.
6. Number of demonstrations completed.

Results-Oriented Measures

1. Sales volume (total or by product or model).
2. Sales volume as a percentage of quota.
3. Sales profitability (dollar gross margin or contribution).
4. Number of new accounts.
5. Number of stockouts.
6. Number of distributors participating in programs.
7. Number of lost accounts.
8. Percentage volume increase in key accounts.
9. Number of customer complaints.
10. Distributor sales-inventory ratios.

Source: Joseph P. Guiltinan and Gordon Paul, *Marketing Management,* 2nd ed., p. 341. © 1988 by McGraw-Hill, Inc. Reprinted by permission of the publisher.

a budgeting standpoint, the firm should use its accounting system to analyze marketing costs as a means of control.

Motivating and Compensating Performance.   The sales manager's personnel function includes more than motivating and compensating the sales force; but from the vantage point of sales force productivity, these two tasks are of paramount importance. Operationally, it means that the sales manager has the responsibility of keeping the morale and efforts of the sales force at high levels through supervision and motivation.

These closely related tasks are accomplished through interaction with the sales force (1) by contacts with supervisors, managers, or sales executives individually or in group meetings; (2) through communication by letters or telephone; and (3) through incentive schemes by which

HIGHLIGHT 9–5
Characteristics Related to Sales Performance in Different
Types of Sales Jobs

Type of Sales Job	Characteristics That Are Relatively Important	Characteristics That Are Relatively Less Important
Trade selling	Age, maturity, empathy, knowledge of customer needs and business methods.	Aggressiveness, technical ability, product knowledge, persuasiveness.
Missionary selling	Youth, high energy and stamina, verbal skill, persuasiveness.	Empathy, knowledge of customers, maturity, previous sales experience.
Technical selling	Education, product and customer knowledge—usually gained through training, intelligence.	Empathy, persuasiveness, aggressiveness, age.
New business selling	Experience, age and maturity, aggressiveness, persuasiveness, persistence.	Customer knowledge, product knowledge, education, empathy.

Source: Gilbert A. Churchill, Jr.; Neil M. Ford; and Orville C. Walker, *Sales Force Management: Planning Implementation and Control,* 3rd ed. (Homewood, Ill.: Richard D. Irwin, 1990), p. 404.

greater opportunity for earnings (as in sales contests) or job promotion may be achieved.

Compensation is a principal method by which firms motivate and retain their sales forces. Devising a compensation plan for a company is a technical matter, but there are some general guidelines in formulating such a plan. First, a firm should be mindful of any modifications necessary to meet its particular needs when adopting another company's compensation plan. Second, the plan should make sense (i.e., should have a logical rationale) to both management and the sales force. Third, the plan should not be so overly complex that it cannot be understood by the average salesperson. Fourth, as suggested in the section on quotas, the plan should be fair and equitable to avoid penalizing the sales force because of factors beyond their control; conversely, the plan should ensure rewards for performance in proportion to results. Fifth, the plan should allow the sales force to earn salaries that permit them to maintain an acceptable standard of living. Finally, the plan should attempt to minimize attrition by giving the sales force some incentive, such as a vested retirement plan, for staying with the company.

There are two basic types of compensation: salary and commission. Salary usually refers to a specific amount of monetary compensation at an agreed rate for definite time periods. Commission is usually monetary compensation provided for each unit of sales and expressed as a percentage of sales. The base on which commissions are computed may be: volume of sales in units of product, gross sales in dollars, net sales after returns, sales volume in excess of a quota, and net profits. Very often, several compensation approaches are combined. For example, a salesperson might be paid a base salary, a commission on sales exceeding a volume figure, and a percentage share of the company's profits for that year.

Some other important elements of sales compensation plans are:

1. *Drawing account.* Periodic money advances at an agreed rate. Repayment is deducted from total earnings computed on a commission or other basis, or is repaid from other assets of the salesperson if earnings are insufficient to cover the advance (except in the case of a guaranteed drawing account).

2. *Special payments for sales operations.* Payments in the nature of piece rates on operations, rather than commissions on results. Flat payments per call or payments per new customer secured can be included in this category. To the extent that these payments are estimated by size of customers' purchases, they resemble commissions and are sometimes so labeled. Other bases for special payments are demonstrations, putting up counter or window displays, and special promotional work.

3. *Bonus payments.* Usually these are lump-sum payments, over and above contractual earnings, for extra effort or merit or for results beyond normal expectation.

4. *Special prizes.* Monetary amounts or valuable merchandise to reward the winners of sales contests and other competitions. Practices vary from firms that never use this device to firms where there is continuous use and almost every member of the sales force expects to get some compensation from this source during

HIGHLIGHT 9–6
The Most Widely Used Sales-Force Compensation Methods

Method	How Often Used	Most Useful	Advantages	Disadvantages
Straight salary	30.3%	When compensating new salespersons; when firm moves into new sales territories that require developmental work; when salespersons need to perform many nonselling activities.	Provides salesperson with maximum amount of security; gives sales manager large amount of control over salespersons; easy to administer; yields more predictable selling expenses.	Provides no incentive; necessitates closer supervision of salespersons' activities; during sales declines, selling expenses remain at same level.
Straight commission	20.8	When highly aggressive selling is required; when nonselling tasks are minimized; when company cannot closely control sales-force activities.	Provides maximum amount of incentive; by increasing commission rate, sales managers can encourage salespersons to sell certain items; selling expenses relate directly to sales resources.	Salespersons have little financial security; sales manager has minimum control over sales force; may cause salespeople to provide inadequate service to smaller accounts; selling costs less predictable.
Combination	48.9	When sales territories have relatively similar sales potentials; when firm wishes to provide incentive but still control sales-force activities.	Provides certain level of financial security; provides some incentive; selling expenses fluctuate with sales revenue.	Selling expenses less predictable; may be difficult to administer.

Source: Adapted from John P. Steinbrink, "How to Pay Your Sales Force," *Harvard Business Review*, July–August 1978, p. 113.

the year, in which case prizes amount to a form of incentive payment.

5. *Profit sharing*. A share of the profits of the business as a whole, figured on the basis of earnings, retail sales, profits in an area, or other factors. Sometimes profit sharing is intended to build up a retirement fund.

6. *Expense allowances*. Provision for travel and other business expenses, which becomes an important part of any compensation plan. No agreement for outside sales work is complete without an understanding about whether the company or the salesperson is to pay travel and other business expenses incurred in connection with work; and, if the company is responsible, just what the arrangements should be. Automobile, hotel, entertainment, and many other items of expense may be included in the agreement.

7. *Maximum earnings or cutoff point*. A limitation on earnings. This figure may be employed for limiting maximum earnings when it is impossible to predict the range of earnings under commission or other types of incentive plans.

8. *Fringe benefits*. Pensions, group insurance, health insurance, and so forth. These are commonly given to sales forces as a matter of policy and become a definite part of the compensation plan.[12]

LESSONS FOR THE MANUFACTURER

Personal selling is an important part of the promotion mix for many products, particularly technically complex ones. However, one mistake some firms make is to underestimate the skills needed to be an effective salesperson and serve customers well. For example, the CEO of IBM was disappointed in the small increase in sales generated by adding 5,000 additional sales and marketing personnel to the IBM staff. The problem, though, was that the additional salespeople were "redeployed" from other IBM units and expected to perform as experienced salespeople. In accord with IBM's production orientation, many of them thought that their job

---

[12]For an excellent review of recruiting, selecting, and motivating sales personnel, see James M. Comer and Alan J. Dubinsky, *Managing the Successful Sales Force* (Lexington, Mass.: D. C. Heath, 1985).

was simply to tell customers what the company was going to do rather than ask customers what they needed and what the company could do for them. In other words, IBM didn't necessarily need *more* salespeople, it needed *better* salespeople who were customer oriented.

The sale of some products may require a team of salespeople to call on customers. This team may include marketing personnel to handle the major selling tasks but also engineering personnel to answer questions about specific product features and benefits that require highly technical expertise. Sales force personnel can also provide valuable information about customer characteristics, customer-desired product modifications, and expected sales information, which can be used to design sales forecasts and production schedules. In addition, engineering and manufacturing personnel should meet customers and see firsthand how their products are being used. This can provide valuable insights for improving existing products or developing new products that better satisfy customers.

ADDITIONAL READINGS

Bellizzi, Joseph A., and Robert E. Hite. "Supervising Unethical Salesforce Behavior." *Journal of Marketing,* April 1989, pp. 36–47.

Brooks, William T. *High Impact Selling: Strategies for Successful Selling.* Englewood Cliffs, N.J.: Prentice Hall, 1988.

Cron, William L. "Industrial Salesperson Development: A Career Stages Perspective." *Journal of Marketing,* Fall 1984, pp. 41–52.

Dubinsky, Alan J., and Thomas N. Ingram. "Salespeople View Buyer Behavior." *Journal of Personnel Selling and Sales Management,* Fall 1982, pp. 6–11.

Honeycutt, Earl D., and Thomas H. Stevenson. "Evaluating Sales Training Programs." *Industrial Marketing Management* 18 (1989), pp. 215–22.

Ingram, Thomas N., and Danny N. Bellenger. "Personal and Organizational Variables: Their Relative Effect on Reward Valences of Industrial Salespeople." *Journal of Marketing Research,* May 1983, pp. 198–205.

Skinner, Steven J.; Alan J. Dubinsky; and James H. Donnelly, Jr. "The Use of Social Bases of Power in Retail Sales." *Journal of Personnel Selling and Sales Management,* November 1984, pp. 48–56.

CHAPTER 10

DISTRIBUTION STRATEGY

Channel of distribution decisions involve numerous interrelated variables that must be integrated into the total marketing mix. Because of the time and money required to set up an efficient channel, and since channels are often hard to change once they are set up, these decisions are critical to the success of the firm.

This chapter is concerned with the development and management of channels of distribution and the process of goods distribution in an extremely complex, highly productive, and specialized economy. It should be noted at the outset that channels of distribution provide the ultimate consumer or industrial user with time, place, and possession utility. Thus, an efficient channel is one that delivers the product when and where it is wanted at a minimum total cost.

THE NEED FOR MARKETING INTERMEDIARIES

A channel of distribution is the combination of institutions through which a seller markets products to the user or ultimate consumer. The need for other institutions or intermediaries in the delivery of goods is sometimes questioned, particularly since the profits they make are viewed as adding to the cost of the product. However, this reasoning is generally falacious, since producers use marketing intermediaries because the intermediary can perform functions *more cheaply and more efficiently* than the producer can. This notion of efficiency is critical when the characteristics of our economy are considered.

For example, our economy is characterized by heterogeneity in terms of both supply and demand. In terms of numbers alone, there are nearly 6 million establishments comprising the supply segment of our economy, and there are close to 90 million households making up the demand side. Clearly, if each of these units had to deal on a one-to-one basis to obtain

---

HIGHLIGHT 10–1
What Intermediaries Add to the Cost of a Compact Disc

Production of disc	.74
Packaging (tuck box, etc.)	1.72
American Federation of Musicians dues	.27
Songwriters royalties	.39
Recording artist's royalties	1.01
Freight to wholesaler	.36
Manufacturer's advertising and selling expenses	1.74
Manufacturer's administrative expenses	1.76
Manufacturer's cost	$7.99
Manufacturer's profit margin	1.10
Manufacturer's price to wholesaler	$9.09
Freight to retailer	.38
Wholesaler's advertising, selling, and administrative expense	.47
Wholesaler's cost	$9.94
Wholesaler's profit margin	.80
Wholesaler's price to retailer	$10.74 $6.90
Retailer's advertising, selling, and administrative expenses	1.76
Retailer's profit margin	3.49
Retailer's price to consumer	$15.99

Source: From *Principles of Marketing,* 3rd ed., by Thomas C. Kinnear and Kenneth L. Bernhardt Copyright © 1990, 1986 by Scott, Foresman and Company. Reprinted by permission of HarperCollins Publishers.

needed goods and services, and there were no intermediaries to collect and disperse assortments of goods, the system would be totally inefficient. Thus, the primary role of intermediaries is to bring supply and demand together in an efficient and orderly fashion.

CLASSIFICATION OF MARKETING INTERMEDIARIES AND FUNCTIONS

There are a great many types of marketing intermediaries, many of which are so specialized by function and industry that they need not be discussed

---

FIGURE 10–1
Major Types of Marketing Intermediaries

Middleman—an independent business concern that operates as a link between producers and ultimate consumers or industrial buyers.

Merchant middleman—an intermediary who buys the goods outright and necessarily takes title to them.

Agent—a business unit that negotiates purchases, sales, or both but does not take title to the goods in which it deals.

Wholesaler—merchant establishment operated by a concern that is primarily engaged in buying, taking title to, usually storing and physically handling goods in large quantities, and reselling the goods (usually in smaller quantities) to retailers or to industrial or business users.

Retailer—merchant middleman who is engaged primarily in selling to ultimate consumers.

Broker—an intermediary who serves as a go-between for the buyer or seller; assumes no title risks, does not usually have physical custody of products, and is not looked upon as a permanent representative of either the buyer or the seller.

Sales agent—an independent channel member, either an individual or company, who is responsible for the sale of a firm's products or services but does not take title to the goods sold.

Distributor—a wholesale intermediary, especially in lines where selective or exclusive distribution is common at the wholesale level in which the manufacturer expects strong promotional support; often a synonym for wholesaler.

Jobber—an intermediary who buys from manufacturers and sells to retailers; a wholesaler.

Facilitating agent—a business firm that assists in the performance of distribution tasks other than buying, selling, and transferring title (i.e., transportation companies, warehouses, etc.)

Source: Based on Peter D. Bennett, ed., *Dictionary of Marketing Terms* (Chicago: American Marketing Association, 1988).

here. Figure 10–1 presents the major types of marketing intermediaries common to many industries. Although there is some overlap in this classification, these categories are based on the marketing functions performed. That is, various intermediaries perform different marketing functions and to different degrees. Figure 10–2 is a listing of the more common marketing functions performed in the channel.

It should be remembered that whether or not a manufacturer utilizes intermediaries to perform these functions, the functions have to be

---

FIGURE 10–2
Marketing Functions Performed in Channels of Distribution

Buying—purchasing products from sellers for use or for resale.

Selling—promoting the sale of products to ultimate consumers or industrial buyers.

Sorting—a function performed by intermediaries in order to bridge the discrepancy between the assortment of goods and services generated by the producer and the assortment demanded by the consumer. This function includes four distinct processes: sorting out, accumulation, allocation, and assorting.

Sorting out—a sorting process that breaks down a heterogeneous supply into separate stocks that are relatively homogeneous.

Accumulation—a sorting process that brings similar stocks from a number of sources together into a larger homogeneous supply.

Allocation—a sorting process that consists of breaking a homogeneous supply down into smaller and smaller lots.

Assorting—a sorting process that consists of building an assortment of products for use in association with each other.

Concentration—the process of bringing goods from various places together in one place.

Financing—providing credit or funds to facilitate a transaction.

Storage—maintaining inventories and protecting products to provide better customer service.

Grading—classifying products into different categories on the basis of quality.

Transportation—physically moving products from where they are made to where they are purchased and used.

Risk-taking—taking on business risks involved in transporting and owning products.

Marketing research—collecting information concerning such things as market conditions, expected sales, consumer trends, and competitive forces.

Source: Based on Peter D. Bennett, ed., *Dictionary of Marketing Terms* (Chicago: American Marketing Association, 1988).

---

performed by someone. In other words, the managerial question is not whether to perform the functions but who will perform them and to what degree.

CHANNELS OF DISTRIBUTION

As previously noted, a channel of distribution is the combination of institutions through which a seller markets products to the user or ultimate

---

FIGURE 10–3
Typical Channels of Distribution for Consumer Goods

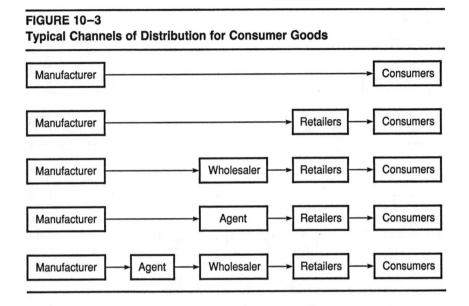

---

consumer. Some of these links assume the risks of ownership; others do not. Some perform marketing functions while others perform nonmarketing or facilitating functions, such as transportation. The typical channel of distribution patterns for consumer goods markets are shown in Figure 10–3.

Some manufacturers use a direct channel, selling directly to the ultimate consumer (e.g., Avon Cosmetics). In other cases, one or more intermediaries may be used. For example, a manufacturer of paper cartons may sell to retailers, or a manufacturer of small appliances may sell to retailers under a private brand. The most common channel in the consumer market is the one in which the manufacturer sells through wholesalers to retailers. For instance, a cold remedy manufacturer may sell to drug wholesalers who, in turn, sell a vast array of drug products to various retail outlets. Small manufacturers may also use agents, since they do not have sufficient capital for their own sales forces. Agents are commonly used intermediaries in the jewelry industry. The final channel in Figure 10–3 is used primarily when small wholesalers and retailers are involved. Channels with one or more intermediaries are referred to as indirect channels.

In contrast to consumer products, the direct channel is often used in the distribution of industrial goods. The reason for this stems from the

FIGURE 10–4
Typical Channels of Distribution for Industrial Goods

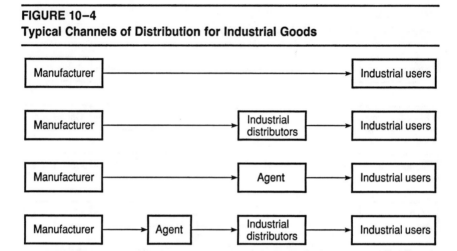

structure of most industrial markets, which often have relatively few but extremely large customers. Also, many industrial products, such as computers, need a great deal of presale and postsale service. Distributors are used in industrial markets when the number of buyers is large and the size of the buying firm is small. As in the consumer market, agents are used in industrial markets in cases where manufacturers do not wish to have their own sales forces. Such an arrangement may be used by small manufacturers or when the market is geographically dispersed. The final channel arrangement in Figure 10–4 may also be used by a small manufacturer or when the market consists of many small customers. Under such conditions, it may not be economical for sellers to have their own sales organization.

SELECTING CHANNELS OF DISTRIBUTION

General Considerations

Given the numerous types of channel intermediaries and functions that must be performed, the task of selecting and designing a channel of distribution may at first appear to be overwhelming. However, in many industries, channels of distribution have developed over many years and

---

HIGHLIGHT 10–2
"Are Channels of Distribution What the Textbooks Say?"

The middleman is not a hired link in a chain forged by the manufacturer, but rather an independent market, the focus of a large group of customers for whom he buys. Subsequent to some market analysis of his own, he selects products and suppliers, thereby setting at least one link in the channel.

After some experimentation, he settles upon a method of operation, performing those functions he deems inescapable in the light of his own objectives, forming policies for himself wherever he has freedom to do so. Perhaps these methods and policies conform closely to those of a Census category of middleman, but perhaps they do not.

It is true that his choices are in many instances tentative proposals. He is subject to much influence from competitors, from aggressive suppliers, from inadequate finances and faulty information, as well as from habit. Nonetheless, many of his choices are independent.

As he grows and builds a following, he may find that his prestige in his market is greater than that of the suppliers whose goods he sells. In some instances his local strength is so great that a manufacturer is virtually unable to tap that market, except through him. In such a case the manufacturer can have no channel policy with respect to that market.

Source: Phillip McVey, "Are Channels of Distribution What the Textbooks Say?" *Journal of Marketing,* January 1960, pp. 61–65. This article can be considered a classic in the field of marketing. Reprinted by permission of the American Marketing Association.

have become somewhat traditional. In such cases, the producer may be limited to this type of channel to operate in the industry. This is not to say that a traditional channel is always the most efficient and that there are no opportunities for innovation, but the fact that such a channel is widely accepted in the industry suggests it is highly efficient. A primary constraint in these cases and in cases where no traditional channel exists is that of *availability* of the various types of middlemen. All too often in the early stages of channel design, executives map out elaborate channel networks only to find out later that no such independent intermediaries exist for the firm's product in selected geographic areas. Even if they do exist, they may not be willing to accept the seller's products. In general, there are six basic considerations in the initial development of channel strategy. These are outlined in Figure 10–5.

FIGURE 10–5
Considerations in Channel Planning

---

1. *Customer characteristics.*
   a. Number.
   b. Geographical dispersion.
   c. Purchasing patterns.
   d. Susceptibilities to different selling methods.
2. *Product characteristics.*
   a. Perishability.
   b. Bulkiness.
   c. Degree of standardization.
   d. Installation and maintenance services required.
   e. Unit value.
3. *Intermediary characteristics.*
   a. Availability.
   b. Willingness to accept product or product line.
   c. Strengths.
   d. Weaknesses.
4. *Competitive characteristics.*
   a. Geographic proximity.
   b. Proximity in outlet.
5. *Company characteristics.*
   a. Financial strength.
   b. Product mix.
   c. Past channel experience.
   d. Present company marketing policies.
6. *Environmental characteristics.*
   a. Economic conditions.
   b. Legal regulations and restrictions.

It should be noted that for a particular product any one of these characteristics may greatly influence choice of channels. To illustrate, highly perishable products generally require direct channels, or a firm with little financial strength may require middlemen to perform almost all of the marketing functions.

Specific Considerations

The above characteristics play an important part in framing the channel selection decision. Based on them, the choice of channels can be further refined in terms of (1) distribution coverage required; (2) degree of control desired; (3) total distribution cost; and (4) channel flexibility.

Distribution Coverage Required.   Because of the characteristics of the product, the environment needed to sell the product, and the needs and expectations of the potential buyer, products will vary in the intensity of distribution coverage they require. Distribution coverage can be viewed along a continuum ranging from intensive to selective to exclusive distribution.

Intensive distribution. Here the manufacturer attempts to gain exposure through as many wholesalers and retailers as possible. Most convenience goods require intensive distribution based on the characteristics of the product (low unit value) and the needs and expectations of the buyer (high frequency of purchase and convenience).

Selective distribution. Here the manufacturer limits the use of intermediaries to the ones believed to be the best available. This may be based on the service organization available, the sales organization, or the reputation of the intermediary. Thus, appliances, home furnishings, and better clothing are usually distributed selectively. For appliances, the intermediary's service organization could be a key factor, while for better clothing and home furnishings, the intermediary's reputation would be an important consideration.

Exclusive distribution. Here the manufacturer severely limits distribution, and intermediaries are provided exclusive rights within a particular territory. The characteristics of the product are a determining factor here. Where the product requires certain specialized selling effort and/or investment in unique facilities or large inventories, this arrangement is usually selected. Retail paint stores are an example of such a distribution arrangement.

Degree of Control Desired.   In selecting channels of distribution, the seller must make decisions concerning the degree of control desired over the marketing of the firm's products. Some manufacturers prefer to keep as much control over the policies surrounding their product as possible. Ordinarily, the degree of control achieved by the seller is proportionate to the directness of the channel. One Eastern brewery, for instance, owns its own fleet of trucks and operates a wholly owned delivery system direct to grocery and liquor stores. Its market is very concentrated geographically, with many small buyers, so such a system is economically

HIGHLIGHT 10-3
Intensive, Selective, and Exclusive Distribution: Market Coverage

Strategy	Exclusive	Selective	Intensive
Number of retail intermediaries	One →	Some →	As many as available →
Outlets	Use one outlet to sell or install product	Use a limited number of outlets in a given territory	Place product in every outlet in territory
Consumer goods	Gucci clothes, Oldsmobile cars, Rolex watches	Scott lawn fertilizer, Litton microwave ovens	Coke and Pepsi
Industrial goods	Trane air-conditioning unit	Rockwell flange systems for lathes	Office supplies (Scovill paper clips)

Source: Reprinted from *Principles of Marketing*, 3rd ed., by Thomas C. Kinnear and Kenneth L. Bernhardt. Copyright © 1990, 1986 by Scott, Foresman and Company. Reprinted by permission of HarperCollins Publishers.

feasible. However, all other brewers in the area sell through wholesalers or distributors.

When more indirect channels are used, the manufacturer must surrender some control over the marketing of the firm's product. However, attempts are commonly made to maintain a degree of control through some other indirect means, such as sharing promotional expenditures, providing sales training, or other operational aids, such as accounting systems, inventory systems, or marketing research data on the dealer's trading area.[1]

Total Distribution Cost.   The total distribution cost concept has developed out of the more general topic of systems theory. The concept suggests that a channel of distribution should be viewed as a total system composed of interdependent subsystems, and that the objective of the system (channel) manager should be to optimize total system performance. In terms of distribution costs, it generally is assumed that the total system should be designed to minimize costs, other things being equal. The following is a representative list of the major distribution costs to be minimized.

1. Transportation.
2. Order processing.
3. Cost of lost business (an "opportunity" cost due to inability to meet customer demand).
4. Inventory carrying costs, including:
   a. Storage-space charges.
   b. Cost of capital invested.
   c. Taxes.
   d. Insurance.
   e. Obsolescence and deterioration.
5. Packaging.
6. Materials handling.

---

[1]For further discussion, see John Gaski, "The Theory of Power and Conflict in Channels of Distribution," *Journal of Marketing,* Summer 1984, pp. 9–29; Gul Butaney and Lawrence H. Wortzel, "Distributor Power versus Manufacturer Power: The Customer Role," *Journal of Marketing,* January 1988, pp. 52–63.

HIGHLIGHT 10–4
Franchising: An Alternative to Traditional Channels of Distribution

A franchise is a means by which a producer of products or services achieves a direct channel of distribution without wholly owning or managing the physical facilities in the market. In effect, the franchiser provides the franchisee with the franchiser's knowledge, manufacturing, and marketing techniques for a financial return.

Ingredients of a Franchised Business

Six key ingredients should be included within a well-balanced franchise offered to a franchisee. These are given in order of importance:

- *Technical knowledge* in its practical form is supplied through an intensive course of study.
- *Managerial techniques* based on proven and time-tested programs are imparted to the franchisee on a continuing basis, even after the business has been started or taken over by the franchisee.
- *Commercial knowledge* involving prescribed methods of buying and selling is explained and codified. Most products to be obtained, processed, and sold to the franchisee are supplied by the franchiser.
- *Financial instruction* on managing funds and accounts is given to the franchisee during the indoctrination period.
- *Accounting controls* are set up by the franchiser for the franchisee.
- *Protective safeguards* are included in the intensive training of the franchisee for employees and customers, including the quality of the product, as well as the safeguards for assets through adequate insurance controls.

Elements of an Ideal Franchise Program

- **High gross margin.** In order for the franchisee to be able to afford a high franchise fee (which the franchiser needs), it is necessary to operate on a high gross margin percentage. This explains the widespread application of franchising in the food and service industries.
- **In-store value added.** Franchising works best in those product categories where the product is at least partially processed in the store. Such environments require constant on-site supervision—a chronic problem for company-owned stores using a hired manager. Owners simply are willing to work harder over longer hours.
- **Secret processes.** Concepts, formulas, or products that the franchisee can't duplicate without joining the franchise program.
- **Real estate profits.** The franchiser uses income from ownership of property as a significant revenue source.
- **Simplicity.** The most successful franchises have been those that operate on automatic pilot: All the key decisions have been thought through, and the owner merely implements the decisions.

Source: Partially adapted from Philip D. White and Albert D. Bates, "Franchising Will Remain Retailing Fixture, but Its Salad Days Have Long Since Gone," *Marketing News*, February 17, 1984, p. 14. Reprinted by permission of the American Marketing Association.

HIGHLIGHT 10–5
Manufacturers and Intermediaries: A Perfect Working Relationship

The Perfect Intermediary

1. Has access to the market that the manufacturer wants to reach.
2. Carries adequate stocks of the manufacturer's products and a satisfactory assortment of other products.
3. Has an effective promotional program—advertising, personal selling, and product displays. Promotional demands placed on the manufacturer are in line with what the manufacturer intends to do.
4. Provides services to customers—credit, delivery, installation, and product repair—and honors the product warranty conditions.
5. Pays its bills on time and has capable management.

The Perfect Manufacturer

1. Provides a desirable assortment of products—well designed, properly priced, attractively packaged, and delivered on time and in adequate quantities.
2. Builds product demand for these products by advertising them.
3. Furnishes promotional assistance to its middlemen.
4. Provides managerial assistance for its middlemen.
5. Honors product warranties and provides repair and installation service.

The Perfect Combination

1. Probably doesn't exist.

Source: William J. Stanton and Charles Futrell, *Fundamentals of Marketing,* 8th ed., p. 350, © 1987 by McGraw-Hill, Inc. Reprinted by permission of the publisher.

The important qualification to the total cost concept is the statement "other things being equal." The purpose of the total cost concept is to emphasize total system performance to avoid suboptimization. However, other important factors must be considered, not the least of which are level of customer service, sales, profits, and interface with the total marketing mix.

Channel Flexibility.   A final consideration relates to the ability of the manufacturer to adapt to changing conditions. To illustrate, in recent years much of the population has moved from inner cities to suburbs and thus make most of their purchases in shopping centers and malls. If a manufacturer had long-term, exclusive dealership with retailers in the inner city, the ability to adapt to this population shift could have been severely limited. In general, the less certain the future seems to be, the less favorable are channel alternatives involving long commitments.

MANAGING A CHANNEL OF DISTRIBUTION

Once the seller has decided on the type of channel structure to use and selected the individual members, the entire coalition should operate as a total system. From a behavioral perspective, the system can be viewed as a social system since each member interacts with the others, each member plays a role vis-à-vis the others, and each has certain expectations of the other.[2] Thus, the behavioral perspective views a channel of distribution as more than a series of markets or participants extending from production to consumption.

A Channel Leader

If a channel of distribution is viewed as a social system comprised of interacting firms with a common set of objectives, then integration among them seems desirable. This is because the channel, as a system, can be conceived as a competitive unit in and of itself; in other words, any success that the product has is determined largely by the effectiveness and efficiency with which human, material, and monetary resources have been mobilized throughout the entire interfirm network.

If the above view is taken, the question arises about who should exert primary leadership in the channel—that is, becomes the "channel captain" or "channel commander." There is little agreement about the answer. Some marketers believe the manufacturer or the owner of the

---

[2]F. Robert Dwyer and M. Ann Welsh, "Environmental Relationships of the Internal Political Economy of Marketing Channels," *Journal of Marketing Research*, November 1985, pp. 397–414; John F. Gaski and John R. Nevin, "The Differential Effects of Exercised and Unexercised Power Sources in a Marketing Channel," *Journal of Marketing Research*, May 1985, pp. 130–42; James C. Anderson and James A. Narus, "A Model of Distributor Firm and Manufacturing Firm Working Partnerships," *Journal of Marketing*, January 1990, pp. 42–58.

HIGHLIGHT 10–6
Pushing or Pulling through the Channel System

A producer has a special challenge with respect to channel systems: How to ensure that the product reaches the end of the channel. Intermediaries—especially retailers—don't have this problem, since they already control that end of the channel.

The two basic methods of recruiting middlemen are *pushing* and *pulling*.

Pushing a product through the channels means using normal promotion effort—personal selling and advertising—to help sell the whole marketing mix to possible channel members. This method is common—since these sales transactions are usually between rational, presumably profit-oriented buyers and sellers. The approach emphasizes the importance of building a channel—and securing the wholehearted cooperation of channel members. The producer—in effect—tries to develop a team that will work well together to get the product to the user.

By contrast, pulling means getting consumers to ask intermediaries for the product. This usually involves highly aggressive promotion to final consumers or users—perhaps using coupons or samples—and temporary bypassing of intermediaries. If the promotion works, the intermediaries are forced to carry the product—to satisfy their customers.

Source: Adapted with permission from E. Jerome McCarthy and William D. Perreault, Jr., *Basic Marketing: A Managerial Approach,* 10th ed. (Homewood, Ill.: Richard D. Irwin, 1990), p. 288.

brand name should be the channel captain. The argument here is that the manufacturer or brand name owner (1) has the most to lose if the system malfunctions or fails; (2) has the most technical expertise; and (3) in many cases has greater resources than other channel members. Others believe the retailer should be the channel captain, since the retailer is the closest link to the consumer and, therefore, can judge better the consumer needs and wants. Still others argue the wholesaler should seek to gain channel control, or that the locus of control should be at the level where competition is greatest.

In some channels of distribution, one member may be large and powerful with respect to other members. It may be a manufacturer, wholesaler, or large retailer. Consider the power Sears, Roebuck has over a small supply manufacturing firm, since 90 percent of Sears products are under its own label. In such cases, the powerful member may assume leadership.

While the issue is certainly not clear, the tendency appears to lean toward channels controlled by the manufacturer, with a few notable exceptions. For example, for their own brands, Sears, Roebuck and Kmart likely play the primary leadership role, while the manufacturer plays a subordinate role. In some cases where wholesalers have their own brands, the manufacturer and retailer probably assume a subordinate role. However, in many cases, manufacturers have absorbed functions previously performed by intermediaries and, thereby, obtained even greater channel control

LESSONS FOR THE MANUFACTURER

Marketing and manufacturing both have important inputs to make concerning the selection of effective channels of distribution. Marketing's major concern is ensuring that the product is available when and where and in the form customers want to purchase it. Achieving this objective, however, can have tremendous influence on the manufacturing process. For example, decisions concerning the location of manufacturing facilities should include the location of customer markets but also the costs in obtaining supplies and other resources, shipping costs of final products, and the differences in costs from one location to another for the land, labor, and other resources needed. In addition, completely avoiding stock-out conditions for consumers often involves greatly increased costs for holding inventory This, of course, is a major advantage of just-in-time production systems, which create more direct shipments, reduce the number of warehouses, and reduce pipeline inventories.

Producing products in different forms to meet the demands of various target markets also can increase manufacturing costs because smaller production runs have lower economies of scale than larger ones.

An important change in channels in recent years is the move toward greater power for retailers and less power for manufacturers. For example, many toy manufacturers will not even produce a toy unless Toys 'R' Us executives agree to sell it in their stores. The power of mass merchandisers, such as Wal-Mart, relative even to large manufacturers like Procter & Gamble, was previously noted in the text. Thus, vertical integration and vertical marketing systems involving manufacturers and retailers may be expected to increase in the future, either through stronger contractual relationships or simply greater mutual dependence. In some cases, particularly since conglomerates have large product lines to offer directly to large retail chains, this may lead to a decrease in the need for other middlemen.

ADDITIONAL READINGS

Achrol, Ravi S., and Louis W. Stern. "Environmental Determinants of Decison-Making Uncertainty in Marketing Channels." *Journal of Marketing Research*, February 1988, pp. 36–50.

Corey, Raymond E.; Frank V. Cespedes; and Kasturi Rangan. *Going to Market*. Boston, Mass.: Harvard Business School Press, 1989.

Dwyer, F. Robert, and Sejo Oh. "A Transaction Cost Perspective on Vertical Contractual Structure and Interchannel Competitive Strategies." *Journal of Marketing*, April 1988, pp. 21–34.

Frazier, Gary L.; James D. Gill; and Sudhir H. Kale. "Dealer Dependence Levels and Reciprocal Actions in a Channel of Distribution in a Developing Country." *Journal of Marketing*, January 1989, pp. 50–69.

Hardy, Kenneth G., and Allan J. McGrath. *Marketing Channel Management*. Glenview, Ill.: Scott, Foresman, 1988.

Justis, Robert, and Richard Judd. *Franchising*. Cincinnati, Ohio: South-Western Publishing, 1989.

Rosenbloom, Bert. *Marketing Channels: A Managerial View*. 3rd ed. Hinsdale, Ill.: Dryden Press, 1987.

Stern, Louis W.; Adel I. El-Ansary; and James R. Brown. *Management in Marketing Channels*. Englewood Cliffs, N.J.: Prentice Hall, 1989.

Stern, Louis W., and Adel I. El-Ansary. *Marketing Channels*. 3rd ed. Englewood Cliffs, N.J.: Prentice Hall, 1988.

CHAPTER 11

PRICING STRATEGY

One of the most important and complex decisions a firm has to make relates to pricing its products or services. If consumers or organizational buyers perceive a price to be too high, they may purchase competitive brands or substitute products, leading to a loss of sales and profits for the firm. If the price is too low, sales might increase, but profitability may suffer. Thus, pricing decisions must be given careful consideration when a firm is introducing a new product or planning a short- or long-term price change.

This chapter discusses demand, supply, and environmental influences that affect pricing decisions and emphasizes that all three must be considered for effective pricing. However, as will be discussed in the chapter, many firms price their products without explicitly considering all of these influences.

DEMAND INFLUENCES ON PRICING DECISIONS

Demand influences on pricing decisions concern primarily the nature of the target market and expected reactions of consumers to a given price or change in price. There are three primary considerations here: demographic factors, psychological factors, and price elasticity.

Demographic Factors. In the initial selection of the target market that a firm intends to serve, a number of demographic factors are usually considered. Demographic factors that are particularly important for pricing decisions include the following:

1. Number of potential buyers.
2. Location of potential buyers.
3. Position of potential buyers (resellers or final consumers).

HIGHLIGHT 11–1
The Meaning of Price

Alternative Terms	What Is Given in Return
Price	Most physical merchandise.
Tuition	College courses, education.
Rent	A place to live or the use of equipment for a specific time period.
Interest	Use of money.
Fee	Professional services: for lawyers, doctors, consultants.
Fare	Transportation: air, taxi, bus.
Toll	Use of road or bridge, or long-distance phone rate.
Salary	Work of managers.
Wage	Work of hourly workers.
Bribe	Illegal actions.
Commission	Sales effort.

Source: From *Principles of Marketing,* 3rd ed., by Thomas C. Kinnear and Kenneth L. Bernhardt. Copyright © 1990, 1986 by Scott, Foresman and Company. Reprinted by permission of HarperCollins Publishers.

4. Expected consumption rates of potential buyers.
5. Economic strength of potential buyers.

These factors help determine market potential and are useful for estimating expected sales at various price levels.

Psychological Factors. Psychological factors related to pricing concern primarily how consumers will perceive various prices or price changes. For example, marketing managers should be concerned with such questions as:

1. Will potential buyers use price as an indicator of product quality?
2. Will potential buyers be favorably attracted by odd pricing?
3. Will potential buyers perceive the price as too high relative to the service the product gives them?

4. Are potential buyers prestige oriented and therefore willing to pay higher prices to fulfill this need?
5. How much will potential buyers be willing to pay for the product?

While psychological factors have a significant effect on the success of a pricing strategy and ultimately on marketing strategy, answers to the above questions may require considerable marketing research. In fact, a review of buyers' subjective perceptions of price concluded that very little is known about how price affects buyers' perceptions of alternative purchase offers and how these perceptions affect purchase response.[1] However, some tentative generalizations about how buyers perceive price have been formulated. For example, research has found that persons who choose high-priced items usually perceive large quality variations within product categories and see the consequences of a poor choice as being undesirable. They believe that quality is related to price and see themselves as good judges of product quality. In general, the reverse is true for persons who select low-priced items in the same product categories. Thus, although information on psychological factors involved in purchasing may be difficult to obtain, marketing managers must at least consider the effects of such factors on their desired target market and marketing strategy.[2]

Price Elasticity.   Both demographic and psychological factors affect price elasticity. Price elasticity is a measure of consumers' price sensitivity, which is estimated by dividing relative changes in the quantity sold by the relative changes in price:

$$e = \frac{\Delta Q/Q}{\Delta P/P}$$

Although difficult to measure, there are two basic methods commonly

---

[1]Kent B. Monroe, "Buyers' Subjective Perceptions of Price," *Journal of Marketing Research,* February 1973, pp. 70–80; also see Donald R. Lichtenstein and Scot Burton, "The Relationship between Perceived and Objective Price-Quality," *Journal of Marketing Research,* November 1989, pp. 429–43.

[2]For a summary of research concerning the effects of price and several other marketing variables on perceived product quality, see Akshay R. Rao and Kent B. Monroe, "The Effect of Price, Brand Name, and Store Name on Buyers' Perceptions of Product Quality: An Integrative Review," *Journal of Marketing Research,* August 1989, pp. 351–57.

HIGHLIGHT 11-2
Some Potential Pricing Objectives

1. Target return on investment.
2. Target market share.
3. Maximum long-run profits.
4. Maximum short-run profits.
5. Growth.
6. Stabilize market.
7. Desensitize customers to price.
8. Maintain price-leadership arrangement.
9. Discourage entrants.
10. Speed exit of marginal firms.

---

used to estimate price elasticity. First, price elasticity can be estimated from historical data or from price/quantity data across different sales districts. Second, price elasticity can be estimated by sampling a group of subjects from the target market and polling them concerning various price/quantity relationships. While both of these approaches provide estimates of price elasticity, the former approach is limited to the consideration of price changes, while the latter approach is often expensive and there is some question as to the validity of subjects' responses. However, even a crude estimate of price elasticity is a useful input to pricing decisions.[3]

SUPPLY INFLUENCES ON PRICING DECISIONS

For the purpose of this text, supply influences on pricing decisions can be discussed in terms of three basic factors. These factors relate to the objectives, costs, and nature of the product.

---

[3]For additional discussion of price elasticity, see Philip Kotler, *Marketing Management: Analysis, Planning and Control,* 6th ed. (Englewood Cliffs, N.J.: Prentice Hall, 1988), pp. 499–501.

Pricing Objectives

Pricing objectives should be derived from overall marketing objectives, which in turn should be derived from corporate objectives. Since it is traditionally assumed that business firms operate to maximize profits in the long run, it is often thought that the basic pricing objective is solely concerned with long-run profits. However, the profit maximization norm does not provide the operating marketing manager with a single, unequivocal guideline for selecting prices. In addition, the marketing manager does not have perfect cost, revenue, and market information to be able to evaluate whether or not this objective is being reached. In practice, then, many other objectives are employed as guidelines for pricing decisions. In some cases, these objectives may be considered as operational approaches to achieve long-run profit maximization.

Research has found that the most common pricing objectives are (1) pricing to achieve a target return on investment; (2) stabilization of price and margin; (3) pricing to achieve a target market share; and (4) pricing to meet or prevent competition.

Cost Considerations in Pricing

The price of a product usually must cover costs of production, promotion, and distribution, plus a profit for the offering to be of value to the firm. In addition, when products are priced on the basis of costs plus a fair profit, there is an implicit assumption that this sum represents the economic value of the product in the marketplace.

Cost-oriented pricing is the most common approach in practice, and there are at least three basic variations: *markup pricing, cost-plus pricing*, and *rate-of-return pricing*. Markup pricing is commonly used in retailing, where a percentage is added to the retailer's invoice price to determine the final selling price. Closely related to markup pricing is cost-plus pricing, where the costs of producing a product or completing a project are totalled and a profit amount or percentage is added on. Cost-plus pricing is most often used to describe the pricing of jobs that are non-routine and difficult to "cost" in advance, such as construction and military weapon development.

Rate-of-return or *target pricing* is commonly used by manufacturers. In this method, price is determined by adding a desired rate of return on

---

HIGHLIGHT 11–3
Basic Break-Even Formulas

The following formulas are used to calculate break-even points in units and in dollars:

$$BEP_{(in\ units)} = \frac{FC}{(SP - VC)}$$

$$BEP_{(in\ dollars)} = \frac{FC}{1 - (VC/SP)}$$

where

FC = Fixed cost
VC = Variable cost
SP = Selling price

If, as is generally the case, a firm wants to know how many units or sales dollars are necessary to generate a given amount of profit, profit (P) is simply added to fixed costs in the above formulas. In addition, if the firm has estimates of expected sales and fixed and variable costs, the selling price can be solved for.

---

investment to total costs. Generally, a break-even analysis is performed for expected production and sales levels and a rate of return is added on. For example, suppose a firm estimated production and sales to be 75,000 units at a total cost of $300,000. If the firm desired a before-tax return of 20 percent, the selling price would be (300,000 + 0.20 × 300,000) ÷ 75,000 = $4.80.

Cost-oriented approaches to pricing have the advantage of simplicity, and many practitioners believe that they generally yield a good price decision. However, such approaches have been criticized for two basic reasons. First, cost approaches give little or no consideration to demand factors. For example, the price determined by markup or cost-plus methods has no necessary relationship to what people will be willing to pay for the product. In the case of rate-of-return pricing, little emphasis is placed on estimating sales volume. Even if it were, rate-of-return pricing involves circular reasoning, since unit cost depends on sales volume but sales volume depends on selling price. Second, cost approaches fail to reflect competition adequately. Only in industries where all firms use this approach and have similar costs and markups can this approach yield similar prices and minimize price competition. Thus, in many industries, cost-oriented pricing could lead to severe price competition, which could eliminate smaller firms. Therefore, although costs are a highly important consideration in price decisions, numerous other factors need to be examined.

Product Consideration in Pricing

Although numerous product characteristics can affect pricing, three of the most important are (1) perishability, (2) distinctiveness, and (3) stage in the product life cycle.

Perishability. Goods that are very perishable in a physical sense must be priced to promote sales without costly delays. Foodstuffs and certain types of raw materials tend to be in this category. Products can be considered perishable in two other senses. High fashion, fad, and seasonal products are perishable not in the sense that the product deteriorates but in the sense that demand for the product is confined to a specific time period. Perishability also relates to consumption rate, which means that some products are consumed very slowly, as in the case of consumer durables. Two important pricing considerations here are that (1) such goods tend to be expensive because large amounts of service are purchased at one time; and (2) the consumer has a certain amount of discretionary time available in making replacement purchase decisions.

Distinctiveness. Products can be classified in terms of how distinctive they are. Homogeneous goods are perfect substitutes for each other, as in the case of bulk wheat or whole milk, while most manufactured goods can be differentiated on the basis of certain features, such as package, trademark, engineering design, and chemical features. Thus, few consumer goods are perfectly homogeneous, and one of the primary marketing objectives of any firm is to make its product distinctive in the minds of buyers. Large sums of money are often invested to accomplish this task, and one of the payoffs for such investments is the seller's ability to charge higher prices for distinctive products.

Life Cycle. The stage of the life cycle that a product is in can have important pricing implications. With regard to the life cycle, two approaches to pricing are skimming and penetration price policies. A *skimming* policy is one in which the seller charges a relatively high price on a new product. Generally, this policy is used when the firm has a temporary monopoly and in cases where demand for the product is price inelastic. In later stages of the life cycle, as competition moves in and other market factors change, the price may then be lowered. Digital watches and calculators are examples of this. A *penetration* policy is one in which the seller charges a relatively low price on a new product. Generally, this policy is used when the firm expects competition to move in rapidly and where demand for the product is, at least in the short run, price elastic. This policy is also used to obtain large economies of scale and as a major instrument for rapid creation of a mass market. A low price and profit margin may also discourage competition. In later stages of the life cycle, the price may have to be altered to meet changes in the market.

ENVIRONMENTAL INFLUENCES ON PRICING DECISIONS

Environmental influences on pricing include variables that are uncontrollable by the marketing manager. Two of the most important of these are competition and government regulation.

Competition

In setting or changing prices, the firm must consider its competition and how competition will react to the price of the product. Initially, consideration must be given to such factors as:

1. Number of competitors.
2. Size of competitors
3. Location of competitors.
4. Conditions of entry into the industry.
5. Degree of vertical integration of competitors.
6. Number of products sold by competitors.
7. Cost structure of competitors.
8. Historical reaction of competitors to price changes.

These factors help determine whether the firm's selling price should be at, below, or above competition. Pricing a product at competition (i.e., the average price charged by the industry) is called "going rate pricing" and is popular for homogeneous products, since this approach represents the collective wisdom of the industry and is not disruptive of industry harmony.[4] An example of pricing below competition can be found in sealed-bid pricing, where the firm is bidding directly against competition for project contracts. Although cost and profits are initially calculated, the firm attempts to bid below competitors to obtain the job contract. A firm may price above competition because it has a superior product or because the firm is the price leader in the industry.

Government Regulations

Prices of certain goods and services are regulated by state and federal governments. Public utilities are examples of state regulation of prices. However, for most marketing managers, federal laws that make certain pricing practices illegal are of primary consideration in pricing decisions. The list below is a summary of some of the more important legal constraints on pricing. Of course, since most marketing managers are not trained as lawyers, they usually seek legal counsel when developing pricing strategies to ensure conformity to state and federal legislation.

1. Price-fixing is illegal per se. Sellers must not make any agreements with *(a)* competitors, or *(b)* distributors concerning the final price of the goods. The Sherman Antitrust Act is the primary device used to outlaw horizontal price fixing. Section 5 of the Federal Trade Commission Act has been used to outlaw price-fixing as an "unfair" business practice.

2. Deceptive pricing practices are outlawed under Section 5 of the Federal Trade Commission Act. An example of deceptive pricing would be to mark merchandise with an exceptionally high price and then claim that the lower selling price actually used represents a legitimate price reduction.

3. Price discrimination that lessens competition or is deemed injurious to it is outlawed by the Robinson-Patman Act (which amends Section 2 of the Clayton Act). Price discrimination is not illegal per se, but sellers cannot charge competing buyers different prices for essentially the same products if the effect of

---

[4]Kotler, *Marketing Management,* p. 510.

such sales is injurious to competition. Price differentials can be legally justified on certain grounds, especially if the price differences reflect cost differences. This is particularly true of quantity discounts.

4. Promotional pricing, such as cooperative advertising, and price deals are not illegal per se; but if a seller grants advertising allowances, merchandising service, free goods, or special promotional discounts to customers, it must do so on proportionately equal terms. Sections 2(d) and 2(e) of the Robinson-Patman Act are designed to regulate such practices so that price reductions cannot be granted to some customers under the guise of promotional allowances.[5]

A GENERAL PRICING DECISION MODEL

From what has been discussed thus far, it should be clear that effective pricing decisions involve the consideration of many factors and, depending on the situation, any of these factors can be the primary consideration in setting price. In addition, it is difficult to formulate an exact sequencing of when each factor should be considered. However, several general pricing decision models have been advanced with the clearly stated warning that all pricing decisions will not fit the framework. Below is one such model, which views pricing decisions as a nine-step sequence.

1. *Define market targets.* All marketing decision making should begin with a definition of segmentation strategy and the identification of potential customers.
2. *Estimate market potential.* The maximum size of the available market determines what is possible and helps define competitive opportunities.
3. *Develop product positioning.* The brand image and the desired niche in the competitive marketplace provide important

---

[5]For further discussion of legal issues involved in pricing, see Louis W. Stern and Thomas L. Eovaldi, *Legal Aspects of Marketing Strategy* (Englewood Cliffs, N.J.: Prentice Hall, 1984), chap. 5.

constraints on the pricing decision as the firm attempts to obtain a unique competitive advantage by differentiating its product offering from that of competitors.

4. *Design the marketing mix.* Design of the marketing mix defines the role to be played by pricing in relation to and in support of other marketing variables, especially distribution and promotional policies.

5. *Estimate price elasticity of demand.* The sensitivity of the level of demand to differences in price can be estimated either from past experience or through market tests.

6. *Estimate all relevant costs.* While straight cost-plus pricing is to be avoided because it is insensitive to demand, pricing decisions must take into account necessary plant investment, investment in R&D, and investment in market development, as well as variable costs of production and marketing.

7. *Analyze environmental factors.* Pricing decisions are further constrained by industry practices, likely competitive response to alternative pricing strategies, and legal requirements.

8. *Set pricing objectives.* Pricing decisions must be guided by a clear statement of objectives that recognizes environmental constraints and defines the role of pricing in the marketing strategy while at the same time relating pricing to the firm's financial objectives.

9. *Develop the price structure.* The price structure for a given product can now be determined and will define selling prices for the product (perhaps in a variety of styles and sizes) and the discounts from list price to be offered to various kinds of intermediaries and various types of buyers.[6]

While all pricing decisions cannot be made strictly on the basis of this model, such an approach has three advantages for the marketing manager. First, it breaks the pricing decision into nine manageable steps. Second,

---

[6]Frederick E. Webster, *Marketing for Managers* (New York: Harper & Row, 1974), pp. 178–79; also see Thomas T. Nagle, *The Strategy and Tactics of Pricing* (Englewood Cliffs, N.J.: Prentice Hall, 1987), Kent B. Monroe, *Pricing: Making Profitable Decisions*, 2nd ed. (New York: McGraw-Hill, 1990).

HIGHLIGHT 11–4
Some Short-Term Price Reduction Tactics

1. Cents-off deals: "Package price is 20¢ off."
2. Special offers: "Buy one, get one free"; "Buy three tires and get the fourth free."
3. Coupons: Store or manufacturer coupons in newspaper, magazines, flyers, and packages.
4. Rebates: Mail in proof-of-purchase seals for cash or merchandise.
5. Increase quantity for same price: "Two extra ounces of coffee free."
6. Free installation or service for a limited time period.
7. Reduce or eliminate interest charges for a limited time: "90 days same as cash."
8. Special sales: "25 percent off all merchandise marked with a red tag."

Source: J. Paul Peter and Jerry C. Olson. *Consumer Behavior and Marketing Strategy*, 2nd ed. (Homewood, Ill.: Richard D. Irwin, 1990), p. 500.

it recognizes that pricing decisions must be fully integrated into overall marketing strategy. Third, it aids the decision maker by recognizing the importance of both qualitative and quantitative factors in pricing decisions.

LESSONS FOR THE MANUFACTURER

The variable cost of manufacturing a product is often a small part of the final price charged to customers. Other costs, including transportation, marketing, profit for the manufacturer, and markups through the channel of distribution, often have a much greater influence on the selling price of a product. For example, retail stores or chains often mark up clothing items several times their original cost. However, setting the manufacturer's selling price involves financial analysis of many of the factors discussed in this chapter, including demand, supply, and environmental considerations. Neither the marketing nor the manufacturing areas have sole responsibility for setting prices, although manufacturing provides cost information, and marketing research should provide information on competitive prices and the price consumers are willing to pay for a given level of product quality and features. New costing systems, such as activity-based costing, are now being used by firms to help get a better understanding of cost drivers and provide insights into pricing decisions.

ADDITIONAL READINGS

Curry, David J., and Peter C. Riesz. "Price and Price/Quality Relationships: A Longitudinal Analysis." *Journal of Marketing*, January 1988, pp. 36–51.

Herr, Paul M. "Priming Price: Prior Knowledge and Context Effects." *Journal of Consumer Research*, June 1989, pp. 67–75.

Lattin, James M., and Randolph E. Bucklin. "Reference Effects of Price and Promotion on Brand Choice Behavior." *Journal of Marketing Research*, August 1989, pp. 299–310.

Lichtenstein, Donald R.; Peter H. Bloch; and William C. Black. "Correlates of Price Acceptability." *Journal of Consumer Research*, September 1988, pp. 243–52.

Mobley, Mary F.; William O. Bearden; and Jesse E. Teel. "An Investigation of Individual Responses to Tensile Price Claims." *Journal of Consumer Research*, September 1988, pp. 273–79.

Monroe, Kent B. *Pricing: Making Profitable Decisions*. 2nd ed. New York: McGraw-Hill, 1990.

Nagle, Thomas T. *The Strategy and Tactics of Pricing*. Englewood Cliffs, N.J.: Prentice Hall, 1987.

Seymour, Daniel T., ed. *Pricing Decisions*. Chicago: Probus Publishing, 1989.

Tellis, Gerard J. "Beyond the Many Faces of Price: An Integration of Pricing Strategies." *Journal of Marketing*, October 1986, pp. 146–60.

Urbany, Joel E.; William O. Bearden; and Dan C. Weilbaker. "The Effect of Plausible and Exaggerated Reference Prices on Consumer Perceptions and Price Search." *Journal of Consumer Research*, June 1988, pp. 95–110.

Zeithaml, Valarie A. "Consumer Perceptions of Price, Quality, and Value: A Means-End Model and Synthesis of Evidence." *Journal of Marketing*, July 1988, pp. 2–22.

PART 4

FUNCTIONAL RELATIONSHIPS IN ORGANIZATIONS

CHAPTER 12
Marketing-Manufacturing Interfaces

CHAPTER 12

MARKETING-MANUFACTURING INTERFACES

So far in this text we have emphasized primarily a marketing viewpoint in the conduct of business. Initially, the focus was placed on the role of marketing in strategic planning. The philosophy underlying that discussion was the marketing concept, which simply means that an organization should seek to make profits by serving the needs and wants of customer groups. The marketing concept is perfectly consistent with the manufacturing idea of total quality management, that is, designing organizations to produce products that satisfy customer wants and needs.

As was pointed out in Part 1, two of the critical marketing planning tasks involve (1) selecting target markets and (2) developing marketing mixes. Part 2 focused on selecting target markets by providing an overview of marketing research, consumer behavior, organizational buyer behavior, and the market segmentation process. Part 3 explained the tools, concepts, and strategies involved in developing the marketing mix.

In Part 4, the focus changes somewhat in that we look at the relationships among marketing and other functional areas in an organization with particular emphasis on marketing-manufacturing interfaces. Naturally, these relationships vary across organizations and may depend on a variety of factors. However, Figure 12–1 provides an overview for the chapter and suggests several of the major determinants of organizational relationships with consumers. We will discuss each element in this model starting with organizational structure.

FIGURE 12-1
Factors Influencing Marketing-Manufacturing Interfaces

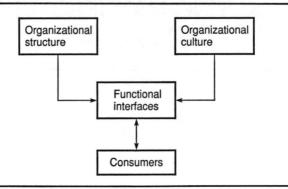

ORGANIZATIONAL STRUCTURE

An organizational structure refers to the formal lines of authority and responsibility as depicted in an organization chart.[1] The structure of an organization can strongly influence relationships among functional areas, such as manufacturing and marketing, since it depicts the formal lines of authority and communication among departments. There are five traditional strategy-driven approaches to organizing a business. These include functional organization structures, geographic organization structures, decentralized business divisions, strategic business units, and matrix structures. These five types are shown in Figure 12-2. In addition to these, a special form of matrix structure, cross-functional management, will also be discussed.

Functional Organizational Structure

A functional organizational structure involves various functional areas reporting to and being coordinated by a chief executive officer or general manager. This approach may boost efficiency by focusing on functional

---

[1]This discussion is based on Arthur A. Thompson, Jr., and A. J. Strickland III, *Strategic Management: Concepts and Cases,* 5th ed. (Homewood, Ill.: BPI/Irwin, 1990), pp. 222–33; and Samuel C. Certo and J. Paul Peter, *Strategic Management: Concepts and Applications,* 2nd ed. (New York: McGraw-Hill, 1991), pp. 136–41.

FIGURE 12–2
Five Common Types of Organizational Structures

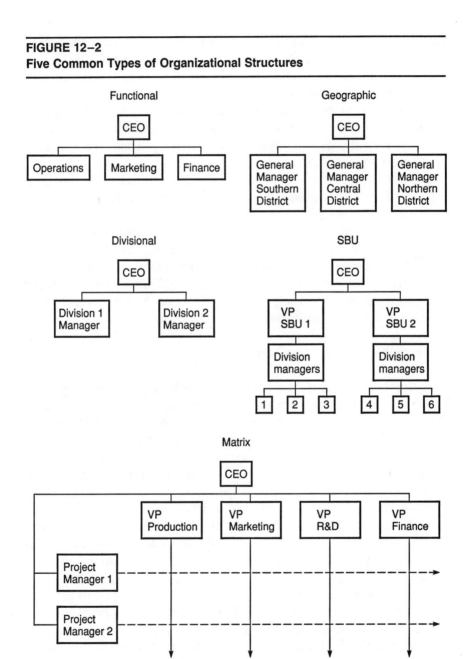

specialization and promoting in-depth functional expertise. It also retains centralized control of strategic planning and decision making, and is well suited for structuring a single business and developing functional-based distinctive competence.

However, there are also several disadvantages to this organizational structure. For example, it promotes narrow specialization and potential functional rivalry and staff-line conflict and may hinder functional coordination and interfunctional decision making.

While many firms are organized along functional lines, a number of large diversified companies have developed additional layers of management within their structures, such as geographic area managers, divisional managers, and strategic business unit (SBU) managers. However, within these divisions, functional structures are still common. It should be noted that within these functional structures there is often no formal line of communication between functional areas. This can make it difficult for an organization to clearly focus its efforts on such things as product quality or customer satisfaction.

Geographic Organization Structure

A geographic organization structure involves having separate geographic areas or territories that serve the particular features and consumer needs of the area. It is commonly used by chain store retailers, power companies, cement firms, restaurant chains, and dairy product companies and often promotes improved performance for the organization. This approach allows strategies to be tailored to the specific needs of each geographic market and delegates profit/loss responsibility to lower strategic levels. It also takes advantage of economies in local operations.

However, there are also several disadvantages to this organization structure. For example, it poses management problems in terms of how much strategic diversity should be allowed across territories and may cause difficulty in maintaining a consistent company and product image if area managers use different strategies. It also adds additional layers of management to the organization. This is particularly a problem when there are both corporate level and geographic level functional departments.

Geographic structures are also used in companies that serve international markets. Organizational structures in such companies may be divided on the basis of different countries or regions or have a separate international division that is divided along these lines.

Divisional Organizational Structure

As firms acquire or develop new products in different industries they may evolve a divisional organizational structure in which each division operates autonomously. Divisions may be formed on the basis of product lines (automotive, motorcycle), markets (consumer, industrial buyers), or channels of distribution (retail store, catalog sales). Each division not only has its own line and staff functions but also formulates and implements its own strategies with corporate approval. Among the advantages of a divisional structure are that it forces coordination and necessary authority down to the appropriate level for rapid response to environmental changes and focuses accountability for performance at the appropriate level. Among the disadvantages of this structure are that it fosters potential dysfunctional conflict for corporate-level resources and may lead to a failure to capitalize on synergies among different divisions.

With the trend toward increased concentration of industry, divisional and SBU-type structures have become more common. While such structures are needed to manage large diversified companies, relationships among functional areas may become more complex since there are usually corporate as well as divisional level functional departments that may need to be coordinated when developing and implementing strategies.

Strategic Business Unit Structure

When a divisional structure becomes unwieldy because a CEO has too many divisions to manage effectively, organizations may reorganize in the form of strategic business units (SBUs) or strategic groups. This structure brings together a number of divisions on the basis of such things as the similarity of product lines or markets. Vice presidents are appointed to oversee the operations of the SBUs and report directly to the CEO. For example, at General Electric, a pioneer in the concept of SBUs, 190 units were grouped into 43 SBUs and then aggregated further into 6 "sectors." This organizational structure can improve coordination between divisions with similar strategic concerns and product/market environments and can tighten strategic management and control of large, diverse business enterprises. It also provides a strategically relevant way to organize the business portfolio of a broad, diversified company.

Among the disadvantages of an SBU structure are that it may create dysfunctional competition for corporate resources and difficulties in defining authority and responsiblity among divisional and SBU level managers. It also adds additional management layers to the organization, which may increase costs.

Many authorities argue that the SBU level is most critical for developing competitive advantage for an organization. However, there can be difficulties in coordinating SBUs effectively. For example, Oscar Mayer, which is part of Kraft General Foods, has a variety of meat and other products that require refrigerated transportation, storage, and display. Kraft Foods, another of the Kraft General Foods companies, has products such as cheese with the same requirements that are sold in the same retail outlets. However, Oscar Mayer and Kraft are separate parts of Kraft General Foods and have their own plants and use their own distribution systems. While it would seem that there could be some synergies in production and distribution between the two, developing a more integrated system would require a considerable change in the organization.

Matrix Organization Structure

A matrix organization structure is used to facilitate the development and execution of various programs and projects. Each of the heads listed at the top of the matrix has *functional* responsibility for all the projects, whereas each of the project managers listed down the side has *project* responsibility for completing and implementing the strategy. This approach allows project managers to cut across departmental lines and can promote the efficient implementation of strategies. This structure accommodates a wide variety of project-oriented business activities and gives formal attention to each dimension of strategy formulation and implementation. It also encourages cooperation, consensus building, conflict resolution, and coordination of related activities. The major disadvantage of this structure is that it can create confusion and contradictory policies by allowing dual accountability between project managers and functional department heads. This structure clearly requires tremendous vertical and horizontal integration and is thus difficult to manage.

It is interesting to note that in their classic study of excellent corporations, Peters and Waterman made the following observation about matrix organization structures:

> Virtually none of the excellent companies spoke of itself as having formal matrix structures, except for project management companies like Boeing. But in a company like Boeing, where many of the matrix ideas originated, something very different is meant by matrix management. People operate in a binary way: they are *either* a part of a project team and responsible to that team for getting some task accomplished (most of the time), *or* they are part of a technical discipline in which they spend some time making sure their technical department is keeping up with the state of the art. When they are on a project, there is no day-in, day-out confusion about whether they are really responsible to the project or not. They are.[2]

Cross-Functional Management

While matrix structures may not be appropriate for all organizations, a variation of them has been pioneered by Japanese managers. This variation is called cross-functional management and involves vertical functions similar to those in a matrix structure. However, the horizontal functions in this approach are not project managers but cross-functional goals such as quality, cost control, and scheduling. Cross-functional committees meet regularly and strive to constantly improve on these goals. At Toyota, all members of the cross-functional committee are board members representing the departments involved in a particular cross function, such as quality. The committee determines the goals and measures for assessing the progress in achieving them. In other companies, the cross-function committee is headed by the president or other senior executive, and meetings are held monthly to work on constantly improving quality, reducing unnecessary costs, and improving scheduling quantity and delivery. A total quality control audit is done annually to evaluate progress in achieving the objectives.

Cross-functional management structures are designed to enhance profits and to constantly improve areas such as employee education, customer satisfaction, customer service, quality assurance, volume and

---

[2]Thomas J. Peters and Robert H. Waterman, Jr., *In Search of Excellence* (New York: Harper & Row, 1982), p. 307.

delivery control, and new product development. These structures were developed to look for ways to improve corporate activities, both vertically and horizontally.[3] As with any organization structure, their success may depend heavily on the prevailing organizational culture.

Unfortunately, there are no hard-and-fast rules for determining which organizational structure is best for a particular company. As shown above, each type of structure has advantages and disadvantages that managers must consider when designing or changing an organization.

It should be clear that different organization structures may lead to different relationships between functional areas. For example, in a functional organization structure, each area is independent and its degree of coordination depends heavily on the judgment and skills of the general manager. In geographic, division, and SBU organization structures, relationships among functional areas may be more complex because both corporate and business levels (geographic area, division, or SBU) have functional specialists working on strategies. In a matrix organization, specific interactions among heads of functional areas and project leaders strongly influence ongoing relationships. In the cross-functional management structure there is a formal, ongoing mechanism for developing interfunctional relationships.

ORGANIZATIONAL CULTURE

Organizational culture or corporate culture refers to more informal aspects of an organization than does organizational structure. Organizational culture can be defined as a set of shared values and beliefs that influences the effectiveness of strategy development and implementation. The significance of organizational culture is that it influences employee behavior, hopefully motivating them to achieve or surpass organizational goals, and it influences the degree and nature of contact across functional departments. Typically the CEO and other present and past leaders of an organization are the key agents influencing organizational culture. Many manufacturing companies have been working hard in recent years to refocus their corporate cultures to emphasize product quality and customer satisfaction.

---

[3]This discussion is based on Masaaki Imai, *Kaizen: The Key to Japan's Competitive Success* (New York: Random House, 1986), pp. 127–34.

Organizational cultures are developed and reinforced in a variety of ways. One authority suggests that there are five primary and five secondary culture development mechanisms.[4] The five primary mechanisms are:

1. *What leaders pay attention to, measure, and control.* Leaders who can communicate effectively what their vision of the organization is and what they want done are more effective at creating the organizational culture they desire. They can do so by emphasizing the same issues in meetings, in casual remarks and questions, and in strategy discussions. For example, if product quality is the dominant value to be inculcated in employees, leaders may consistently inquire about the effect of any proposed changes on product quality.

2. *Leaders' reactions to critical incidents and organizational crises.* The manner in which leaders deal with crises can create new beliefs and values and reveal underlying organizational assumptions. For example, when a firm faces a financial crisis but does not have any layoffs, employees may form the perception that they are members of a family that look out for each other. This may increase their motivation and commitment to the company.

3. *Deliberate role modeling, teaching, and coaching.* The behaviors that leaders perform in both formal and informal settings have an important effect on employee beliefs, values, and behaviors. For example, if the CEO regularly works very long hours and on weekends, other managers may respond by spending more of their time at work.

4. *Criteria for allocation of rewards and status.* Leaders can quickly communicate their priorities and values by consistently linking rewards and punishments to the behaviors they are concerned with. For example, if a weekly bonus is given for exceeding production or sales quotas, employees may recognize the value placed on these activities and focus their efforts on them.

5. *Criteria for recruitment, selection, promotion, and retirement of employees.* The types of people who are hired and who succeed

---

[4]Edgar H. Schein, *Organizational Culture and Leadership* (San Francisco: Jossey-Bass, 1985), pp. 223–43. The discussion that follows is based on this work.

in an organization are those who accept the organization's values and behave accordingly. For example, if managers who are action oriented and who implement strategies effectively consistently move up the organizational ladder, the organization's priorities should come through loud and clear to other managers.

In addition to the five primary mechanisms, there are five secondary mechanisms by which organizational cultures are developed. They are:

1. *The organization's design and structure.* Through the design of an organization's structure, leaders can communicate what they believe are the central tasks of the firm and what they believe about employees in general. For example, a highly decentralized organization suggests that leaders have confidence in the abilities of subordinate managers.

2. *Organizational systems and procedures.* Some visible parts of organization life are the daily, weekly, monthly, quarterly, and annual cycles of routines, procedures, reports to file, forms to fill out, and other tasks that have to be performed repeatedly. For example, if the CEO asks for quarterly reports on all assistant managers, this requirement communicates the message that the organization values and is concerned with this group.

3. *Design of physical space, facades, and buildings.* Leaders who embrace a clear philosophy and management style often make that style manifest in their choice of architecture, interior design, and decor. For example, if a leader believes in open communication, office space may be laid out such that very few private areas or barriers to the flow of traffic exist.

4. *Stories, legends, myths, and parables about important events and leadership behavior.* As an organization develops and accumulates a history, some of it becomes embodied in stories about events and leadership behavior. For example, when the founder of McDonald's restaurants, Ray Kroc, visited a McDonald's franchise in Winnipeg, he found a single fly. Two weeks later the Winnipeg franchisee lost his franchise. After this story made the rounds, many franchisees found ways to eliminate flies from their restaurants. Whether Ray Kroc actually did take away a franchise on this basis is unimportant from a culture development point of view; what is important is that he did do things like that.

HIGHLIGHT 12–1
Building an Organizational Culture: The Company Mission, Values, and Guiding Principles at Ford Motor Company

Mission
Ford Motor Company is a worldwide leader in automotive and automotive-related products and services as well as in newer industries such as aerospace, communications, and financial services. Our mission is to improve continually our products and services to meet our customers' needs, allowing us to prosper as a business and to provide a reasonable return for our stockholders, the owners of our business.

Values
How we accomplish our mission is as important as the mission itself. Fundamental to success for the Company are these basic values:

- *People.* Our people are the source of our strength. They provide our corporate intelligence and determine our reputation and vitality. Involvement and teamwork are our core human values.
- *Products.* Our products are the end result of our efforts, and they should be the best in serving customers worldwide As our products are viewed, so are we viewed.
- *Profits.* Profits are the ultimate measure of how efficiently we provide customers with the best products for their needs. Profits are required to survive and grow.

Guiding Principles
- *Quality comes first.* To achieve customer satisfaction, the quality of our products and services must be our number one priority.
- *Customers are the focus of everything we do.* Our work must be done with our customers in mind, providing better products and services than our competition.
- *Continuous improvement is essential to our success.* We must strive for excellence in everything we do: in our products, in their safety and value—and in our services, our human relations, our competitiveness, and our profitability.
- *Employee involvement is our way of life.* We are a team. We must treat each other with trust and respect.
- *Dealers and suppliers are our partners.* The Company must maintain mutually beneficial relationships with dealers, suppliers, and our other business associates.
- *Integrity is never compromised.* The conduct of our Company worldwide must be pursued in a manner that is socially responsible and commands respect for its integrity and for its positive contributions to society. Our doors are open to men and women alike without discrimination and without regard to ethnic origin or personal beliefs.

Source: Brad Stratton, "The Refined Focus on Automotive Quality," *Quality Progress,* October 1989, p. 49.

5. *Formal statements of organizational philosophy, creeds, and charters*. Explicit statements by leaders of organizations about their values are a final means of shaping organizational culture. For example, posters displayed throughout the successful L.L. Bean Company in Freeport, Maine, constantly remind employees that customers are the most important people to the company.

Ideally organizational cultures should facilitate the accomplishment of organizational goals by motivating employees to work effectively and efficiently. They do so by creating an atmosphere or work climate in which meeting performance targets is valued by employees for both monetary and social rewards.

One of the important functions of organizational culture is that it reinforces the dominant values and positioning within an organization. For example, a company cannot simultaneously produce the lowest cost, highest quality, instantly available, most innovative products. Thus, a company must select a particular strategy, and the culture can reinforce it to create competitive advantage. Such things as product quality, cost efficiency, dependability of delivery, flexibility in product design, and innovativeness should be ranked by companies in terms of their relative importance for success in an industry. Certainly, all are important yet some trade-offs are clearly necessary. An organizational culture also influences the degree to which a company maintains and reinforces ethical decision making.

Organizational culture can strongly influence relationships among functional areas within an organization. For example, an organization that fosters cross-functional informal interactions among managers, such as promoting company softball games or golf outings, may encourage more direct contact across areas than is indicated by the formal organization chart.

FUNCTIONAL INTERFACES

There are many functions within an organization and, as discussed above, the organization structure and corporate culture influence how these functions are organized, managed, and interact. However, there are four major functions in a company, namely finance, human resources, operations, and marketing. These are shown in Figure 12–3.

FIGURE 12–3
Major Organization Functions

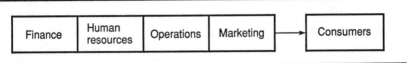

A primary focus of the finance function is to obtain funds for the organization and guide the use of financial resources. Finance specialists also contribute to an organization by assessing the potential profit impact of various strategic alternatives and evaluating the financial condition of the business. The human resources function is concerned with attracting, assessing, motivating, and retaining the number and types of managers and other employees required to run a business effectively. The operations or production function provides product offerings that, hopefully, consumers will find of value. Manufacturing operations generally transform raw materials and other components into tangible products for sale to consumers or organizational buyers. Nonmanufacturing operations provide intangible services, such as entertainment, education, and health care. As discussed throughout this text, the marketing function is primarily concerned with creating exchanges for the organization's product offerings with consumers.

Of particular concern to this text are the relationships between manufacturing and marketing. However, these relationships cannot be considered meaningfully without also considering the consumer. A number of systems have been developed to facilitate profitable interactions among manufacturing, marketing, and consumers. These systems are known as quality function deployment (QFD) and will be discussed at the end of the chapter. However, it is useful to first examine marketing, manufacturing, and consumer relationships from a conceptual viewpoint called consumer means-ends chain analysis.

Consumer Means-Ends Chain Analysis

The basic idea underlying means-ends chains is that products mean more to consumers than simply a set of product attributes.[5] Product attributes

---

[5]This discussion is based on J. Paul Peter and Jerry C. Olson, *Consumer Behavior and Marketing Strategy,* 2nd ed. (Homewood, Ill.: Richard D. Irwin, 1990), Chapter 4.

are the tangible features of a product that are created in the manufacturing process. In addition to these, products also have consequences that may be connected to important consumer values. Product consequences are the direct risks or benefits of using the product, and values are even more abstract beliefs about the consequences of using the product.

Figure 12–4 presents a conceptual model of a means-ends chain. As suggested in this figure, often manufacturing determines the product attributes (hopefully, with the aid of sound marketing research) and has a strong influence on the consequences of product usage. Marketing influences the consequences and develops ties between these consequences and values that are important to consumers. For example, Cadillac and Chevrolet automobiles have many of the same components and features, yet Cadillacs command a premium price because they tie to important values for some consumers, such as self-esteem.

FIGURE 12–4
Functional Relationships and Consumer Means-Ends Chains

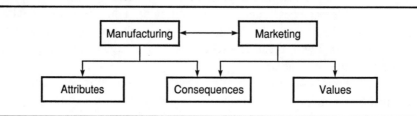

FIGURE 12–5
An Illustration of a Consumer Means-Ends Chain

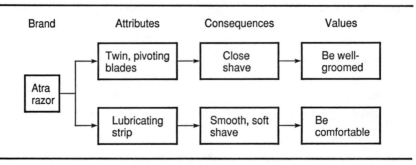

Figure 12–5 presents a simple example of a means-ends chain for an Atra razor. The razor's attributes of interest to this consumer were that it had twin, pivoting blades and a lubricating strip. These attributes led to consequences that included having a close shave and also a smooth, soft shave. The desired values associated with the product were that the consumer would be well-groomed and comfortable. Analysis of consumers through means-ends chains gives manufacturing and marketing important strategic direction for designing and promoting products. Product attributes can be designed to lead to desired consequences and priced, promoted, and distributed to tie to values that are important to consumers.

Often a means-ends chain analysis can be done effectively using the three levels: attributes, consequences, and values. However, more detailed analyses can be accomplished by dividing each into two sublevels. Attributes can be divided into concrete and abstract types. Concrete attributes are those that are perceived directly through the five senses, such as color and taste. Abstract attributes are not directly sensed but are inferred by the consumer, for example, that the product is stylish, durable, or reliable. Consequences can also be divided into functional and psychosocial types. Functional consequences are what the product does for the consumer in a usage sense, such as, how well a car handles. Psychosocial consequences concern how consumers feel about themselves and how they feel others feel about them for using the product. For example, driving a Porsche may make the consumer feel special and attractive to other people. Values can be divided into instrumental and terminal types. Instrumental values refer to preferred modes of conduct, such as being the center of attention or having a good time, while terminal values refer to preferred end states, such as being happy, wealthy, or tranquil.

Figure 12–6 provides several examples of expanded means-ends chains. Note that some products for some consumers do not necessarily tie to high-level values but are evaluated only through the consequence level. However, it seems likely that products that are tied to high-level values would have greater meaning for consumers and be more important to them. Brands of products with attributes that tie to high-level values may well be more successful in the marketplace. For example, Tide detergent at the concrete attribute level is a chemical formulation much like many other laundry detergents. However, for some consumers Tide represents good cleaning power, which means their children will have cleaner clothes, which means they are good parents, which leads to higher

FIGURE 12–6
Examples of Means-Ends Chains at the Product Level

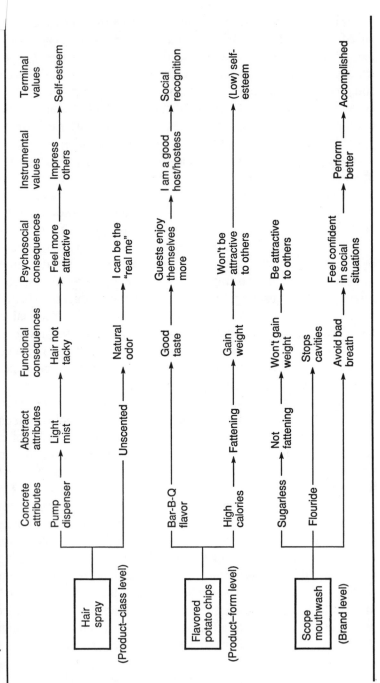

self-esteem. Ties to these higher-level consequences and values may explain why Tide is the market leader while generic brands, which are cheaper but arguably as effective, have only limited market share.

Means-ends chain analysis is a relatively new development in the marketing literature. However, it has important implications for relationships between manufacturing and marketing. First, this analysis suggests that products and brands often mean more to consumers than simply a bundle of product attributes. While marketing research is required to develop better understandings of consumers' means-ends chains, such analysis can aid in focusing operations on the meanings, values, and uses

---

HIGHLIGHT 12–2
Marketing Strategies Associated with Various Types of Operations

Type of Operation	Type of Product	Typical Process Characteristics	Typical Characteristics of Market Strategy
Service Project Job shop	Make to order as customer specifies.	Use of broadly skilled workers and general purpose equipment; emphasis on good initial planning of work, quality, flexibility.	Selling diversity of capabilities and ability to provide features customers desire, ability to perform a quality job, ability to achieve reasonable delivery times.
Continuous process	Make for inventory product designed to have features desired by many potential customers.	Use of workers with narrower skills, specialized equipment, perhaps automation; emphasis on efficiency and cost control; good distribution system to make items readily available.	Selling the desirability of features that are already designed into the product plus the desirability of the price, availability, service. Market research is important to ensure that product features are appropriate for the market.

Source: Reprinted with permission from *Production and Operations Management,* 4/e, by James B. Dilworth, p. 55. © 1989 by McGraw-Hill, Inc.

products have for consumers. For example, through the use of technology such as digital chips, manufacturers have been capable of providing a long list of features and options on electronic equipment like VCRs, telephones, fax machines, and copiers. However, product operation and instructions for such equipment have become so complicated that consumers often cannot figure out how to use the products.[6] A means-ends chain analysis of what these products mean to consumers might have been able to focus technology more directly on benefits and values rather than on an overabundance of unneeded and unwanted product features.

Second, this analysis highlights the importance of a close, continuing relationship between marketing and manufacturing, including design and engineering. While manufacturing and marketing personnel often do not relate well because of differences in training, objectives, language, and views of their own relative importance, means-ends chain analysis, by including strategic concerns for both areas, may provide a useful bridge between the two.

Quality Function Deployment

Quality function deployment (QFD) is a relatively recent development in organizations. It was pioneered by Kobe Shipyard, Mitsubishi Heavy Industries, Ltd., and has been used successfully by companies such as Toyota, Nissan, Ford, General Motors, Digital Equipment, Hewlett-Packard, AT&T, Polaroid, and ITT. It is a developing area and much of the design of QFD systems in organizations remains priority information since company executives believe that these systems are a foundation for competitive advantage.

The basic transformations in quality function deployment are shown in Figure 12–7. QFD starts with marketing research to determine customer requirements for products. These are translated in turn into systems requirements, part requirements, part characteristics, manufacturing operations, and production requirements to make a product that satisfies what customers say they want in the product. In essence, QFD focuses on coordinating skills across functions in an organization in order to design, manufacture, and market products that meet consumer needs, wants, quality requirements, and desired product attributes. These sys-

---

[6]For an excellent discussion of this issue, see "I Can't Work This Thing!" *Business Week*, April 29, 1991, pp. 58–66.

FIGURE 12-7
A General Model of Quality Function Deployment

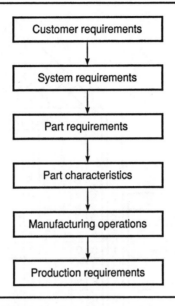

Source: Reprinted from P. J. Ross, *The Taguchi Techniques for Quality Engineering,* © 1988 by McGraw-Hill, Inc. Reproduced with permission of the publisher.

tems attempt to make products that are right the first time for specific target markets. Among the advantages of QFD are:

1. It focuses the organization on satisfying customer needs and wants.
2. It allows for greater interaction across functional areas.
3. It can reduce or eliminate engineering changes.
4. It can reduce design time.
5. It can reduce start-up problems.
6. It can reduce warranty claims.
7. It can increase consumer acceptance of products.[7]

---

[7]This list is combined from Richard G. Newman, "QFD Involves Buyers/Suppliers," *Purchasing World,* October 1988, pp. 91–93; and Dennis De Vera, Tom Glennon, Andrew A. Kenny, Mohammed A. H. Khan, and Mike Mayer, "An Automotive Case Study," *Quality Progress,* June 1988, pp. 35–38.

FIGURE 12–8
House of Quality Applied to a Blend Door Actuator

Customer Needs		Rankings	Durable	Low noise	Fast replacement	Low price	Low repair rate	Small size	Movable tabs	Adaptable output	Low weight	Positive fastening	Tough material
Primary	Secondary												
Comfortable	Quiet	5	5	5	0	3	3	1	0	0	0	1	0
Convenient	Easy to service	1	0	0	5	0	0	1	1	1	0	0	0
Low cost	Inexpensive	3	3	3	0	5	1	1	0	0	3	3	3
Low cost	Low warranty	5	5	3	5	5	5	0	0	0	0	0	0
Fit	Small size	3	0	1	0	3	0	5	0	0	5	0	0
Fit	Universal mounting	5	0	0	1	3	0	5	5	5	0	0	0
Reliable	Drop integrity	1	3	0	0	3	0	3	0	0	5	5	5
Reliable	Long life	5	5	5	0	3	5	0	0	0	0	0	0
Ratings			87	77	35	97	68	52	25	25	29	19	14
Target Values			50 M cycles	38 dB max.	10 min. max.	< $X.XX	< X.X R/100	3" x 4" x 1.0"		3 shafts	X oz. max.	Drop test	

Comparative Analysis: Worse — Same — Better

Source: Dennis De Vera, Tom Glennon, Andrew A. Kenny, Mohammed A. H. Khan, and Mike Mayer, "An Automotive Case Study," *Quality Progress*, June 1988, p. 37. Reprinted by permission of Andrew Kenny.

Figure 12–8 shows an example of one type of QFD called House of Quality as applied to an automotive air-conditioning control device, a blend door actuator that maintains a selected air temperature. House of Quality starts with marketing research to define a target market based on the importance of various product attributes desired by consumers, called customer needs on the left side of Figure 12–8. Actual consumer statements regarding attributes are interpreted and classified in terms of primary, secondary, and in some cases, tertiary needs.

Customer needs are then translated into engineering characteristics or design features as shown on the top of Figure 12–8. This task involves a number of decisions regarding appropriate level of attributes and, in some cases, trade-offs between attributes. For example, making the unit more durable may increase the price. The roof of the house specifies the relationships between various design features: P stands for a positive relationship and N for a negative one. After these decisions are made, the company's product is compared with those of competitors on customer needs as shown on the right-hand side of Figure 12–8.

After comparisons with competitive products, decisions are made concerning the appropriate levels for each design feature. The process may then move to other tasks. For example, parts specifications to achieve the design features may be determined. Then planning can be done to determine the appropriate operations process and, finally, production planning and the specification of production requirements. Hopefully, the output of the system is a product that results in customer satisfaction.

QFD systems offer companies an excellent method for incorporating customer needs and wants into the design of products. However, implementing such systems is a major challenge for many companies since increased coordination across functional areas is critical, and most traditional organizational structures were not designed with this in mind. Many companies are refocusing their corporate cultures to try to overcome this problem. In addition, such systems might be improved by taking a consumer means-ends analysis viewpoint. Thus, rather than focusing only on product attributes, marketing research could be used to investigate product consequences and values as well as inputs into QFD.

In sum, QFD approaches attempt to develop products that are consistent with desired consumer attributes. They focus on breaking down traditional function boundaries in an organization and encourage teamwork among functional employees, such as marketing and manufacturing personnel. While the success of these systems often depends on the corporate culture of the organization, many firms believe they are superior to traditional methods of product design and marketing.

LESSONS FOR THE MANUFACTURER

Relationships among functional areas are determined primarily by the organizational structure and organizational culture of a firm. Organizational structures present the formal lines of authority and communication in a firm. Alternative organizational structures have various advantages and disadvantages for the organization; however, there is clearly a need to carefully coordinate the activities of various functional areas. Cross-functional management systems are designed to do so.

Organizational culture refers to the shared beliefs and values within an organization, and one of the differential advantages of successful firms is an effective culture. For example, leaders of organizations such as Merck and Wal-Mart have been credited with designing organizational cultures that have led to effective design and implementation of strategies. Often an organizational culture will be dominated by a particular functional area such as engineering, manufacturing, or marketing, which may strongly influence relationships among functional areas and determine the real power in the organization.

Perhaps the most important lesson from this chapter is the importance of effective relationships between manufacturing and marketing as illustrated in the discussion of quality function deployment. Inputs from consumers, obtained through well-designed and well-executed marketing research, are critical for designing, engineering, and manufacturing products that consumers will want, purchase, and continue to purchase. Inputs from manufacturing on what products and product features can be produced with the required level of quality and cost effectiveness are critical for the success of the firm. Effective decision making for the selection of target markets and the design of marketing mixes depend on clear communication and coordination between marketing and manufacturing. Although marketing personnel and manufacturing personnel sometimes speak at each other instead of to each other, it is critical for each functional area to understand the approaches taken by the other, to appreciate the other area's problems, and to work together to obtain overall corporate objectives.

ADDITIONAL READINGS

Hall, Robert W. *Attaining Manufacturing Excellence*. Homewood Ill: Business One Irwin, 1987.

Porter, Michael E. *Competitive Advantage*. New York: Free Press, 1985.

Schnaars, Steven P. *Marketing Strategy: A Customer-Driven Approach*. New York: Free Press, 1991.

PART 5

CASES IN MARKETING MANAGEMENT

CASE 1

TIMEX CORP.*

Timex Corp. was one of the first companies to offer low-cost, durable mechanical watches. These watches were mass produced with hard-alloy bearings which were less costly than jeweled bearings. They were also much longer lasting than nonjeweled watches had been before. Timex attempted to sell these watches in jewelry stores offering a 30 percent markup. However, jewelers commonly received 50 percent markup on merchandise and therefore many refused to stock them. The company then began selling direct to drugstores, hardware stores, and even cigar stands. At one point the company had a distribution system of nearly a quarter of a million outlets. This mass-distribution strategy was coupled with heavy TV advertising demonstrating the durability of the watches. For example, one of the ads showed a Timex watch being strapped to an outboard motor propeller and continuing to work after the engine had been run for several minutes. Such ads were used to support the contention that Timex watches could "take a licking and keep on ticking." In order to keep dealers and prices firmly in line, Timex limited production to about 85 percent of anticipated demand, making them somewhat scarce.

This strategy was extremely successful. By the late 1960s Timex had 50 percent market share in America and as much as 20 percent of worldwide sales. In 1970, Timex had after-tax profits of $27 million on sales of $200 million.

After a quarter of a century of dominance in the low-price watch market, Timex began to face serious competition by the mid-1970s. One of the major technological advances was the development of electronic

---

*This case was prepared by the author from the following sources: "Timex Takes the Torture Test," *Fortune*, June 27, 1983, pp. 112–20; "Can Timex Take a Licking and Keep on Ticking?" *Business Week*, February 20, 1984, p. 102; and "The Swiss Put Glitz in Cheap Quartz Watches," *Fortune*, August 20, 1984, p. 102.

watches, which Timex executives initially judged to be unimportant. By the time they recognized the importance of this technological change and introduced an electronic watch, competitors had already developed and marketed much-improved models. In fact, the Timex electronic watches were so big and clumsy that employees nicknamed them "quarter pounders" and prices ended up 50 percent above competitive, much more attractive watches.

By 1983 Timex's U.S. market share had plummeted to about 17 percent and operating losses approached $100 million. Distribution outlets had declined to 100,000 outlets. Timex ranked fifth in volume behind Japan's Seiko, Citizen, and Casio, and a Swiss combine, ASUAG-SSIH Ltd. Digital and quartz analog watches dominated the market and even the successful Japanese companies faced increased price competition from manufacturers in Hong Kong. In fact, the export price of the average digital watch dropped from $5 in 1981 to less than $2 and many companies were forced out of business with margins of only a few cents per watch.

At this point Timex decided to attempt to rebuild its watch market. (It also decided to make itself less vulnerable by diversifying into home health care products and home computers.) To rebuild its timekeeping business, the company invested over $100 million to retool and redesign its watch and clock lines. Timex's marketing vice president supported this investment by stating that "We were thick, fat, ugly, overpriced, and behind in technology." The strategy then became to produce watches that were just as attractive as higher-priced brands and keep the major portion of the line priced at under $50. Of course, this forced Timex to compete in a world already overloaded with too many inexpensive watch brands. In addition to watches from Japan and Hong Kong, Swiss manufacturers scored a big hit with a trendy timepiece called Swatch, which was brightly colored plastic and sold for $30. Sales soared to 100,000 units per month and swatches could not be produced fast enough.

Timex also attempted to compete in the over $100 price range with its superthin quartz analog Elite collection, which was sold in department and jewelry stores for up to $120. However, as one competitor summed it up in evaluating the market potential of the Timex Elite collection, "It's got one disadvantage; it's got a $12.95 name on it."

LESSONS FOR THE MANUFACTURER

Through the early 1970s, Timex Corp. clearly had a sound business strategy. It had engineered and manufactured watches with hard-alloy bearings that were more durable than other nonjeweled watches and less expensive than watches with jeweled bearings. The company pioneered the development of new channels of distribution for watches that included drug and hardware stores. The company's pricing strategy allowed it to make excellent profits, in part because it offered lower markups for retailers. Its promotion strategy focused on positioning Timex watches as low-cost, durable timepieces, and its "takes a licking and keeps on ticking" theme is still remembered by many consumers. Certainly, obtaining 50 percent of the American market and 20 percent of the world market for watches is an outstanding accomplishment.

One way of thinking about Timex's downfall by the early 1980s is to consider the meanings of product quality. Clearly, Timex produced a quality, low-priced watch when considered from the point of view of traditional manufacturing objectives. That is, the watches had few defects, were very durable, and performed their functional task very effectively. However, from the point of view of consumers, the products were not quality merchandise, not because they didn't work well, but because they were outdated in technology and styling.

Timex management can be blamed on two counts. First, it underestimated the demand for electronic watches, which became very popular. Second, it had not carefully analyzed the competitive environment and the potential for foreign-made electronic watches to challenge them in the low-priced market segment. In general, as with many other companies then and now, Timex apparently was too internally focused on production efficiencies and margins and did not pay enough attention to consumer wants and competitive offerings.

Finally, as noted in the case, Timex recognized its problems and retooled and redesigned its watch and clock lines. It has scored a number of successes since, most notably the Timex Ironman, a multifunction sports watch that sells for under $40, millions of which have been sold.

CASE 2

TSR HOBBIES, INC.— "DUNGEONS AND DRAGONS"*

TSR (Tactical Studies Rules) Hobbies, Inc., had grown rapidly since its start in 1973 to sales of $27 million in fiscal 1983. TSR's star product responsible for this rapid growth was "Dungeons and Dragons," a unique fantasy/adventure game. The game was unique because it happened largely in the minds of its players. Its emphasis on cooperation among players and dependence on their imaginative powers set it apart from traditional board games.

OVERVIEW

Company History

TSR Hobbies, Inc., was founded by E. Gary Gygax in a small Wisconsin resort town. Gygax never graduated from high school, but pursued his passion for fantasy in the forms of war games and science fiction books. When Gygax lost his job as an insurance underwriter in 1970, he started developing fantasy games almost full-time, while supporting his family with a shoe repair business in his basement. In 1973 Gygax pursuaded a boyhood friend and fellow war game enthusiast, Donald Kaye, to borrow $1,000 against his life insurance, and TSR Hobbies, Inc., was founded.

The two gamers published a popular set of war games rules for lead miniatures called "Cavaliers and Roundheads." In January of 1974 another inveterate gamer friend, Brian Blume, invested $2,000 in the company, and the three partners printed the first set of rules for "Dungeons and Dragons." The game was assembled in the Gygax home and was sold

---

*This case was prepared by Margaret L. Friedman, Assistant Professor, School of Business, University of Wisconsin–Whitewater.

EXHIBIT 1
TSR Hobbies Sales

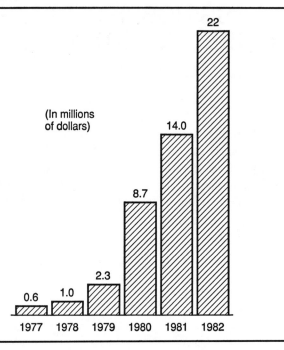

Source: Adapted from *The Wall Street Journal*, January 7, 1983.

---

through an established network of professional gamers. In 1974, 1,000 sets of the "Dungeons and Dragons" game were sold. Eight years later it was selling at the rate of 750,000 per year. The sales history for the product is shown in Exhibit 1.

The rapid growth of TSR was not necessarily a reflection of keen and experienced management skill. The three top officers in the company all lacked formal management training, but felt they could remedy this deficiency by taking management courses and seminars. Although TSR wanted to attract older, experienced toy and game managers to their ranks, most of their recruits came from outside the toy/game/hobby industry.

Between 1977 and 1982 the TSR work force grew from 12 to more than 250 employees. Gygax's original partner, Donald Kaye, died of a heart attack in 1975, and so the partnership was assumed by Gygax and brothers Brian and Keven Blume. Gygax was president of TSR, Kevin was chief executive, and Brian was executive vice president. All company decisions were directed through Kevin Blume, from major decisions down to authorization for a $12 desk calendar for a secretary. There was some personnel turnover and evidence of employee dissatisfaction due to nepotism in the company's hiring policies. It was reported that between 10 and 20 of Brian Blume's relatives were on the company's payroll.

The "Dungeons and Dragons" Game

"Dungeons and Dragons" represented a significant innovation in the game and hobby industry. A basic set for a "Dungeons and Dragons" game consisted of a lengthy instruction book, dice, and a wax pencil, all of which sold for $12.

The game begins when each player generates a mythical character with a roll of the dice. The personality profile for each character is determined according to rigorous guidelines given in the instruction booklet. For example, there is a Dungeon Master role in each game. It is the Dungeon Master who develops a map of the dungeon layout as there is no game board. Each character has particular spells and powers which are critical in negotiating the game's adventure. The goal is to navigate through a treacherous dungeon, arrive at a particular destination, and depart alive with the treasure. The combination of mythical characters and adventure is why "Dungeons and Dragons" is called a role-playing/ fantasy/adventure game. No two "Dungeons and Dragons" games are alike since the way the game unfolds depends upon the players' imaginations.

To survive, players must work together, rather than against one another, winding their way through a dangerous path to the treasure. Players are confronted with conquest after conquest involving ghouls, monsters, dragons, and other obstacles to finding the treasure and escaping with it. The instruction booklet describes the various powers and spells available to the different characters and general rules for behaving in the dungeon. The crayon is used to keep track of pathways taken and used-up spells. The game can last from two hours to weeks on end—it is all up to the imaginative powers of the players.

MARKETING STRATEGY

TSR's goal was to double sales every year. The strategy used to achieve this goal was based heavily on target market expansion, product line expansion, expansion of promotional activities, and more intensive distribution.

Expansion of Target Market

When "Dungeons and Dragons" was first introduced, it was targeted solely to experienced gamers. The first edition of the game came in a plain brown bag and the rules were so complex that only experienced gamers could decipher them. Word of the game spread to college campuses with the help of publicity involving a Michigan State University student who was rumored to be lost in the steam tunnels under the campus while playing a "live" "Dungeons and Dragons" game. This potentially negative publicity for "Dungeons and Dragons" turned into an advantage for the company since it created word-of-mouth advertising and interest among college students.

As the product matured, the median age of new buyers dropped from college age to the 10–14-year-old bracket. Typically, these consumers were boys described as introverted, intelligent, nonathletic, and very imaginative. The game provided an outlet for such boys to join in a group activity and helped bring them out of their shells. In fact, educators noted that "Dungeons and Dragons" welds a group of players into an ongoing joint project that teaches participation, assertiveness, and cooperation.

To further increase sales of the product, TSR targeted the product to new consumer groups. For example, at one point, women made up only 12 percent of the total number of purchasers. TSR conducted consumer research and found that women felt the game was created as a release for "macho" fantasies. Many women also stated that the lengthy instruction manual (63 pages) would take too long to read and be wasteful of their time. In response to such perceptions, TSR (1) publicized the fact that the game is not cutthroat and competitive, (2) reduced the length of the instruction manual, and (3) created a game which can be played in a limited amount of time. TSR also targeted downward to the younger children's market with a product that transferred the "Dungeons and Dragons" theme to a more conventional board game called "Dungeons!"

Expansion of Product Lines

Initially, the basic "Dungeons and Dragons" set was marketed as a hobby, rather than as a game. A hobby involves a starter toy, which is enhanced with a myriad of add-ons. For example, a miniature train is considered a hobby since the engine and track form the basis for building an entire railroad system, including special cars, track, scenery, stations, and so on over time. Similarly, for each $12 basic "Dungeons and Dragons" set sold, retailers could expect an additional $150 in satellite or captive product purchases in the form of modules that provide supplemental adventures of varying complexity. There were at least 50 such satellite products on the market.

Since TSR management recognized that their short product line was vulnerable to competition from such toy and game giants as Mattell, Parker Brothers, Milton Bradley, and Ideal, several other new products were introduced to extend the line. Most of these new introductions followed the role-playing, fantasy theme. For example, since each fantasy world in a "Dungeons and Dragons" game has its own set of characters and monsters, a line of miniature lead figurines of these creatures was introduced. These included miniature dragons, wizards, and dwarfs. Although these figures are not necessary to play the game, it was hoped that a market of figurine collectors would develop.

TSR also marketed a number of other role-playing games, including "Top Secret," a spy adventure game; "Boot Hill," a western adventure game; "Gamma World," a futuristic game; and "Star Frontiers," a science fiction game, all of which were quite successful. Somewhat less successful have been TSR's other board game entrants, "Snit's Revenge," "The Awful Green Things from Outer Space," "Escape from New York," and "Dungeons!" These more conventional board games were intended to change the company's image from that of a producer of complex, esoteric games to a producer of a broader range of game products.

TSR also added new lines to their product mix. For example, they produced a feature-length film using a "Dungeons and Dragons" theme, as well as a successful Saturday morning cartoon program for children and an hour-long pilot for a radio-theater program.

TSR's other ventures included purchase of *Amazing* magazine, the oldest science fiction magazine on the market (since 1926), and publishing *Dragon* magazine, which began in 1976 and obtained a circulation of over 70,000 copies per issue. The Dragon Publishing division of TSR also produced calendars and anthologies of fiction, nonfiction, and humor. TSR's most popular publications included *Endless Quest* books. Young readers determine the plot of these stories by making choices for the main character. Depending on the choices made, the reader is directed to different pages in the book. Therefore, each book contains a number of different adventure stories. TSR also developed a line of books called

Heart Quest, which are romance novels for teenagers in this same create-your-own-plot format. TSR had performed consulting services for a failing needlework company owned by a friend of Gygax. To further its diversification efforts TSR acquired this company briefly, realizing soon, however, that it was a poor investment.

TSR found licensing to be a profitable form of product line expansion. Arrangements were made to permit 14 companies to market products that displayed the TSR and "Dungeons and Dragons" name. For example, Mattel, Inc., was sold a license for an electronic version of "Dungeons and Dragons," and St. Regis Paper Company was sold a license for a line of notebooks and school supplies.

Expansion of Promotional Activities

In the beginning, TSR relied on word-of-mouth advertising among gamers to sell the "Dungeons and Dragons" game. As their markets expanded, TSR employed other promotional methods, including television commercials and four-color magazine ads. TSR's ad budget in 1981 was $1,194,879, which was divided as follows: 13 percent on trade magazines, 28 percent on consumer magazines, and 59 percent on spot television. During the Christmas season of 1982, $1 million was spent on a television campaign for the "Dungeons!" board game.

The company's logo and accompanying slogan were updated in 1982. Formerly, the logo showed a wizard next to the letters TSR and the slogan "The Game Wizards." The updated logo included a stylized version of the letters "TSR" and the slogan "Products of the Imagination." This updated logo and slogan were designed to convey an image with broader market appeal.

TSR sponsored an annual gamers convention, which attracted dozens of manufacturers and thousands of attendees to Kenosha, Wisconsin. This became the largest role-playing convention is the world, which included four days of movies, demonstrations, tournaments, seminars, and manufacturers' exhibits. The company also sponsored the Role Playing Game Association. This association offered newsletters and informational services and was responsible for calculating international scoring points to rate players in official tournaments. It also provided a gift catalog of premiums available only to RPGA members.

In the beginning, the printing and artwork needed for the "Dungeons and Dragons" instruction booklet were contracted with suppliers outside of TSR. The company has since engaged in backward vertical integration into the manufacturing process by hiring a staff of artists and purchasing its own printing facility.

Expansion of Distribution Channels

Retail distribution was originally concentrated in hobby stores but expanded rapidly into department stores and bookstores, although some mass market retailers such as Sears, Penney, and Kmart were reluctant to stock all of the satellite products generated by the basic "Dungeons and Dragons" set. This evolution from exclusive distribution through hobby stores to intensive distribution followed naturally from the concomitant expansion of target markets and product lines.

Over time TSR employed as many as 15 manufacturers' representatives who marketed the product through independent wholesalers in nine territories. One problem with this distribution system was that the company did not have close contact with its wholesalers, and hence, was not able to offer much merchandising assistance.

TSR opened its own retail hobby shop for a brief period. However, this outlet attracted a lot of mail order business, creating channel conflict among other retail hobby outlets, and the shop was closed in 1984.

EXPANSION PROBLEMS

TSR obviously grew quickly and expanded in many different directions, which caused several problems. For example, TSR announced it would hire over 100 new employees and 50 new hires were actually made in June of 1983. However, by April of 1984, over 230 employees were laid off. The rapid loss of personnel resulted in coordination problems. For example, two different products were packaged in boxes with identical graphics on the covers. The layoffs also created morale problems.

In an effort to "tighten the reigns," Keven Blume eliminated half of the company's 12 divisions to streamline accounting, reporting, and general decision making. TSR was then divided into four separate companies: TSR Inc. for publishing games and books, TSR Ventures Inc. for supervising trademark licensing, TSR Worldwide Ltd. for managing international sales, and Dungeons and Dragons Entertainment Corporation for producing cartoons. Each company functioned independently of the

EXHIBIT 2
Positioning Map

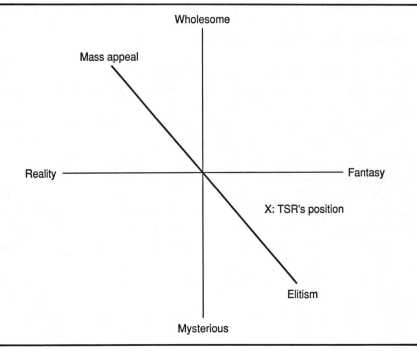

others, with its own stock and board of directors. Still, the three partners sat on all four boards in order to maintain tight control over the company.

TSR's full-fledged entry into the mass market also drained their cash reserves, creating cash flow problems for the company. Business practices in the mass market were different than what TSR was accustomed to in the specialized hobby market. For example, it is common to cater to mass retailers by allowing six months for payment, whereas 30 days or less is more usual for small hobby shops. Also, demand is relatively smooth in the hobby market unlike the mass market, which experiences a Christmas buying rush. Thus, TSR was not prepared for the retail Christmas buying rush and many items ordered were out of stock.

TSR also faced an image problem in the mass market, illustrated in the positioning map shown in Exhibit 2. The early success of "Dungeons and Dragons" depended largely upon its image as a mysterious hobby that was not for just anyone, but only for an elite few. Because of this image, many consumers in the mass market were convinced that the "Dungeons and Dragons" game was "bad for the mind" because it involved hours and hours of make-believe. Dr. Joyce Brothers was engaged to endorse the product and to legitimize its role-playing format. In supporting the product she pointed to research results illustrating that children who played "Dungeons and Dragons" developed better reading skills, math skills, and basic logic and problem-solving skills.

TSR faced formidable competition in the mass market. Large companies such as Milton Bradley, Mattel, and Parker Brothers spent more on advertising each year than TSR earned in profits. However, TSR's fantasy/role-playing concept was unique. Only Mattel's "He Man" and "Masters of the Universe" could be remotely compared to TSR's product concept. While the other traditional toy and game giants had no comparable fantasy/role-playing games, they dominated the northwest quadrant of the map in Exhibit 2, the market TSR wanted to enter. Though TSR was a market leader in fantasy/role-playing games in the hobby market, it remained to be seen whether this type of product could gain a respectable share of the mass market.

LESSONS FOR THE MANUFACTURER

TSR Hobbies, Inc., made a big splash in the specialized hobby market Upper management's intimate understanding of the product and hobby enthusiasts contributed to TSR's tremendous initial success. However, entry into the mass market resulted in serious problems for an inexperienced management team.

Many of the problems the company faced can be understood by examining the differences between manufacturing and marketing to specialized hobby shops versus large discount stores. In terms of products, a full product line is beneficial for attracting middlemen and large retailers, whereas a few specialized items are sufficient for small hobby shops. However, manufacturing a broader line of products requires greater skill in organizing, scheduling production runs, and managing inventory.

In terms of pricing and channels, the indirect channel, which included distributors, wholesalers, and retailers, required changes in pricing strategy to accommodate margins at each level. In addition, large retailers often exact greater demands for financing, discounting, and other services than small retailers. Selling through large discount stores likely caused channel conflict with the small hobby shops and invited direct competition with large toy manufacturing companies.

In terms of promotion, more broadcast and more expensive advertising that reaches a broader market is needed to reach the mass market, and in-store promotions and displays are also required. In addition, when the company sold directly to hobby shops, its salespeople could explain games carefully to hobby shop owners and employees, who could then answer any questions consumers might have. With the indirect channels used, store personnel likely knew little or nothing about the games. Finally, the games doubtless lost some of their mysterious and elitist nature once they were promoted to the mass market.

The expansion into the mass market also caused a number of problems internally for TSR. For example, the organizational structure changed dramatically, causing operating inefficiencies. Employee turnover increased and employee morale plummeted due to mismanagement and nepotism. Production became less dependable, leading to problems such as 90,000 copies of a board game being folded the wrong way and two games being packed in boxes with identical graphics. Production and inventory problems also increased since demand fluctuated greatly as discount stores stocked up to meet the Christmas buying rush.

Overall, this case is an excellent example of what can happen when a company grows too fast with an inexperienced management team. Serious problems arose in marketing, manufacturing, finance, and human resources. Although the company obtained huge sales increases during these years as shown in Exhibit 1, it has not maintained its presence in the mass market. The case makes clear the importance of careful planning and coordination between functional areas, particularly when a company is making a radical strategy change.

CASE 3

CATERPILLAR TRACTOR COMPANY*

INTRODUCTION

In January 1984, Caterpillar Tractor Co. Chairman Lee L. Morgan was actively involved in corporate-wide planning efforts. These efforts were directed at reestablishing Caterpillar's tradition of profitability and world leadership in the heavy equipment and machinery industry. Looking to the coming year, he reported:

> 1984 should be a markedly better year. The 1983 loss of $345 million reflected the deep recession in most of the world's economies. Current indicators suggest . . . strong sales increases for our kinds of products. Sales should be significantly higher in 1984, and we expect to be profitable.

By year end, it was anticipated, specific plans detailing actions on new business opportunities would be completed and long-term sales and profit strategies would be identified, effective through 1995.

HISTORY

Headquartered in Peoria, Illinois, and currently the largest multinational company that designs, manufactures, and markets construction equipment, machinery, engines, and parts, Caterpillar's roots date back to the

*This case was prepared by Donald W. Eckrich, Associate Professor and Chairman, Department of Marketing, Ithaca College, as the basis for class discussion rather than to illustrate either effective or ineffective handling of administrative situations and problems. A special thanks for their invaluable assistance throughout the preparation of this case is due Charles F. Maier and Barbara A. Wright.

late 19th century and the evolution of mechanized agricultural equipment. In February 1889, Daniel Best introduced the first steam-powered harvester, replacing the 40-horse-drawn combine with an 8-man, 11-ton, self-propelled tractor using 8-foot wheels. Shortly thereafter, Benjamin Holt began field testing the first crawler-type equipment, built simply by replacing the wheels on existing equipment with new "track" structures— pairs of treads comprised of wooden slats linked loosely together.

Driven by increasing demand in agriculture, road building, military equipment, and industrial construction, the two companies prospered. The introduction of the internal combustion engine provided yet another boost for the evolving heavy equipment industry.

In 1925, the Holt and Best Companies merged to form Caterpillar Tractor Co., thereby setting the stage for several decades of dramatic and systematic growth through technological leadership and new applications in the emerging equipment and machinery industry. Agricultural applications quickly gave way to forestry opportunities, which in turn gave way to oil field and highway operations.

In 1931, the first Caterpillar Diesel Tractor was introduced. This product initiated an incredible six-year sales growth spurt from $13 million to $63 million and launched the track-type tractor into prominence as the single largest user of diesel power.

Caterpillar's growing reputation for industry leadership and technological superiority was further strengthened during World War II by U.S. government defense contracts. These contracts included demand for both existing equipment (e.g., bulldozers and graders) and special government requests for revolutionary and sophisticated equipment such as air-cooled diesel engines for advanced military operations.

Throughout the postwar years, the Korean conflict, and into the 1970s, Caterpillar generally concentrated on the development of large, industrial-sized machines and engines. In 1944, Caterpillar announced its plans to build a line of matched earthmoving equipment, and quickly found a receptive and profitable market. Later, in 1951, the Trackson Company of Milwaukee was purchased to produce hoists, pipe layers, and hydraulically operated tractor shovels for Caterpillar crawlers. In 1965, Towmotor Corporation was acquired, continuing the expansion into heavy equipment with forklift trucks and straddle carriers for a wide range of materials handling in industrial, shipping, warehousing, and other markets. Thus, by the early 1970s, Caterpillar had achieved at least foothold positions in a variety of heavy equipment product lines, with the objective of achieving industry leadership in each of the new areas.

In 1977, Caterpillar unveiled the single-largest, most technologically advanced tractor in the world—the D-10. Foremost among its advantages were (1) an elevated drive sprocket and (2) modular-designed major components. The elevation of the drive sprocket removed it from high-wear and shock-load areas, reduced overall stress on the undercarriage, and produced a smoother ride. The modular design of major components not only permitted faster and more efficient servicing, but also provided the opportunity to pretest components before final assembly. Modular designs thereby reduced repair and overall downtime in some cases by as much as 80 percent. Perhaps most significant regarding the D-10 and its modular-designed components was the extent to which they reflected the intense product quality and service orientations adhered to throughout Cat's history. It had long been assumed by management that industrial users' needs would best be served through the progress of technology, largely irrespective of the effects on pricing.

Only four years later, in 1981, several more years of research and development were capped off with the introduction of a 16-cylinder, 1,600 horsepower, 1,200 kilowatt engine—also stressing modular design and repair convenience. In early 1982, a new D8L crawler tractor was introduced, the third in a series of crawler tractors to employ the elevated sprocket. Finally, several other technological advances previously introduced on smaller, track-type loaders were extended to larger models, thereby permitting the relocation of the engine to the rear and, correspondingly, improving balance, operator visibility, and serviceability.

Thus, over several decades, Caterpillar Tractor Co. managed to establish a pace-setting position in the heavy equipment industry by focusing directly on state-of-the-art technology and continuous product redesign. Specifically, concern for increased *user productivity* through greater equipment capacities, enhanced reliability, and quicker serviceability contributed most heavily to Cat's success and superior image. Maintenance of this leadership position across numerous product lines has also translated into the industry's highest prices.

MANUFACTURING AND WAREHOUSING

Caterpillar manufactures products in two principal categories: (1) machines and parts (M&Ps), which includes track-type machinery like bulldozers, tractors, rippers, and track-loaders, as well as several wheel-type machines such as motor graders, loaders, off-highway trucks, and tractor-

EXHIBIT 1
Consolidated Sales and Profit Data

	1983	1982	1981	1980	1979
Sales	$5,424	$6,469	$9,154	$8,598	$7,613
Profit (loss) for year-consolidated	$ (345)	$ (180)	$ 579	$ 565	$ 492
Profit (loss) per share of common stock	$ (3.74)	$ (2.04)	$ 6.64	$ 6.53	$ 5.69
Return on average common stock equity	(10.1)%	(4.9)%	15.9%	17.4%	16.9%
Dividends paid per share of common stock	$ 1.50	$ 2.40	$ 2.40	$2,325	$ 2.10
Current ratio at year-end	2.15 to 1	2.87 to 1	1.50 to 1	1.71 to 1	1.88 to 1
Total assets at year-end	$6,968	$7,201	$7,285	$6,098	$5,403
Long-term debt due after one year at year-end	$1,894	$2,389	$ 961	$ 932	$ 952
Capital expenditures for land, buildings, machinery, and equipment	$ 324	$ 534	$ 836	$ 749	$ 676
Depreciation and amortization	$ 506	$ 505	$ 448	$ 370	$ 312

Source: Caterpillar Tractor Company Annual Report, 1983.

284

scrapers; and (2) engines, used to power a variety of equipment for highway, marine, petroleum, agricultural, industrial, and electric power generation applications, ranging from diesel to natural gas and turbines. The category of M&Ps, it should be noted, includes all related parts and equipment for all of the machines. Exhibits 1, 2, 3, and 4 present sales, profit, and other financial data for the years 1979 to 1983.

EXHIBIT 2
Total Sales by Category (billions)

	1983	1982	1981	1980	1979
Inside the United States					
Machines and parts	$2.08	$1.84	$2.62	$2.84	N/A
Engines and parts	.85	.96	1.35	.85	N/A
Total inside	$2.93	$2.80	$3.97	$3.69	$3.51
Outside the United States					
Machines and parts	$2.08	$2.92	$4.48	$4.36	N/A
Engines and parts	.41	.75	.70	.55	N/A
Total outside	$2.49	$3.67	$5.28	$4.91	$4.10
By country (millions)					
Africa/Mid East	$ 680	$1,062	$1,886	$1,282	$ 960
Europe	771	927	993	1,267	1,153
Asia/Pacific	515	800	927	922	764
Latin America	266	637	903	879	716
Canada	262	239	472	563	505
Combined totals	$5.42	$6.47	$9.15	$8.60	$7.60

EXHIBIT 3
Research and Engineering Costs (in millions)

	1983	1982	1981	1980	1979	1978
New product development and major project improvements	n.a.*	$230	$227	$200	$191	$160
Other—general	n.a.*	$146	$136	$126	$ 92	$ 96
Total	$340	$376	$363	$326	$283	$256
Percent of sales	6.3%	5.8%	3.9%	3.8%	3.7%	3.6%

*n.a. = Not available.

EXHIBIT 4
Heavy Equipment and Machinery Manufacturer Earnings (in millions)

	1983	1982	1981	1980	1979
Caterpillar Tractor Co.	($ 345)	($ 180)	$ 579	$ 565	$ 492
International Harvester*	($ 539)	($1,738)	($ 393)	($ 397)	$ 369
Deere*	($.052)	($ .039)	$.250	$.228	$.310
Allis-Chalmers	($ 133)	($ 207)	($ 28)	$ 47	$ 81
Clark Equipment	($.012)	($ .155)	$.029	$.051	$.106

---

*Fiscal year ends October 31—latest year's figures are estimates. Losses indicated in ( ).
Source (in part): Harlan S. Byrne, "For Heavy Equipment Makers, Recovery to Be Delayed Another Year," *The Wall Street Journal*, November 3, 1982.

Manufacturing and warehousing activities take place worldwide through 22 plants in the United States and several wholly or partly owned subsidiaries located in Australia, Belgium, Brazil, Canada, France, Japan, India, Indonesia, Mexico, and the United Kingdom. Each international location has been carefully selected to provide significant cost advantages by reducing global transportation costs, eliminating duty applicable to U.S.-built machinery, and by capitalizing on the manufacturing cost advantage derived from lower foreign wage levels. Such trends, it should be noted, have not been without some repercussions. The United Automobile Workers, for instance, representing over 80 percent of Cat's stateside hourly employees, is ever alert to this threat to their jobs and has become vitally concerned and quite vocal regarding possible extensions of foreign plants.

In addition, major warehouses and emergency parts depots are strategically located throughout the world. As a result, these combined facilities form a worldwide organizational network that attempts to maximize Caterpillar's flexibility and customer responsiveness. All parts manufactured by any one plant are completely interchangeable with the same parts manufacturerd by any other plant. Thus, replacement parts are generally available on extremely short notice wherever Caterpillar machines are deployed throughout the world. In short, all dealers and customers recognize Cat's parts and distribution as one of the two or three major advantages of owning Cat equipment. Heavy equipment purchasers widely acknowledge that no other firm in the industry can touch Cat in this category.

DEALERS

Recognized as the strongest in the industry, Caterpillar's dealer network handles all sales and service worldwide, with the exception of direct sales to the U.S. government, the Soviet Union, and the People's Republic of China, which are handled by a subsidiary division of Cat known as CIPI (Caterpillar Industrial Products, Inc.). Comprised of 213 independent dealers (84 in the United States), Caterpillar dealers represent an enterprise almost as large as the company. They operate 1,050 sales, parts, and service outlets in more than 140 countries, employ about 75,000 people, and have a combined net worth of approximately $3.1 billion. A typical dealership sells and services Caterpillar equipment exclusively, represents an average net worth of approximately $12 million, and is likely in a second or third generation of affiliation. Industry estimates place the capitalization of Caterpillar's dealer network at 10 times that of any competitor.

With Caterpillar's sales and service activities outside the direct control of Caterpillar executives, increasing efforts have been directed at improving service to dealers and informing users of the advantages of Caterpillar products. In 1978, a computerized dealer terminal system was completed, which linked dealers and Caterpillar facilities to the European parts distribution department in Belgium. Essentially it provided direct computer access for ordering and locating parts for dealers in Europe, Africa, and the Middle East. In 1979, more than 3,000 consumers and dealer personnel attended Caterpillar-sponsored seminars, 47,000 visitors viewed Caterpillar products and manufacturing operations, and representatives from 26 countries attended a week-long International Agricultural Seminar.

Comparable levels of seminar and visitation activity can be noted throughout the past few years, further promoting selective demand to both engine and equipment users. In one instance, 400 representatives of energy-related mining operations attended a seminar held at a West Virginia coal mine, which not only highlighted the use of Cat machines, but, perhaps more importantly, the dealers' capabilities to support special needs of mine operators. In another instance, in order to demonstrate dealer commitment to servicing the on-highway truck industry, Cat co-sponsored the National Fuel Economy Challenge, a competition open to owners of new trucks equipped with Caterpillar 3406 and 3408 Economy Engines. Results confirmed impressive fuel economy statistics for

Caterpillar engines and provided hands-on exposure to dealer support facilities.

In what was called "target marketing" by Cat executives, the predominant dealer support theme during the past few years has begun to focus dealer efforts on special end-user groups. U.S. dealers brought over 1,000 owners of competitive equipment to Peoria to learn about Cat equipment, its advantages and capabilities, as well as to actually operate Cat equipment. In another program, "Build Your Future," small machine owners, unfamiliar with the differential advantages of Caterpillar equipment and dealer support capabilities, were instructed on various general business topics and specific Caterpillar operations capabilities including equipment maintenance. Factory tours and machine demonstrations were also provided.

In 1983, the continuing efforts to improve service to users and dealers achieved a milestone with a major restructuring of the company's marketing organizations in the United States and Far East. The changes generally consisted of moving from a centralized, functional organization to a geographically dispersed, marketing-oriented team structure. As a result, the new structure recognizes the growing diversity of competition and product applications and the need for more individually tailored programs. It is more responsive to dealer needs and opportunities, shortens the lines of communication, and speeds up vital decision-making processes. As a result, Caterpillar's dealer organization has become widely regarded and consistently mentioned by customers as a prime reason for purchasing Cat equipment and represents Cat's single largest advantage over all competitors, both in the United States and internationally.

RESEARCH AND ENGINEERING

Improving quality and technological leadership have long been key ingredients of Caterpillar's long-term growth strategy. In a 1983 statement to stockholders, Chairman Morgan asserted, "We will not allow our product leadership to be diminished." Expenditures for research and engineering (R&E) have consistently ranked number one in the industry, and have permitted Caterpillar to develop state-of-the-art products, manufacturing processors, and apparatus. In 1982, for example, expenditures for R&E reached a record $376 million (data on other recent research and engineering expenditures appear in Exhibit 3). As a result, Caterpillar's product leadership is not only widely recognized, but manufacturing facilities, as well, are considered the most modern and best equipped in the industry.

A carryover of this commitment to product leadership is the general practice of passing along specific product advances as soon as reliably feasible rather than accumulating several modifications and incorporating them all simultaneously in periodic model changes. Not only would the latter fail to permit the entire line to be completely up-to-date at all times, but it would also fail to ensure maximum sales opportunities for existing, but aging, products. As an example of the success of this market penetration strategy, a simple addition of rubber grousers on tractors used primarily for log skidding created 200 immediate new machine sales for other agricultural users.

COMPETITION

As a result of decades of domination of the heavy equipment and construction industry, Caterpillar has an estimated 45–50 percent share for earthmoving machinery in the U.S. market and roughly 30–35 percent of the market worldwide. Mr. Morgan readily admits the toughest competition facing Caterpillar is from Komatsu Ltd., of Tokyo, which has rapidly grown to second place in worldwide sales. In addition, considerable domestic competitive pressures come from J. I. Case, Inc., and Deere & Company, considered number two and number three, respectively.

In 1981, the president of Komatsu Ltd. stated a goal of achieving 20 percent of the U.S. market within five years; the company has succeeded in boosting market share from approximately 2 percent in 1974 to 15 percent in 1983. Komatsu is gaining sales basically in selected markets such as specialty bulldozers (i.e., including amphibians and remote-controlled units especially for underground use), and in equipment larger than Caterpillar's largest. Number one in terms of the latter is Komatsu's 1,000 Hp. tractor bulldozer, which far surpasses Cat's biggest, the D-10 with only 700 Hp. In these specialty areas, Komatsu does particularly well. Projections are that Komatsu Ltd., as a result of aggressiveness, adaptability, and a number of complex economic factors, will continue to encroach into the U.S. market largely at the expense (or demise) of many smaller competitors. As one industry analyst put it, "When elephants fight, the grass dies."

Nevertheless, despite claims of durability and efficiency that rival Caterpillar, Komatsu probably will not match the current sales of Cat in the United States. With approximately 670 part-time dealerships in America (i.e., those who sell Komatsu and other manufacturers' equipment simultaneously), and several competitive handicaps in the United States, such as ocean freight costs and narrow product lines, Komatsu cannot compete head-to-head with Cat. Thus the company initially adopted a strategy of allying itself, through joint-venture subsidiaries, with International Harvester (IH) and Bucyrus-Eire (B-E) to manufacture wheeled vehicles and excavators. In 1980, Komatsu bought out B-E with financial assistance provided directly by Japan's Fair Trade Commission and, in 1982, IH's share of the joint venture was also purchased. Thus, domestic entrance for Komatsu has been achieved through limited and well-conceived flanking attacks providing American-based manufacturing facilities and distribution links.

The U.S. presence of Komatsu, however, is considered by industry analysts more a matter of competitive visibility than an operational threat to Caterpillar's leadership position. The most direct threats to Caterpillar's domestic markets are J. I. Case and John Deere & Co. J. I. Case has an estimated 35 percent share of the earthmoving equipment market and John Deere has an estimated 30 percent share of the farm-machinery market.

However, each of these organizations, as well as several others (Allis-Chalmers, Clark Equipment, Harnischfeger Corp., IH, and Massey-Ferguson), has been undergoing considerable upheaval as a result of the early 1980s worldwide recession (see Exhibit 4 for performance data from selected competitors). As one analyst put it:

> Producers of construction, farm, and other heavy equipment have been in varying degrees of recession . . . and had expected recovery to start by now. Instead, widespread weakness is showing up, and companies are awash in red ink.
>
> Executives and analysts have been surprised by the depths and breadth of the slump. In past recessions, declines in some markets have been at least partly offset by strengths in others. Not so today. Practically all major markets are weak. For instance, the collapse of the oil and gas drilling boom and the financial problems of many countries weren't anticipated.

And the farm depression has been deeper and more prolonged than machinery makers expected.[1]

Thus, although Caterpillar has probably fared better than the other firms, the most significant domestic problem for Caterpillar is the delay in the recovery of the market.

Internationally, and despite the worldwide slump, Komatsu Ltd. is Caterpillar's single largest and growing competitor with 15 percent share of the *world market* (second only to Caterpillar), and 60 percent of the Japanese market. Cat accounts for roughly 50 percent of the world market but only 30 percent of the Japanese market (Caterpillar Mitsubishi).

Typical of many Japanese manufacturing firms, Komatsu's competitive thrust focuses directly on a long-term strategy to equal or exceed Caterpillar's position. Considering Cat vulnerable to superior managerial efficiency and operating flexibility, Komatsu's broad marketing strategy has emphasized expanding market share, largely on the basis of lower prices and efforts to match Caterpillar's follow-up service and parts capabilities. The slogan "Maru-C," is widely acknowledged as one of Komatsu's greatest challenges—to "engulf Caterpillar." Komatsu offers customers prices up to 15 percent below Caterpillar and endeavors to accommodate every conceivable special heavy equipment need through continual *adaptation* of existing products. In one instance, special equipment was developed exclusively for the particular needs of Australian coal miners. In another instance, an electric-powered bulldozer was developed for a small number of contractors whose special needs required them to operate equipment within legal noise limits.

Determined to produce the world's best earthmoving equipment, Komatsu executives lay claim to offering superior equipment in terms of power, durability, and lower fuel consumption.[2] Indeed, considerable evidence is available to support such claims, and industrial customers have responded to Komatsu's discount pricing and manufacturing flexibility. In terms of follow-up support, Komatsu maintains a crew of salespeople (engineers), ready to fly anywhere in the world to solve Komatsu

---

[1]Harlan S. Byrne, "For Heavy Equipment Makers, Recovery to Be Delayed Another Year," *The Wall Street Journal,* November 3, 1982.

[2]Bernard Krisher, "Komatsu on the Track of Cat," *Fortune,* April 20, 1981, pp.14–74.

equipment problems. Within the United States, Komatsu maintains five regional centers to directly support dealer efforts.

OTHER PROBLEMS

The suddenness of Caterpillar's 1982 $180 million loss, the first in 50 years, found President Robert E. Gilmore and Chairman Lee Morgan stunned and hopeful of a quick return to profitability. In a 1983 joint address to stockholders they reported:

> We hope that the worldwide economic malaise is coming to an end, and that people will soon be able to return to more normal lives.
>
> The economy will recover, and the world will need capital goods of the kinds made by Caterpillar. Roads will be built . . . ore and coal will be mined . . . fields will be cleared and dams constructed . . . oil and gas will be produced. These and other applications for our products are essential to a growing world population.
>
> Our concern isn't whether demand will revive and grow. It will.

However, by early 1984 Caterpillar's troubles were beginning to prove far more pervasive and devastating than first thought.

In retrospect, several contributing factors began emerging as much as five years earlier, and not without Caterpillar's awareness. For instance, as the only manufacturer of pipelayers in the United States, Caterpillar was particularly hard hit by President Carter's 1979 "high tech" export control measures against the Soviet Union. Caterpillar was on the verge of a multimillion (perhaps billion) dollar contract with the Soviet Union for 2,000 heavy tractors at approximately $500,000 each and hundreds of pipelayers at $250,000 each. However, the export control measures ended this opportunity and the sale went to Komatsu.

Later in 1979, additional clouds surfaced. As a result of ever increasing oil prices, worldwide economic growth abruptly halted. Adding to the U.S. problems, the growing and unprecedented international trade deficits of the 1970s prompted ever higher interest rates and greater uncertainty regarding the future of the international trading system, and contributed significantly to inflation. The Consumer Price Index in 1979 was up 13 percent and Chairman Morgan noted, "inflation has become deeply embedded," and "solutions will neither be simple nor quick."

By 1981, effects of the world's economic recession began to appear at Caterpillar as physical sales volume declined "moderately"—as the company called it. Slowdowns in the world markets, considered the most significant long-term growth opportunities for heavy construction equipment manufacturers, were particularly difficult to manage insofar as the U.S. competitive posture was slumping in general. Unlike the embargo against the Soviet Union, some developing world markets were being diminished by a variety of anti-U.S. export/import restrictions issued by developing countries themselves. Loss of accessibility to such markets, restricted information flows, and the growing trend in foreign government subsidies were leaving Caterpillar in a hopeful, but retrospective, position, as noted in a joint letter to stockholders by Chairman Morgan and President Gilmore:

> We have a competitive edge. . . . Outside authorities frequently confirm that ours is the preferred product.
>
> Our very substantial capital investment and research and engineering programs . . . should help us maintain a technological lead . . . .
>
> Toward that end, we seek the renewed commitment of Caterpillar people everywhere.

Unfortunately, throughout 1982, conditions continued to deteriorate. After the first quarter of operations, management began imposing numerous temporary plant shutdowns and indefinite layoffs. Domestic interest rates were sufficiently high to cause most U.S. capital spending to be abandoned. Worldwide, the previous decade of accelerated oil explorations and refinement had resulted in overproduction such that oil prices also began to slump, which further resulted in reduced energy development and construction. Facing the unprecedented reduction in practically all markets simultaneously, Caterpillar experienced a 29 percent sales decline, and reported the first loss in common stock prices in 50 years. Common stock prices plunged from $55–$60 per share in 1981 to $35 per share in 1982.

On October 1, 1982, the United Auto Workers Union struck (20,400 members or roughly 80 percent of Cat's active, U.S. hourly employees), seeking an extension of the existing contract. For almost 30 years, the UAW labor contract had established a pattern that provided workers with automatic annual 3 percent wage increases. Management now resisted these increases because the increase in labor costs would make it even more difficult to compete. Recent data, for instance, placed Cat's per capita U.S. labor costs at roughly twice those of Japanese firms.

Throughout 1983, even well after the labor settlement, ripple effects of the dispute continued to emerge. Inventory shortages of both parts and equipment resulted in lost sales, lost good will, and a considerable strain on efforts to return to profitability. These efforts included reductions in expenditures for perhaps Cat's most sacred budget item—research and engineering—as well as the second annual cut in the capital expenditures budget—from $836 million in 1981, down to $324 million in 1983. These cost-cutting efforts resulted in layoffs and plant closings leaving employment figures at the end of 1983 markedly reduced from previous years. Hourly employees, reduced in 1982 by 21,501, dropped another 624 in 1983, while the number of salaried employees was cut 3,077 and 2,585 in these two years.

The combination of a deteriorating worldwide economic climate and postsettlement reconstruction efforts required management to assume an adaptive posture while long-term solutions were worked out. Perhaps most noteworthy in this regard is the Cost Reduction Program (CRP), aimed at positioning Cat's 1986 cost levels more than 20 percent below those of 1981 (in constant dollars adjusted for volume). These cost reductions were intended to be *permanent* and included plant closings, new applications of computer and scientific technology, inventory reduction programs, and faster deliveries from suppliers. At the end of 1983 considerable efforts were being directed at achieving a scaled-down, more efficient organization.

The achievement of a long-term, strategic growth perspective has captured management's attention. Beginning in late 1982, management initiated efforts to focus planning specifically on future opportunities in diesel, natural gas, and turbine engines, and to review the basic role of the lift truck in Cat's product mix. In 1983, Caterpillar management held a Business Strategy Conference, which developed specific objectives along with a timetable for activities through 1995. The plan involves what are designed to be the most productive means of "establishing, confirming, or modifying current strategies for . . . existing business; developing, evaluating, recommending, and selecting for implementation 'new' strategic growth opportunities; and developing corporate goals consistent with the findings and decisions produced by the conference."

Based on this planning, U.S. dealers recently launched a marketing program targeted at non-Caterpillar owners. Recognizing the strategic growth opportunities associated with market development, this program, called PLUS 3, provided a means for end users of competitors' equipment to gauge the superiority of CAT *dealers* in after-sales parts support and service. Specifically, the program guaranteed a 48-hour repair turnaround or the customer would be given a machine to use from the dealer's rental fleet, and a 48-hour parts delivery or the customer would receive the part free! It also included one of the most extensive power train warranties in the industry—36 months or 5,000 hours, whichever came first. Results of PLUS 3 were quite favorable, most notably among small- and medium-sized machine owners.

As a result of additional analyses regarding the role of the lift truck to Caterpillar, at least one U.S. plant was closed and management began labor negotiations with two non-U.S. production facilities. Indications were quite strong that more and more production throughout the product mix would be moved overseas in the future (e.g., lift trucks to Korea). Identifying future growth opportunities and detailing appropriate marketing strategies for the next decade were seen as becoming more critical as no significant upturn had been experienced through mid-1984, and the future seemed to be even more unstable and uncertain.

LESSONS FOR THE MANUFACTURER

Although Caterpillar Tractor Company might have better anticipated and planned for the tumultuous changes in the environment that led to its huge sales and profit losses, many of the changes were beyond its control. For example, the unprecedented U.S. trade deficits, record levels of inflation, unfavorable foreign exchange differentials and protectionist attitudes in several world markets, financial inadequacies of developing countries, President Carter's "high tech" export control measures, and increased competition from Komatsu were not problems the company brought on itself. While the case does not describe in detail the problems the company has had with labor unions, some question could be raised as to why it has not been able to solve these problems, even today.

The company's business strengths should not be overlooked. Caterpillar produced a technologically superior product line and immediately integrated the latest advances on existing machines. It had the most extensive dealer-service-parts network in the industry, which was recognized by buyers as an important reason for buying Cat equipment. The company held the largest share of domestic and international markets for earth-moving machinery and held the price leadership position in the industry.

However, while the company's introspective and technologically oriented growth philosophy was responsible for many decades of success, the dramatic changes in the external environment in the early 1980s might have signaled a need for change. For example, Komatsu, to a greater degree than Caterpillar, was practicing the marketing concept and total quality management philosophy in that it built custom equipment that met the specialized needs of particular customers and markets.

Overall, this case demonstrates the fact that even a company that produces the best quality products in the industry and has the best service network for them can be threatened by environmental changes. Perhaps the most important lesson to be learned is that no matter how successful an organization is, it must be forward looking and constantly vigilant and prepared for environmental threats and opportunities.

CASE 4

HARLEY-DAVIDSON, INC.—
MOTORCYCLE DIVISION*

Harley-Davidson, Inc. is a diversified company with corporate head-quarter at 3700 Juneau Avenue, Milwaukee, Wisconsin. Its three major business segments include (1) motorcycles and related products, (2) transportation vehicles including both recreational and commercial vehicles, and (3) defense and other businesses. In 1990, the company experienced another record year of growth. In the *Business Week 1000* ranking of the top U.S. companies, Harley-Davidson, Inc., with a market value of $515 million, moved from the 973d to the 865th largest U.S. company. Richard F. Teerlink, president and chief executive officer of the company, offered the following introduction to the company's 1990 annual report:

> Fellow Shareholder: I am again pleased to announce a record year at Harley-Davidson, Inc. in terms of revenues, profits, and earnings. I'm especially proud this year because we were able to deliver very impressive results despite the fact that 1990—the third and fourth quarters, especially—was tough on most American manufacturers.
>
> Revenues for 1990 totaled $864.6 million, an increase of 9.3 percent over 1989. Net income was $37.8 million, a 14.8 percent increase and net earnings per share increased 11.0 percent to $2.12. Since 1987, revenues, net income, and net earnings per share have increased 33.8, 78.3, and 29.3 percent, respectively. Considering where we were as recently as five years ago, these are tremendous results.

Indeed, these were tremendous results given that the company is the only U.S. motorcycle manufacturer still in business, although there were once more than 140 competitors. In addition, the company had tremendous difficulties surviving the 1970s and early 80s and few analysts

---

*This section is based on "How Harley Beat Back the Japanese," *Fortune*, September 25, 1989, pp. 155–64.

thought it would survive. In fact, the company would have gone bankrupt in 1985 had it not gotten refinancing with only days to spare.

COMPANY BACKGROUND AND OPERATIONS

Harley-Davidson was established in 1903 and had a virtual monopoly on the heavyweight motorcycle market by the 1960s.[1] In the early 60s Japanese manufacturers entered the marketplace with lightweight motorcycles that did not directly compete with Harley-Davidson. The influx of the Japanese products backed by huge marketing programs caused the demand for motorcycles to expand rapidly.

Recognizing the potential for profitability in the motorcycle market, American Machine and Foundry (AMF, Inc.) purchased Harley-Davidson in 1969. AMF almost tripled production to 75,000 units annually over a four-year period to meet the increases in demand. Unfortunately, product quality deteriorated significantly as over half the cycles came off the assembly line missing parts, and dealers had to fix them up in order to make sales. Little money was invested in improving design or engineering. The motorcycles leaked oil, vibrated, and could not match the excellent performance of the Japanese products. While hard-core motorcycle enthusiasts were willing to fix up their Harleys and modify them for better performance, new motorcycle buyers had neither the devotion nor skill to do so. If Harley-Davidson was to remain in business, it desperately needed to improve quality and update its engine designs. Japanese manufacturers also moved into the heavyweight motorcycle market and began selling Harley look-alike motorcycles. Yamaha was the first company to do so and was soon followed by the three other major Japanese manufacturers, Honda, Suzuki, and Kawasaki. Their products looked so similar to Harley's that it was difficult to tell the difference without reading the name on the gas tank. The Japanese companies also copied the style of the Harley advertisements. As one Harley executive put it, "We weren't flattered."

In late 1975 AMF appointed Vaughn Beals in charge of Harley-Davidson. He set up a quality control and inspection program that began

---

[1]This section is based on "How Harley Beat Back the Japanese," *Fortune,* September 25, 1989, pp. 155–64.

to eliminate the worst of the production problems. However, the cost of the program was high. For example, the company had to spend about $1,000 extra per bike to get the first hundred into shape for dealers to sell at around $4,000. Beals along with other senior managers began to develop a long-range product strategy—the first time the company had looked 10 years ahead. They recognized the need to upgrade the quality and performance of their products to compete with the faster, high-performance Japanese bikes. However, they also recognized that such changes would require years to accomplish and a huge capital investment.

In order to stay in business while the necessary changes in design and production were being accomplished, the executives turned to William G. Davidson, Harley's styling vice president. Known as "Willie G." and a grandson of one of the company founders, he frequently mingled with bikers and with his beard, black leather, and jeans was well accepted by them. Willie G. understood Harley customers and stated that:

> They really know what they want on their bikes: the kind of instrumentation, the style of bars, the cosmetics of the engine, the look of the exhaust pipes and so on. Every little piece on a Harley is exposed, and it has to look just right. A tube curve or the shape of a timing case can generate enthusiasm or be a total turnoff. It's almost like being in the fashion business.[2]

Willie G. designed a number of new models by combining components from existing models. These included the Super Glide, the Electra Glide, the Wide Glide, and the Low Rider. Each model was successful and other Harley executives credit Davidson's skill with saving the company. One senior executive said of Willie G., "The guy is an artistic genius. In the five years before we could bring new engines on-stream, he performed miracles with decals and paint. A line here and a line there and we'd have a new model. It's what enabled us to survive."

Still Harley-Davidson was losing market share to its Japanese competitors who continued to pour new bikes into the heavyweight market. By 1980, AMF was losing interest in investing in the recreational market and decided to focus its efforts on its industrial product lines. Since AMF could not find a buyer for Harley-Davidson, it sold the company to 13 senior Harley executives in an $81.5 million leveraged buyout financed by Citicorp on June 16, 1981.

---

[2]Ibid., p. 156.

In 1982 things turned worse than ever for Harley-Davidson. Overall demand for motorcycles dropped dramatically and Harley's market share of this smaller market also continued to drop. The company had a large inventory of unsold products and could not continue in business with its level of production and expenses. Production was cut drastically and more than 1,800 of the 4,000 employees were let go.

The Japanese manufacturers continued producing and exporting to the United States at rates well above what the market could endure. Harley-Davidson was able to prove to the International Trade Commission (ITC) that there was an 18-month finished-goods inventory of Japanese motorcycles that fell well below fair market value and asked for protection. The ITC can offer protection to a U.S. industry being threatened by a foreign competitor. In 1983, President Reagan increased the tariffs on large Japanese motorcycles from 4.4 percent to 49.4 percent, but these would decline each year and be effective for only five years. While this did decrease the imports somewhat and gave Harley some protection, Japanese manufacturers found ways to evade most of the tariffs, for example, by assembling more of their heavyweight bikes in their U.S. plants. Harley-Davidson's market share in the 1983 heavyweight motorcycle market slipped to 23 percent, the lowest ever, although it did earn a slight profit. By 1984, it had sales of $294 million and earned $2.9 million; it has continued to increase sales and profits through the early 1990s.

Manufacturing Changes

From the late 1970s Harley-Davidson executives recognized that the only way to achieve the quality of Japanese motorcycles was to adopt many of the manufacturing techniques used by them. The manufacturing systems changes that were instituted included a just-in-time manufacturing program and a statistical operator control system.[3]

The just-in-time manufacturing program was renamed MAN, which stood for Materials As Needed. When the program was discussed with managers and employees at the York, Pennsylvania, manufacturing facility, many of them reacted in disbelief. The York plant already had a

---

[3]This section is based on Thomas Gelb, "Overhauling Corporate Engine Drives Winning Strategy, *Journal of Business Strategy*, November/December 1989, pp. 8–12.

modern computer-based control system with overhead conveyors and high-rise parts store and the new system would replace all of this with push carts! However, the MAN system eliminates the mountains of costly parts inventory and handling systems, speeds up set-up time, and can solve other manufacturing problems. For example, parts at the York facility were made in large batches for long production runs. They were stored until needed and then loaded on a 3.5 mile conveyor that rattled endlessly around the plant. In some cases, parts couldn't be found, or when they were, they were rusted or damaged. In other cases, there had been engineering changes since the parts were made and they simply no longer fit. The MAN system consists of containers that travel between the place where the parts are made and where they are to be used. The containers serve as a signal at each end to either "feed me" or "empty me." This system is credited with reducing work-in-process inventory by $22 million.

The statistical operator control (SOC) system allows continuous process improvements to reduce costs. The system involves teaching machine operators to use simple statistics to analyze measurements taken from parts to determine dimensional accuracy and quality. The system helps identify problems that occur during production early enough that they can be corrected before many parts are produced.

Human Resource Changes

In designing the new manufacturing processes, Harley executives recognized the importance of employee involvement.[4] In 1978 the company was among the first in the United States to institute a companywide employee involvement program. Harley-Davidson was the second U.S. company to begin a quality circles program, which permits employees to contribute their ideas, solve problems, and improve the efficiency and quality of their work. Prior to these changes, engineers would figure out how to improve the manufacturing process and then tell operating employees what changes they needed to make. Naturally, the engineering plans were not flawless but the operating employees would not lift a finger to help solve the problems and would simply blame the engineers for screwing up again.

---

[4]*Fortune*, September 25, 1989, pp. 155–64.

The changes in manufacturing and human resource strategy were credited with a 36 percent reduction in warranty costs; a 46 percent increase in defect-free vehicles received by dealers since 1982; inventory turnover up 500 percent; and productivity per employee up 50 percent.

Marketing Changes

By 1983 Harley executives recognized that they had become too internally oriented and needed to pay greater attention to customers.[5] They recognized that they would not be able to compete effectively with the Japanese manufacturers by offering a complete product line of motorcycles but rather would have to find a niche and defend it successfully. They decided to focus all of their efforts on the superheavyweight motorcycle market (850cc or greater) and adopted a "close-to-the-customer" philosophy. This involved several unique marketing strategies. First, Harley executives actively sought out and discussed motorcycle improvement issues with customers. Second, it started the Harley Owner Group (HOG) to bring together Harley riders and company management in informal settings to expand the social atmosphere of motorcycling. The club is factory-sponsored and is open to all Harley owners. It sponsors national rallies and local events and gives customers a reason to ride a Harley and involves them in a social group whose main activities revolve around the product.

Third, it began a Demo Ride program in which fleets of new Harleys were taken to motorcycle events and rallies and licensed motorcyclists were encouraged to ride them. This program was felt to be critical for convincing potential new customers that Harley-Davidson motorcycles were of excellent quality and not the rattling, leaking bikes of the 1970s. The program was renamed SuperRide and $3 million was committed to it. A series of TV commercials was purchased to invite bikers to come to any of Harley's over 600 dealers for a ride on a new Harley. Over three weekends, 90,000 rides were given to 40,000 people, half of whom owned other brands. While sales from the program did not immediately cover costs, many of the riders came back a year or two later and purchased a Harley.

Fourth, the company invited several manufacturing publications to visit the plant and publish articles on quality improvement programs.

---

[5]Ibid.

These articles reached the manufacturing trade audience and the national media as well. Finally, recognizing that many dealers viewed their business as a hobby and did not know how to sell, the company increased its sales force by 50 percent to give sales representatives more time to train dealers in how to sell Harleys.

Financial Changes

Although Harley-Davidson was improving its quality, reducing its break-even point, catching up with competitors in the superheavyweight market, and marketing more aggressively, Citicorp was concerned about the economy and what would happen to Harley-Davidson when the tariffs on Japanese bikes were lifted in 1988.[6] The bank decided it wanted to recover its loans and quit being a source of funds for the company. After a number of negotiations, Citicorp took a $10 million write-off, which might have facilitated Harley obtaining new financing. However, other bankers felt that the company must have been in really bad shape if Citicorp took a write-off and refused financial assistance. While lawyers were drawing up a bankruptcy plan, Harley executives continued to seek refinancing. Finally, several banks did agree to pay off Citicorp and refinance the company with $49.5 million.

Harley-Davidson went public with a stock sale on the American Stock Exchange in 1986. The company hoped to raise an additional $65 million and obtained over $90 million with the sale of common stock and high-yielding bonds. It then was in an excellent cash position and purchased Holiday Rambler Corporation, at that time the largest privately held recreational vehicle company in the United States. Holiday Rambler is similar to Harley-Davidson in that it is a niche marketer that produces premium-priced products for customers whose lives revolve around their recreational activities. In 1987 the company moved to the New York Stock Exchange and made two additional stock market offerings. Selected financial data for Harley-Davidson is contained in Exhibits 1 through 4.

By 1987, Harley-Davidson was doing so well that it asked to have the tariffs on Japanese bikes removed a year ahead of schedule. On its 85th birthday in 1988, the company held a huge motorcycle rally involving over 40,000 motorcyclists from as far away as San Francisco and Orlando,

---

[6]Ibid.

EXHIBIT 1

Harley-Davidson, Inc. Selected Financial Data (In Thousands, Except Share and per Share Amount)

	1990	1989	1988	1987	1986
Income statement data:					
Net sales	$864,600	$790,967	$709,360	$645,966	$295,322
Cost of goods sold	635,551	596,940	533,448	487,205	219,167
Gross profit	229,049	194,027	175,912	158,761	76,155
Selling, administrative, and engineering	145,674	127,606	111,582	104,672	60,059
Income from operations	83,375	66,421	64,330	54,089	16,096
Other income (expense):					
Interest expense, net	(9,701)	(14,322)	(18,463)	(21,092)	(8,373)
Lawsuit judgment	(7,200)	—	—	—	—
Other	(3,857)	910	165	(2,143)	(388)
	(20,758)	(13,412)	(18,298)	(23,235)	(8,761)
Income from continuing operations before income taxes and extraordinary items	62,617	53,009	46,032	30,854	7,335
Provision for income taxes	24,309	20,399	18,863	13,181	3,028
Income from continuing operations before extraordinary items	38,308	32,610	27,169	17,673	4,307
Discontinued operation, net of tax	—	3,590	(13)	—	—
Income before extraordinary items	38,308	36,200	27,156	17,673	4,307
Extraordinary items	(478)	(3,258)	(3,244)	3,542	564
Net income	$ 37,830	$ 32,942	$ 23,912	$ 21,215	$ 4,871
Weighted average common shares outstanding	17,787,788	17,274,120	15,912,624	12,990,466	10,470,460

Per common share:					
Income from continuing operations	$2.15	$1.89	$1.70	$1.36	$0.41
Discontinued operation	—	0.21	—	—	—
Extraordinary items	(.03)	(.19)	(.20)	0.28	0.05
Net income	$2.12	$1.91	$1.50	$1.64	$0.46
Balance sheet data:					
Working capital	$ 50,152	$ 51,313	$ 74,904	$ 64,222	$ 38,552
Total assets	407,467	378,929	401,114	380,872	328,499
Short-term debt, including current maturities of long-term debt	23,859	26,932	33,229	28,335	18,090
Long-term debt, less current maturities	48,339	74,795	135,176	178,762	191,594
Total debt	72,198	101,727	168,405	207,097	209,684
Stockholders' equity	198,775	156,247	121,648	62,913	26,159

In December 1986, the Company acquired Holiday Rambler Corporation. Holiday Rambler Corporation's results of operations are not included in the income statement data for 1986.
Source: Harley-Davidson, Inc. Annual Report 1990, p. 29.

EXHIBIT 2
Harley-Davidson, Inc. Consolidated Statement of Income (In Thousands, Except per Share Amounts)

Years Ended December 31	1990	1989	1988
Net sales	$864,600	$790,967	$709,360
Operating costs and expenses:			
Cost of goods sold	635,551	596,940	533,448
Selling, administrative, and engineering	145,674	127,606	111,582
	781,225	724,546	645,030
Income from operations	83,375	66,421	64,330
Interest income	1,736	3,634	4,149
Interest expense	(11,437)	(17,956)	(22,612)
Lawsuit judgment	(7,200)	—	—
Other–net	(3,857)	910	165
Income from continuing operations before provision for income taxes and extra-ordinary items	62,617	53,009	46,032
Provision for income taxes	24,309	20,399	18,863

Income from continuing operations before extraordinary items	38,308	32,610	27,169
Discontinued operation, net of tax:			
Income (loss) from discontinued operation	—	154	(13)
Gain on disposal of discontinued operation	—	3,436	—
Income before extraordinary items	38,308	36,200	27,156
Extraordinary items:			
Loss on debt repurchases, net of taxes	(478)	(1,434)	(1,468)
Additional cost of 1983 AMF settlement, net of taxes	—	(1,824)	(1,776)
Net income	$ 37,830	$ 32,942	$ 23,912
Earnings per common share:			
Income from continuing operations	$2.15	$1.89	$1.70
Discontinued operation	—	.21	—
Extraordinary items	(.03)	(.19)	(.20)
Net income	$2.12	$1.91	$1.50

The accompanying notes are an integral part of the consolidated financial statements.
Source: Harley Davidson, Inc. Annual Report 1990, p. 34.

EXHIBIT 3

Harley-Davidson, Inc. Consolidated Balance Sheet (In Thousands, Except Share Amounts)

December 31	1990	1989
Assets		
Current assets:		
Cash and cash equivalents	$ 14,001	$ 39,076
Accounts receivable, net of allowance for doubtful accounts	51,897	45,565
Inventories	109,878	87,540
Deferred income taxes	14,447	9,682
Prepaid expenses	6,460	5,811
Total current assets	196,683	187,674
Property, plant, and equipment, net	136,052	115,700
Goodwill	63,082	66,190
Other assets	11,650	9,365
	$407,467	$378,929

Liabilities and Stockholders' Equity

Current liabilities:		
Notes payable	$ 22,351	$ 22,789
Current maturities of long-term debt	1,508	4,143
Accounts payable	50,412	40,095
Accrued expenses and other liabilities	72,260	69,334
Total current liabilities	146,531	136,361
Long-term debt	48,339	74,795
Other long-term liabilities	9,194	5,273
Deferred income taxes	4,628	6,253
Commitments and contingencies (Note 6)		
Stockholders' equity:		
Series A Junior Participating preferred stock, 1,000,000 shares authorized, none issued	—	—
Common stock, 18,310,000 and 9,155,000 shares issued in 1990 and 1989, respectively	183	92
Additional paid-in capital	87,115	79,681
Retained earnings	115,093	77,352
Cumulative foreign currency translation adjustment	995	508
	203,386	157,633
Less:		
Treasury stock (539,694 and 447,091 shares in 1990 and 1989, respectively), at cost	(771)	(112)
Unearned compensation	(3,840)	(1,274)
Total stockholders' equity	198,775	156,247
	$407,467	$378,929

Source: Harley-Davidson, Inc. Annual Report 1990, p. 33.

EXHIBIT 4

Harley-Davidson, Inc. Business Segments and Foreign Operations (In Thousands)

A. Business Segments

	1990	1989	1988
Net sales:			
Motorcycles and related products	$595,319	$495,961	$397,774
Transportation vehicles	240,573	273,961	303,969
Defense and other businesses	28,708	21,045	7,617
	$864,600	$790,967	$709,360
Income from operations:			
Motorcycles and related products	$ 87,844	$ 60,917	$ 49,688
Transportation vehicles	825	12,791	20,495
Defense and other businesses	2,375	2,236	755
General corporate expenses	(7,669)	(9,523)	(6,608)
	83,375	66,421	64,330
Interest expense, net	(9,701)	(14,322)	(18,463)
Other	(11,057)	910	165
Income from continuing operations before provision for income taxes and extraordinary items	$ 62,617	$ 53,009	$ 46,032

	Motorcycles and Related Products	Transportation Vehicles	Defense and Other Businesses	Corporate	Consolidated
1988					
Identifiable assets	$180,727	$215,592	$ 2,863	$ 1,932	$401,114
Depreciation and amortization	10,601	6,958	3	396	17,958
Net capital expenditures	14,121	6,693	66	29	20,909
1989					
Identifiable assets	192,087	176,813	7,018	3,011	378,929
Depreciation and amortization	9,786	7,282	1,125	1,814	20,007
Net capital expenditures	18,705	3,524	1,190	200	23,619
1990					
Identifiable assets	220,656	177,498	7,163	2,150	407,467
Depreciation and amortization	13,722	6,925	1,166	618	22,431
Net capital expenditures	34,099	2,547	1,257	490	38,393

There were no sales between business segments for the years ended December 31, 1990, 1989, and 1988.

B. Foreign Operations (In Thousands)

	1990	1989	1988
Assets	$ 25,853	$ 18,065	$ 6,557
Liabilities	17,717	15,814	3,761
Net sales	82,811	39,653	22,061
Net income	5,555	2,281	1,941

Export sales of domestic subsidiaries to nonaffiliated customers were $93.0 million, $75.4 million, and $56.8 million in 1990, 1989, and 1988, respectively.
Source: Harley-Davidson, Inc. Annual Report 1990, p. 43.

Florida. All attenders were asked to donate $10 to the Muscular Dystrophy Association and Harley memorabilia was auctioned off. The event raised over $500,000 for charity. The final ceremonies included over 24,000 bikers whose demonstration of product loyalty is unrivaled for any other product in the world.

MOTORCYCLE DIVISION—EARLY 1990S

Exhibit 5 shows the motorcycle division's growth in unit sales. In 1990, Harley-Davidson dominated the superheavyweight motorcycle market with a 62.3 percent share while Honda had 16.2 percent, Yamaha had 7.2 percent, Kawasaki had 6.7 percent, Suzuki had 5.1 percent, and BMW had 2.5 percent. Net sales for the division were $595.3 million with parts and accessories accounting for $110 million of this figure. Production could not keep up with demand for Harley-Davidson motorcycles although a $23 million paint center at the York, Pennsylvania, plant was nearing completion and would increase production to 300 bikes per day.[7]

Approximately 31 percent of Harley-Davidson's 1990 motorcycle sales were overseas. The company worked hard at developing a number of international markets. For example, anticipating the consolidation of Western European economies in 1992, a European parts and accessories warehouse was established in Frankfurt, Germany, in 1990. After entering a joint venture in 1989 with a Japanese distributor, the company bought out all rights for distribution in Japan in 1990. Revenue from international operations grew from $40.9 million in 1986 to $175.8 million in 1990.

Product Line

For 1991, Harley-Davidson offered a line of 20 motorcycles shown in Exhibit 6. Other than the XLH Sportster 883 and XLH Sportster 883 Hugger, which had chain drives, all models were belt driven; all models had a five-speed transmission. Three of the Sportster models had an 883cc engine and one had a 1200cc engine; all of the remaining models had

---

[7]Harley-Davidson, Inc. Annual Report 1990, p. 12.

EXHIBIT 5
Harley-Davidson Motorcycle Unit Sales, 1983–1990

Year	Total Units	Domestic Units	Export Units	Export Percentage
1990	62,458	43,138	19,320	30.9
1989	58,925	43,637	15,288	25.9
1988	50,517	38,941	11,576	22.9
1987	43,315	34,729	8,586	19.8
1986	36,735	29,910	6,825	18.6
1985	34,815	29,196	5,619	16.1
1984	39,224	33,141	6,083	15.5
1983	35,885	31,140	4,745	13.2

Source: Adapted from Harley-Davidson, Inc. Annual Report 1990, p. 20.

1340cc engines. The first five models listed in Exhibit 6 were touring models, while the remaining bikes were standard and cruising types. All of the models exhibited impressive painting and classic styling attributes visually reminiscent of Harley-Davidson motorcycles from the 50s and 60s.

Motorcycle magazine articles commonly were favorable toward Harley-Davidson products but pointed out weaknesses in various models. For example, a review of the XLH Sportster 1200 in the December 1990 edition of *Cycle* reported:

> But Harley undeniably has its corporate finger on the pulse of Sportster owners, and knows what they want. All of the complaints—poor suspension, high-effort brakes, awkward riding position, short fuel range, engine vibration, and poor seat—have echoed through the halls of 3700 Juneau Ave. for more than a decade, yet have had seemingly little effect on XL sales. H-D sold 24,000 Sportsters over the past two years, and these complaints have been common knowledge to anyone who's cared enough to listen.[8]

The article, however, was very complimentary of the newly designed engine and new five-speed transmission and concluded that "This is the best Sportster ever to roll down an assembly line."

[8]"Harley-Davidson 1200 Sportster," *Cycle*, December 1990, p. 90.

EXHIBIT 6
Harley-Davidson, Inc. 1991 Product Line and Suggested Retail Prices

Model	Suggested Retail Price
FLTC Tour Glide Ultra Classic	$13,895
FLHTC Electra Glide Ultra Classic	$13,895
FLTC Tour Glide Classic	$11,745
FLHTC Electra Glide Classic	$11,745
FLHS Electra Glide Sport	$10,200
FXDB Sturgis	$11,520
FLSTC Heritage Softail Classic	$11,495
FLSTF Fat Boy	$11,245
FXSTS Springer Softail	$11,335
FXSTC Softail Custom	$10,895
FXLR Low Rider Custom	$10,295
FXRT Sport Glide	$10,595
FXRS Low Rider Convertible	$10,445
FXRS SP Low Rider Sport Edition	$10,295
FXRS Low Rider	$10,195
FXR Super Glide	$ 8,995
XLH Sportster 1200	$ 6,095
XLH Sportster 883 Deluxe	$ 5,395
XLH Sportster 883 Hugger	$ 4,800
XLH Sportster 883	$ 4,395

Source: Adapted from *Cycle World's 1991 Motorcycle Buyer's Guide*, pp. 76–82.

A review of the same model in *Cycle World's 1991 Motorcycle Buyer's Guide* pointed out a number of the same problems but concluded that

> Yet the bike's appeal is undeniable. A stab at the starter button rumbles it into instant life, and as the engine settles into its characteristically syncopated idle, the bike is transformed into one of the best platforms anywhere from which to Just Cruise. And that means anything from cruising your immediate neighborhood to cruising (with appropriate gas and rest stops) into the next state.

This the bike is more than willing to do, with its premium tires and seemingly bullet-proof reliability. The important thing is to not ask the Sportster 1200 to be something it isn't. What it is is a Sportster, much as Sportsters always have been.

This is merely the best one yet.[9]

Pricing

The suggested retail prices for 1991 Harley-Davidson motorcycles are also shown in Figure 6. These products were premium priced although the low-end XLH Sportster 883 and XLH Sportster 883 Hugger were less so in order that new motorcyclists could buy them and then trade up at a later time to larger, more expensive models. In fact, in 1987 and 1988, the company offered to take any Sportster sold in trade on a bigger Harley-Davidson at a later time.

The prices for Harleys can be compared with competitive products.[10] For example, the three 1991 Honda Gold Wing touring models with larger 1520cc engines had suggested retail prices of $8,998, $11,998, and $13,998. A Harley look-alike, the Kawasaki Vulcan 88, had a 1470cc engine and a suggested retail selling price of $6,599; a Kawasaki Voyager XII with a 1196cc engine had a suggested retail selling price of $9,099. Another Harley look-alike, the Suzuki Intruder 1400, had a 1360cc engine and a suggested retail selling price of $6,599. The Yamaha Virago 1100, another Harley look-alike, had a 1063cc engine and also had a suggested retail selling price of $6,599.

Promotional Activities

Kathleen Demitros, vice president—marketing for the Motorcycle Division, discussed a problem in designing advertising for Harley-Davidson motorcycles:

> One of the problems was that we had such a hard-core image out there that it was turning off a lot of people, even though people basically approved

---

[9]"Harley-Davidson Sportster 1200—Improving on Tradition," *Cycle World 1991 Motorcycle Buyer's Guide,* April–May 1991, p. 27.

[10]All prices are taken from *Cycle,* December 1990.

of Harley-Davidson. We had to find a way to balance our image more, without turning it into "white bread" and making it bland. Our goal was to get as close to our Harley riders as possible and communicate with them very personally.[11]

In addition to print advertising in general magazines, and Harley's own quarterly magazine, called *Enthusiast,* Harley has its own catalogs with full color pictures and descriptions of each model and discussions of Harley-Davidson products. For example, below is an excerpt from the 1991 Harley-Davidson catalog:

> To the average citizen, it's a motorcycle. To the average motorcyclist, it's a Harley. To the Harley owner, it's something else entirely, something special. Once you've got your Harley, it's much more than a piece of machinery or a way to get around. In a sense, it actually owns you. It occupies you even when you're not riding it. It's part of your life. And while you might not ever be able to explain it to anyone who doesn't know, you know. The trip certainly doesn't end after the road does. Different? Most wouldn't have it any other way.

In 1990 the Harley Owner Group had 650 chapters and 134,000 members with expected growth in 1991 of 15 percent and an additional 55 chapters.[12] In addition to national, regional, and state rallies and other events, meetings between HOG members and Harley management continued to provide suggestions for product improvements. HOG groups have "adopted" various scenic highways and have taken responsibility for their upkeep. In the 10 years Harley-Davidson and its owner groups have been involved, they have raised over $8.6 million for the Muscular Dystrophy Association.

Dealer Improvements

Several years earlier Harley-Davidson instituted a Designer Store program to improve the appearance, image, and merchandising of its products at the retail level. By the end of 1990, more than 310 of the company's 851 domestic and international motorcycle dealerships had completed

---

[11]Kate Fitzgerald, "Kathleen Demitros Helps Spark Comeback at Harley-Davidson," *Advertising Age,* January 8, 1990, p. 3.

[12]This discussion is based on Harley-Davidson, Inc. Annual Report 1990, pp. 15–26.

major store renovation projects or had agreed to do them in 1991. Some dealers reported receiving full return on the renovation investment within 12 to 18 months due to increased sales brought about by a more inviting shopping environment.

Market Information

The traditional U.S. motorcyclist is an 18- to 24-year-old male.[13] Since 1980, the number of men in this age group has declined from 42.4 million to 35.3 million. By 2000 the number is expected to be only slighly higher, at 36.1 million. Women are buying motorcycles in increasing numbers and sales to them have doubled. However, they still account for only 6 percent of the total motorcycles purchased. Motorcycle manufacturers have responded to this market, however, by designing bikes that are lower slung and easier for women to ride. The Harley-Davidson XLH Sportster 883 Hugger was designed in part for this market.

The sale of motorcycles, including three- and four-wheel off-road vehicles, peaked in 1984 at 1,310,240 units. Five years later sales had dropped to 483,005 units. Sales dropped in all categories, although dirt bikes had the largest sales losses. Sales of larger motorcycles, which tend to be purchased by older buyers for use on highways, represented 12.2 percent of sales in 1984 but increased to 21.3 percent of sales five years later.

As less affluent young men have drifted away from motorcycling, the sport has been taken up by professionals and businesspeople in their 40s and 50s. Likely, the late Malcolm S. Forbes, motorcycle enthusiast and wealthy magazine publisher, influenced this market, which is older and more conservative, and often rides long distances with their spouses on luxury vehicles.

There is some evidence that many motorcycle owners do not use their bikes very often, some only for a ride or two in the summer. Although the number of fatal accidents involving motorcylces declined 9 percent in a recent year, this decrease was likely because of decreased usage. The Insurance Institute for Highway Safety reported that in a crash, a person was 17 times more likely to die on a motorcycle than in a car.

---

[13]This discussion is based on Doron P. Levin, "Motorcycle Makers Shift Tactics," *The New York Times,* September 16, 1989.

EXHIBIT 7
U.S. Motorcycle Market Shares for Major Manufacturers

Company	1985	1987	1989
Honda	58.5%	50.8%	28.9%
Yamaha	15.5	19.8	27.7
Kawasaki	10.2	10.2	15.6
Suzuki	9.9	11.6	14.2
Harley-Davidson	4.0	6.3	13.9

Source: R. L. Polk & Co., as reported in "That 'Vroom!' You Hear Is Honda Motorcycles," *Business Week*, September 3, 1990, p. 74.

Competition

Exhibit 7 shows changes in overall market share percentages for the five major competitors in the U.S. motorcycle market.[14] Honda clearly lost the greater share and its sales decreased from $1.1 billion in fiscal 1985 to $230 million in fiscal 1990. However, motorcycle sales represent less than 1 percent of Honda's worldwide revenues.

Honda's plan to battle its sagging sales involved the introduction of more expensive, technologically advanced bikes. However, with an increase in the value of the yen from 250 to the dollar in 1987 to 120 by 1988, all Japanese competitors had to raise prices. Honda had to raise their prices even more to cover their new expensive models and became less price competitive. In fact, nearly 600 Honda motorcycle dealers went out of business since 1985, leaving the company with 1,200 dealers in North America. Honda's Maryville, Ohio, plant had so much excess capacity that executives considered transforming much of it to production of auto parts.

Honda's 1990 strategy included cutting back prices and a $75 million advertising campaign to reintroduce the "wholesome" angle of cycling to reach new market segments. Promotional emphasis was also given to encouraging Americans to use motorcycles for commuting as an alter-

---

[14]This discussion is based on "That 'Vroom!' You Hear Is Honda Motorcylces," *Business Week*, September 3, 1990, pp. 74, 76.

native to cars as is done in Europe and the Far East. High levels of air pollution, increased traffic, and rising fuel costs supported Honda's strategy. The advertising campaign was oriented less to selling individual products than to selling the idea that motorcycling is fun. Honda also offered free rides in shopping malls, sponsored races, and paid for Honda buyers to be trained at Motorcycle safety centers throughout the country.

In 1991, Honda's motorcycle product line included 25 models with displacements from 49 to 1520cc's including sportbikes, touring, cruisers, standards, and dual-purpose types. It also included 4 models of four-wheel all terrain vehicles (ATVs). Kawasaki's line included 23 motorcycle models in a variety of types and 4 four-wheel models. Suzuki offered 24 models of motorcycles and 8 four-wheel models. Yamaha offered 25 motorcycle models and 7 four-wheel models. Other smaller competitors in the U.S. market included ATK, BMW, Ducati, Husqvarna, KTM, and Moto Guzzi.

LESSONS FOR THE MANUFACTURER

The ability of Harley-Davidson, Inc. to come back from the brink of bankruptcy to market-share leadership in the superheavyweight motorcycle industry is a testimony to both "doing the right things" and "doing things right" across a variety of functional areas. This does not mean that the company today is free from difficult problems and stiff competition. However, it does demonstrate how changing a company and focusing on integrated efforts across functional areas can result in corporate success.

When the company was failing, it was clearly important to obtain financing that did not require large interest payments. The initial asset-based refinancing and then equity capital gave the company the funds necessary to continue in business while other changes were being made. The changes in manufacturing to a just-in-time inventory system, statistical operator controls, and greater attention to product quality were clearly important for enhancing the product's reliability and desirability for consumers. The changes in marketing to paying close attention to customer wants in styling and other attributes, particularly through the Harley Owner Group, and other changes in the marketing mix were critical for communicating with customers and designing and manufacturing market-sensitive products. The changes in human resources to get employees involved in improving the product were also critical for the success of the company. Lastly, the strategy of getting increased tariffs placed on Japanese bikes should not be ignored as it facilitated survival until the company could improve its operations.

While different functional specialists often point to their own area as the most important for the dramatic turnaround of Harley-Davidson, it should be clear that all of the changes were critical for the survival and success of the company. While the financial changes were important for bringing needed capital, such changes alone could not save the company. While the manufacturing changes were critical for producing a quality product, such changes would not be effective without consideration of consumer wants and communication of the changes to consumers. While the marketing changes, including improved marketing research, promotion, and channels were helpful, such changes alone could not account for the success without a reliable product. The human resource changes were critical for improving product quality; but, again, without the changes in other functional areas, they cannot stand alone as the single source of success.

Overall, then, the major lesson that should be learned from this case is the need for excellence and cooperation across functional areas. While the company has had some labor problems and difficulties getting its new paint plant functioning flawlessly, there remains a strong demand for the products in both domestic and international markets. For 1992, several changes were made in the product. These include the oil filter relocated to the front of the engine for easier maintenance, a new steel oil line, new brake pad and brake disc material, and recalibrated carburetors for better cold starts. While these may seem like small changes, they are consistent with a philosophy of continuous improvement.

NAME INDEX

SUBJECT INDEX

OTHER TITLES OF INTEREST TO YOU FROM THE BUSINESS ONE IRWIN/APICS LIBRARY OF INTEGRATED RESOURCE MANAGEMENT . . .

INTEGRATED DISTRIBUTION MANAGEMENT
Competing on Customer Service, Time, and Cost
Cristopher Gopal and Harold Cypress

Manufacturing professionals who strive to maximize the efficiency of their companies' distribution systems will instantly recognize the wealth of knowledge this guide provides. Gopal and Cypress direct you toward satisfying internal and external customer expectations and provide strategies for improving efficiency and service using the powerful Integrating Link.

ISBN: 1-55623-578-X

MANAGING INFORMATION
How Information Systems Impact Organizational Strategy
Gordon B. Davis and Thomas R. Hoffmann

Whether your company is considering implementing an information system or it is still untangling the technical applications of a newly administered one, *Managing Information* is a vital resource for grasping IS concepts. Those who strive for a workable information system in an integrated manufacturing environment will appreciate the book's outline for an effective program that, by touching each function of the organization, will increase precision in scheduling, inventory control, and marketing data management.

ISBN: 1-55623-768-5

FIELD SERVICE MANAGEMENT
An Integrated Approach to Increasing Customer Satisfaction
Arthur V. Hill

How do companies like 3M and Whirlpool consistently rate high with customers in areas of field service repair? Hill, an established researcher and consultant in service operations management, examines their tactics while offering you practical strategies to solidify the customer-vendor bond. By utilizing Hill's advice on customer response time management, service delivery performance, advanced technology control, and other timely topics, your customers will receive the maximum value from your company's products.

ISBN: 1-55623-547-X

WORLD-CLASS ACCOUNTING AND FINANCE
Carol J. McNair

Even if you're not responsible for numbers-crunching and accounting, a working knowledge of finance and accounting will heighten your understanding of the company and increase your contribution and value. Addressing nonfinancial readers, McNair reviews basic and advanced accounting and finance principles and shows how they affect the performance of the manufacturing, distribution, and marketing functions of an organization.
ISBN: 1-55623-550-X

INTEGRATED PROCESS DESIGN AND DEVELOPMENT
Dan L. Shunk

When the design and development processes are integrated, productivity improves and costs shrink. Shunk's book is a no-nonsense, reader-friendly guide that not only defines the information requirements for integrated process design, it outlines the procedures you must take to achieve it. In addition, Shunk discusses ways your company can benefit from new and future technological trends, value-adding through design, value-added tracking, and more.
ISBN: 1-55623-556-9